A SEPHIROTHIC

A Journey in Consciousness
with the Golden Dawn Temple Tarot

A SEPHIROTHIC ODYSSEY

A Journey in Consciousness
with the Golden Dawn Temple Tarot

Harry Wendrich and Nicola Wendrich

Wendrich artHouse
www.wendricharthouse.com

Published by Wendrich artHouse, 2016

Wendrich artHouse
1 Brickyard Cottages
Llanelli
Carmarthenshire
SA15 3DL
Wales, UK

www.wendricharthouse.com

Cover image: *A Sephirothic Odyssey,* by Harry Wendrich
Inner front cover image: *The Rosy Cross,* by Harry Wendrich
Inner rear cover image: *Minutum Mundum diagram,* by Nicola Wendrich

Printed in Wales by 4colourdigital.com on FSC Certified and chlorine free paper.

ISBN 978-0-9927479-2-3

As our lives, so this book:
Dedicated to Christ.

To so many figures is our own work indebted, but we would specifically like to acknowledge the contribution to our studies made by Chic and Sandra Tabatha Cicero and Nick Farrell. Our appreciation also extends to the members of the Horus-Hathor Temple with whom we have shared ritual, learning and friendship over the years.

Our thanks to Sandra Tabatha Cicero for permission to reference her Colour Scales, and also to Aaron Leitch for allowing us to share his inspired work on the Shem ha-Mephoresh within these pages. Thank you to Don Jusko for his good-humoured advice over the years regarding the colour wheel and for allowing us to include his Real Color Wheel here. Our appreciation to Gareth Knight for advice concerning articles within the public domain, and also to Llewellyn Worldwide for kind permission to use content from Israel Regardie's *Golden Dawn*.

This book could not have been published by Wendrich artHouse if it were not for the generosity of Geraint Webley from 4colourdigital.com, who unreservedly gave of his time and expertise to assist and enable the publication and print of both the Tarot cards and this book.

Finally, a big thank you to our four sons, Joseph, Noah, Shiloh, and Arthur for their patience through our long hours of writing and editing, and for sharing this magical journey of life with us.

The Golden Dawn

The Hermetic Order of the Golden Dawn, founded in 1888 by William Wynn Westcott, Samuel Liddell MacGregor Mathers, and William Robert Woodman, formulated a structured system of magical study in the Western Mystery Tradition, which included the Kabbalah, Tarot, Astrology, Geomancy, Enochian magic, and Hermeticism. Its history as an Order is a complex and fascinating story. Members included Dion Fortune, W.B. Yeats, A.E. Waite, Aleister Crowley, and Israel Regardie, and while it ceased to exist under that name in 1903 (its members spawning the organizations of the Stella Matutina and Alpha et Omega), the HOGD can be considered the original source of several other Orders which have since been established to further the study and survival of these esoteric teachings.

One such Order, appropriately, the modern-day Hermetic Order of the Golden Dawn, claims initiatory lineage to the original Order through the late Dr. Israel Regardie, who, along with Chic Cicero, resurrected this branch of the original Order in 1977, in Georgia, U.S.A., following its traditional teachings, grade structure and ethos. In 1997, Nick Farrell visited Chic and Sandra Tabatha Cicero, joined the Hermetic Order of the Golden Dawn, and proceeded to co-found a Temple of the HOGD in the UK, of which Harry Wendrich became a member in 2004. It is from within this Order that the *Golden Dawn Temple Tarot* was birthed. While the Tarot project was underway, Nick Farrell left the HOGD to set up The Magical Order of the Aurora Aurea (MOAA) – a modern magical Order which incorporates techniques drawn from Golden Dawn, Whare Ra, and Dion Fortune's tradition. Harry Wendrich continued as an Adept of the HOGD, his work entailing the construction of the Vault of the Adepti according to updated colour theory.

There are differences in opinion in many areas of Golden Dawn Tarot study, including the naming and placement of Kings/Knights/Princes, the subtleties of the Colour Scales, even the assignment of the Major Arcana Keys to the Paths of the Tree of Life themselves. Despite all the debates and reasons put forward, it is of our humble opinion that there is no fixed and hard rule regarding such things: that which is important when working with the Tree of Life is one's intention. While the images of the *Golden Dawn Temple Tarot* were based upon the Golden Dawn's *Book T* and designed in collaboration with Nick Farrell, this book represents our own work upon the subject and does not necessarily reflect the teachings of any specific Order.

Prologue

By Nicola Wendrich

As anybody who has embarked upon a journey with the Tarot knows, the journey never actually ends, as the Tarot cards hold within their symbolism the mysteries of Creation in their telling of the tale of the soul's return to its original home. In some ways, this book is a magical grimoire – an Odyssey of our own Tarot education experienced through three separate practices of meditation, painting, and writing, spanning decades of continual focus.

Early on in his spiritual journey, Harry met with the 22 archetypes of the Major Arcana in meditation, under the direction of his inner guide, working through the system presented by Edwin C. Steinbrecher in his book *The Inner Guide Meditation*.[1] Harry spent years balancing the archetypes according to their placement within his astrological natal chart on seven levels, as a prerequisite for personal kundalini work. Seven years later, we revisited the archetypes as a married couple throughout five years of joint meditations, the conversations from which are shared in Appendix I. Whilst this sequence of meditations was underway, we began work upon the *Golden Dawn Temple Tarot*.

Harry and Nick Farrell worked out the Major Arcana images between them, Nick careful to keep the structure true to Golden Dawn ritual symbolism, and Harry keen to observe and portray that which was communicated via the Tarot archetypes in meditations. Through painting the Minor Arcana in accordance with the symbolism of *Book T*, my continuing voyage led me from Kether of Atziluth (Ace of Wands) to Malkuth of Assiah (Ten of Pentacles) – the Ten Sephiroth through the Four Worlds of Emanation. Harry and I painted the Court Cards together.

Throughout the painting of the deck, invisible agencies would magnetically draw toward us the energies which needed to be expressed. Synchronicities existed within our dreams and events of our outer life, and parallels also occurred within the Golden Dawn Temple of which both Nick and Harry were members. It was clear that the Golden Dawn Temple Tarot was to be much more than a pictorial representation of words and symbols in a manuscript – the paintings were a response to and conduit of both the archetypal energies of the Tree of Life and the modern-day Golden Dawn current. The deck took seven years to complete, during which time several insights were brought to light, such as the need to revise and update the traditional Golden Dawn Colour Scales, and an

---

1   Steinbrecher, Edwin C. *The Inner Guide Meditation: a Spiritual Technology for the 21st Century.* York Beach, ME: Samuel Weiser, 1988.

additional method of interpreting the astrological associations within the Minor Arcana as archetypal influences, which we have presented within this study.

Throughout the years of painting I gave birth, experienced the loss of a loved one, knew illness, heartbreak, and more. I was amazed at how such major events were synchronistic with specific paintings – some paintings took two months to complete, others over a year, but one followed another in sequence, a relentless progression down the Tree, manifesting on canvas in harmony with the other aspects of my daily reality.

Beginning with the Ace of Wands, followed by the Ace of Cups, Ace of Swords, and finally the Ace of Pentacles, the four Aces took almost one year to complete and corresponded with the four seasons. I received dreams during the sketching stage of both Wands and Cups in which I was presented with a wand and a cup, respectively, which I took to be good omens for the painting of such. While painting the Ace of Swords I felt the continual presence of my Higher Self around me, which correlated with connecting this card to one's True Will.

Upon completion of the four Aces I had a dream in which I was instructed by an angel to continue painting the remaining cards using only the three primary colours (magenta, yellow and cyan) and white on my palette. At the same time, Harry dreamt that an angel presented him with an empty colour wheel and told him to fill it. Given that Harry was also painting the first panel of the Vault of the Adepti at this time, it was clear to us that the traditional colour theory of the Golden Dawn was to be updated in the light of modern colour theory, which places magenta as the true primary instead of red. This will be examined in the final chapter: *The Colour Magic of the Golden Dawn.*

Using a palette of the three primary colours and white allows one to experience the magic of mixing colours. The formula given in the *Path of the Chamaeleon*[2] shows how the colours of Queen Scale are formed following a logical mixing sequence which increases in complexity as one descends the Tree. For example, to produce the colours of Malkuth, firstly primaries are mixed to produce secondary colours, which are in turn mixed in four combinations to produce the colours of the Malkuth quadrant, a process which is a vital step in ascertaining the correct colours, as the colours of Malkuth (citrine, olive, russet, and black) cannot be determined from a worded description alone. Mixing colours takes time, and time is an essential component of experiencing the density of the Sephiroth on the Tree of Life. If one were to simply select a tube of pre-mixed paint, one would not only run the risk of an inaccurate colour choice, but "convenience" would effectively cause the artist to miss the crucial experiential, and thus magical, aspect of generating through colour, in this case, the slow and dense fields of Malkuth and the Element of Earth.

Similarly, the Prince Scale is produced through the mixing of King and Queen Scales, allowing colour to beautifully demonstrate how the Prince holds the energies of both King and Queen, yet is a new creation in his own right.

The currents within Kether and Chokmah were expressed to me through dreams.

---

2   A Golden Dawn document entitled "Ritual W – Hodos Chamelionis"

The Twos of Chokmah are the Field of Force, and it was in the pearl-hued mist of these Sephiroth that the primaries and white commenced their command of the palette.

In painting the Threes of Binah (the Greater Mother and the Field of Form), I intuitively felt it important to apply the background colour with brushstrokes that reflected the nature of the element – quick, upward, flame-like strokes for Fire, smooth, flowing ribbons of colour for Water, a misty effect for Air, and blocks of intersecting shapes for Earth. The black background of Three of Cups was of course generated through mixing the three primaries of magenta, cyan and yellow, the ribbons of which tangibly and powerfully held the hidden potential of all colours. While painting Three of Swords (Lord of Sorrow), Harry was painting Death beside me. A founding member of the Temple passed away during these paintings, and although I had not met him, I dreamed of the man three nights before his passing (the study of this dream in hindsight predicted his death). Upon completion of the Threes I became pregnant. These were my main experiences while painting the Supernals of the Tree of Life.

With the Fours of Chesed came the sensation of moving down the Tree into the denser fields of the Lower Sephiroth. I began to paint cards two at a time, as canvases required time to dry between coats, and although until then I had been following the sequence of Wand, Cup, Sword, Pentacle, I found it impossible to paint a Wands card along with a Cups card. Their conflicting energies proved their incompatibility; conversely, Wands with Swords were comfortable together, as were Cups and Pentacles.[3] Four of Swords (Lord of Rest from Strife) brought an unusual experience. As I commenced the painting I felt an extraordinary sense of being the object of negative thinking cast by a person whom I knew of but had never met. There was no question of being able to paint until I had dealt with the problem, so I went immediately into an inner guided meditation, summoned the archetype of the person concerned as it existed within me, and commanded it to submit before Yeheshua. Not without a struggle, it did so, leaving me free to continue with the painting feeling a very definite rest from strife. Painting slowed as I suffered acute morning sickness, which Four of Cups (Lord of Blended Pleasure) summed up perfectly – the joy of carrying life coupled with the difficulty of such.

The Fives brought many challenging situations, as one might expect from Geburah. The painting of Five of Wands (Lord of Strife) and Five of Swords (Lord of Defeat) paralleled various struggles encountered when Nick left the Temple to commence work upon what was to become, at that time, a new Golden Dawn Order – the Magical Order of the Aurora Aurea. Five of Cups (Lord of Loss in Pleasure) held all the pain of relationships that could not be. Five of Cups is painted with the primary magenta of Queen Scale Geburah, according to the revised colour scales which came about as we painted this deck. Magenta is a strong feminine colour which carries well the emotional and sexual angst of the Five of Cups. The majority of work upon Five of Pentacles (Lord of Material Trouble) felt like toil, an enforced trudging through the motions due to the weight of a heavy depression, which, once recognised as part of the Sephira's field of force, could become consciously

---

3   see p.59, Ain Soph: *YHVH and the Four Elements*, for further reference.

manifested in paint on canvas. Painting continued as I experienced the long period of physical heaviness, inaction, and seemingly stagnant passage of time through the later stages of pregnancy, and the painting was completed as I sat through the slow healing of a Caesarian operation.

In stark contrast, the Sixes of Tiphareth were all painted with the pure and sweet energy of our new-born child in the studio, often while at his mother's breast or asleep in her lap. The golden and pastel colours of Tiphareth were fully in tune with this scenario. While painting Six of Pentacles (Lord of Material Gain), funds became available to build a new studio, timed to perfection for our requirement of a space large enough to accommodate the assembly of the Vault of the Adepti in order to continue its construction.

In passing through the Veil of Paroketh the paintings began to take an increasingly longer time to complete, most obviously because seven and eight of anything takes longer to paint than three or four, particularly the Pentacles which were ringed with Celtic knotwork and painted in the colours of Malkuth. This was fitting with the increasing density of the Sephiroth as I worked my way down the Tree. The Sevens, famous for their negative influences, brought some rather depressing energies of "Unstable Effort," "Illusionary Success," and "Success Unfulfilled" into the studio. Procrastination seemed to prevail, and Seven of Cups hung around unfinished even as I began the Eights, which I would not normally have felt comfortable with. However, Eight of Cups (Lord of Abandoned Success) matched my mood exactly as we discovered that some of the stored canvases had become victims of mould – I felt like throwing the paintings into a skip! At which point, I recognised the link with the negative energies of the Sephiroth, and could then apply myself to persevere and overcome the troubles. This seemed to be the pattern for 'negative' cards – I would experience problems, often affecting me emotionally, which did not dissipate until I had become conscious of the connection between the negative situation and the painting in question. There was also much disappointment and delusion in the plans of friends who visited us in our studio at that time, and the only way out of that disappointment seemed to be perseverance and hope, which we hinted at through the depiction of a rainbow in the background of the Sevens – the sevenfold prismatic band that emanates from the Sephira of Netzach.

Harry and I had been painting the Tarot almost every day for four years with a drive to see its completion, and this sense of urgency at times knocked other aspects of our life out of balance. Yet the painting of certain cards would restore the imbalance, when it related to their sphere of influence. One such example was Eight of Pentacles (Lord of Prudence), which refused to be completed until every job that needed doing upon our estate had been attended to, including the construction and renewal of several paths, fences, a new chicken run and chicken house, and the planting and tending of the vegetable garden.

By this point, I understood that the cards would bring with them situations linked to their spheres of influence, and I wondered what the Nines would have in store – I wasn't particularly looking forward to Nine of Swords (Lord of Despair), seeing as my every experience of it in a reading had surmised depression and illness. As I drafted the sketch, an old friend, who had not been in touch with me for three years, telephoned to say that her incurable illness was driving her crazy and that she had tried to end her life. I knew then that somehow the energy of the card had magnetized her into my sphere of being. We remained in contact throughout the painting of that card, and for that time only. The weight of her depression and despair was so overwhelming that I would have to spend some time in prayer both before and after working upon the painting in order to function outside of it.

I painted Ten of Wands (Lord of Oppression) and Ten of Swords (Lord of Ruin) to the backdrop of a dying mother-in-law and a father diagnosed with melanoma. I hardly need to describe the weighty, oppressive feeling within the studio at this time. Harry's mother died during the painting of Ten of Swords. Her passing brought the end of our trips to the home in Germany that Harry had been born in, and the position of the crossed swords within the card seemed to carry this energy of finality. Indeed, our world seemed to come to a standstill at this point. Harry could not paint for some time afterwards, and it was a separate commission to paint the alchemical plate *"Emerging from the Swamp"*[4] which motivated the return to his palette, eventually resuming his work upon the High Priestess. In due course, the painting of Ten of Pentacles (Lord of Wealth) brought an inheritance.

Ten of Cups (Lord of Perfected Success) took over a year to complete, and all the while we witnessed our family life blossom. All areas of our life seemed to be brought into their highest potential at that time, including the business direction (commencing the opening of our studio/gallery to the public), our home (being literally gifted with a bigger home), the material needs of our children, and our personal magical work (within the operation of a new Temple). We were blessed with an overflowing abundance which did not cease while this painting was underway.

Painting the Court Cards demonstrated a similar experiential magnetism – a combination of drawing into our environment individuals who displayed the qualities of each card, and our personal experience of first negative, then positive traits of the card in question.

We decided that these aspects of our Tarot education should be documented in a book. Our original intention was to relate the experiential painting phenomenon, elaborate upon a series of articles upon the Major Arcana that Harry had written for the magazine Hermetic Virtues between 2007 and 2013, and expound upon the colour theory and other insights gained along the way. However, as we began to construct this book, it soon became apparent that it was not to simply be a matter of assimilating information previously gained. The writing of this book has been as illuminating, challenging, and humbling as was the painting of the deck, because both were literally lived through, at times requiring sacrifice for initiation into the area being studied. Once again, our focus upon each card would cause its energy to permeate our life, producing various effects in the physical, mental, emotional, and spiritual bodies which, once understood, would

---

4   Splendor Solis No. 8: Emerging from the Swamp; Accessed February 1st, 2016.
http://www.wendricharthouse.com/study/splendor-solis/

enable the writing to take place. These experiences would last only for as long as each Path was in focus, then the energy dynamic would shift into that of the proceeding Path. This time, our journey began in Malkuth and followed each Path and Sephira in sequence up to Kether and even into *Ain Soph*, before descending through the vehicles of the Court Cards.

Our written study focuses mainly upon the changes in consciousness as one's soul follows the Path of the Serpent up the Tree. As we travelled upwards from Malkuth to Chesed, the energy intensified, each Path bringing an aspect of purification and preparation for the very definite shift of energy which awaited us in the crossing of the Abyss into the Supernal Realm. A most notable event of this stage was our acquisition of an electronic device which, when connected to a plant, allows the energy of the plant to generate music. Through nine months of a continual aural and auric connection to the energy of plants was the Supernal Realm engaged. I encountered several devic spirits of trees in our garden, and we became acutely aware of the field of Universal Consciousness during this time. The influence of the High Priestess began as soon as Tiphareth had been written upon – she demanded a fast, from which I was not released until we had written upon, and therefore crossed over, Da'ath. The Empress brought the call for active service as a carer/meal provider to a friend who had at that time become chronically ill, and as nurse to our son who was incapacitated during the same period. Her influence also infused our bountiful summer garden, which saw many visitors sharing in the wonderful Music of the Plants experience.

Each Sephira was fully absorbing. The experience of Kether led me to lie down daily in a white room, as this was the place in which I could most harmoniously assimilate the experience of the vast and cloud-like field of potential which we both sensed continually – it was like walking around with one's head in a cloud, feeling that we were standing at the threshold of a momentous change which could not yet be perceived. A long break ensued, until all thought of writing had left us, following which I experienced an initiation into the phenomenon of Living on Light[5] and subsequently realized how this sacrifice had been the prerequisite for being granted access to writing upon *Ain Soph*.

We have endeavoured to retain the sense of the magical journey which unfolded through the act of writing this book so that the sense of increasing intensity that we felt in approaching *Ain Soph* and the transition of consciousness en route can also be experienced by the reader. The journey itself has been formatted into three main parts: Part I taking the journey of the Major Arcana, Part II journeying through the Sephiroth, and Part III as the experience of the Court Cards through the gradation of their magnetism within *Ain Soph* from the Kings to the Princessess. The introductions to each section work together to provide a fuller picture of the Tree of Life and *Ain Soph*, and the final chapter on Colour Theory together with the Appendices delves deeper into some of the symbolism and techniques used within this study.

---

5 Jasmuheen, *Pranic Nourishment: Living on Light*. (Buderim, Australia: Self Empowerment Academy, 2012)

It is our sincere hope that in venturing into these pages,
the Spirit behind the written word will inspire you within your own
Sephirothic Odyssey...

CONTENTS

A SEPHIROTHIC ODYSSEY
Part I: The 22 Keys

A SEPHIROTHIC ODYSSEY
Part II: The Sephirothic Gates
The Minor Arcana

A SEPHIROTHIC ODYSSEY
Part III: The Royal Court

APPENDICES

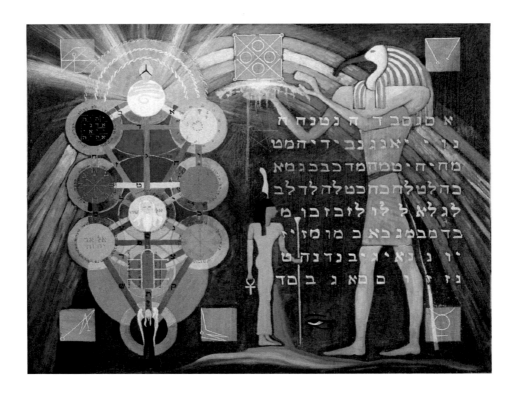

Introduction

The Tree of Life and the Golden Dawn

Around the world in various forms exists an ancient sacred knowledge hidden within the symbolism of a World Tree or Cosmic Tree. One such example is the Kabbalistic Tree of Life as used by the Hermetic Order of the Golden Dawn in the structure of its initiatory system.[1]

The Hermetic Order of the Golden Dawn uses a hierarchical system based around three distinct Orders. The grading system of these Orders allows for a sustained exploration within a region of consciousness corresponding with the Paths and Sephiroth of the Tree of Life. Through initiation into a grade and with the commitment to study and commit to memory the rudimentary knowledge of the grade, the aspirant/magician can explore and examine these different levels of consciousness, which at times can be difficult to work through. The Tarot Keys are employed as portals into each Path that needs to be

1   Kabbalists have constructed the Tree of Life in various different arrangements over the centuries. The *Golden Dawn Temple Tarot* is based upon the most common depiction of the Tree of Life in Hermetic Kabbalah, called the Kircher Tree: Athanasius Kircher's portrayal of the Tree of Life, based on Philippe d'Aquin's version, both in the year 1625.

experienced and balanced within the individual.

The Golden Dawn initiations open up inner potential and help a magician understand the inner workings of his/her own mind, while the Knowledge Papers provide an outline of the alchemical processes occurring. Another aspect of initiation into the Golden Dawn current is that the magician enters into an egregore which enlivens the magical persona, and allows for interaction with other sincere practitioners who may be further advanced within the system and able to hold out a hand when the need arises.

The Golden Dawn works with the four-fold elemental pattern within its elemental grading system. The Outer Order is the Golden Dawn proper. The Outer Order Grades are:

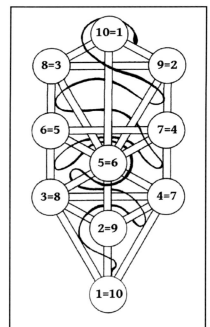

Neophyte	0=0	Probationary
Zelator	1=10	Malkuth/Earth
Theoricus	2=9	Yesod/Air/Moon
Practicus	3=8	Hod/Water/Mercury
Philosophus	4=7	Netzach/Fire/Venus

Portal: Probationary between Outer and Inner Orders

If invited, the aspirant then passes through the Vault of the Adepti into the Inner Order, named the *Rosae Rubeae et Aureae Crucis* (Ruby Rose and Cross of Gold).

The Inner Order Grades are:
Adeptus Minor	5=6	Tiphareth/Sun
Adeptus Major	6=5	Geburah/Mars
Adeptus Exemptus	7=4	Chesed/Jupiter

An obscure or theoretical Third Order is said to be linked to the Secret Chiefs who direct the spiritual current of the other two Orders.

The Third Order 'Theoretical' Grades:
Magister Templi	8=3	Binah/Saturn
Magus	9=2	Zodiac/Chokmah
Ipsissimus	10=1	Kether

The opening of a great book to find a mirror within conveys the idea that there are no great mysteries to be found in these Orders except the mystery of the Self. It is easy to lose sight of this simple truth in the face of grading structures and Inner and Outer Orders which, whilst serving to safeguard the minds of the students as they become informed of the inner alchemical processes occurring, also bring the risk that the ego becomes fixed upon the academic understanding of the particular systems being examined rather than seeking greater depths of awareness. And although the Knowledge Papers introduce the concepts of both the Qlippothic Realms or Underworld below, and the Veils of Negative Existence above, the Golden Dawn grading system placed on the glyph of the Tree of Life gives the impression that there is nothing to explore beyond its grading structure. It also suggests that one must travel upwards to ever-greater heights of knowledge and power, yet, although there is a feeling of rising up into the higher grades, upon entering the Vault there is a definite shift in perspective: we do not actually travel upwards but rather inwards, towards one's centre and also towards the Earth and its centre – the journey to the heart of hearts. This study explores the changes in consciousness on such a journey.

The Serpent on the Tree

There are in fact two Kabbalistic Trees, as mentioned in the Biblical Book of Genesis – the Tree of Life and the Tree of the Knowledge of Good and Evil. In some ways these two Trees are but one Tree representing two aspects of itself, showing the dynamic of both a downward movement of the Divine Will in Creation and an upward movement of the consciousness of the soul.

The Tree of Life is a glyph which reveals the Law of *Ain Soph*, crystallizing the Divine Light into the Four Worlds of the Kabbalah. The Tree of Life reveals the divine process of Creation, via the Lightning Flash which draws out the 10 Sephiroth on its downward journey. Each Sephira holds within it another Tree of Life, and each Sephira also has four levels or densities which are attributed to the Four Worlds/Four Elements, revealing the multi-dimensional quality of these immense areas of consciousness. Light/Consciousness becomes increasingly structured as it descends the Tree of Life. As consciousness lowers, it passes into a Sephira, through its four levels, and into the next Sephira, and so on, from Kether to Malkuth. The 22 Paths linking the 10 Sephiroth are aspects of Divine Will, encapsulated in the 22 letters of the Hebrew alphabet.

The four-fold division of the 10 Sephiroth is represented by the Minor Arcana. The Paths on the Tree of Life are represented by the Major Arcana. They have a seven-fold division corresponding to the spectrum of light and the related seven levels of consciousness.[2]

The glyph of the Tree of the Knowledge of Good and Evil depicts a serpent, as from this Tree was Eve tempted, resulting in man's exile from Eden – the fall of man or the fall of consciousness and the fragmentation of the soul. The serpent fixes one's focus upon the reality of the outer manifested creation, locking one's consciousness into many and various illusions, and thus hindering the soul's knowledge of its divine nature. The resulting forces of imbalance within the Tree are depicted in the twisting, rising movement of the

---

2   This is not apparent within the Golden Dawn's Tree of Life system, which uses the colour system of the Four Worlds to colour the Paths, but it is revealed when entering the Vault of the Adepti, which has seven panels.

serpent, which touches each Path between the two outer Pillars of Severity and Mercy (the feminine and masculine polarities) as it climbs from Malkuth to Kether, connecting an underwordly realm with a heavenly realm.

The rising serpent also reveals the path that we need to climb, as this same serpent which entraps the soul within the world/matter can be used as a vehicle of the soul's return to its rightful place within Creation, the Throne in Kether, via the *kundalini*, or 'serpent force'.

The Paths represent the magnetic frequencies within light that interact with us as the archetypal forces of the Major Arcana. Through an inner negotiation with these archetypal forces via meditation, balance may be achieved. As the archetypal forces become balanced through magical work within the seven levels of consciousness, the resultant unified state of consciousness allows for the purifying fire of the kundalini at the base of the spine to ignite. The fire rises slowly, and clears the way for the serpent force to rise, eventually coiling around the Middle Pillar. The rising serpent denotes the breaking of illusions; that is, one's consciousness is no longer bound by an illusion but is able to see beyond it.[3]

We thus experience the Paths and Sephiroth through complex environmental and inward interaction which promotes an evolution of consciousness from individual consciousness or awareness to a Universal or Christ Consciousness. The serpent entwined around the Tree represents a masculine seed that fertilizes greater awareness and higher forms of consciousness, alluding to a second birth. The serpent, then, is a transformative agent. As it rises, the soul becomes free of the spell-binder, regaining its wings to a new birth into Spirit.

---

3   An outward projection of the archetypal forces attracts circumstances into our physical life which enable the archetypal frequencies to become balanced, but achieving balance on all seven levels in this way is likely to take considerably longer and generate more emotional and physical difficulties than focussed inner work, which is able to short-circuit the continuing physical experience of unbalanced archetypes. The kundalini may thus still rise in an individual who is unaware of its existence, and illusions are still broken through the experiences of life without necessarily being aware of these concepts.

PART I: The 22 Keys

THE
MAJOR
ARCANA

THE UNIVERSE
Key 21 (the 32nd Path)

Tau
- cross

 SATURN

The Great One of the Night of Time

"The Thirty-second Path is the Administrative Intelligence, and it is so called because it directs and associates, in all their operations, the seven planets, even all of them in their own due courses."

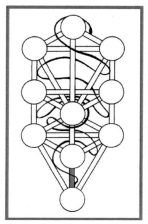

The 32nd Path between the Sephiroth of Malkuth and Yesod marks the beginning of the ascent of the Tree of Life, and in taking this momentous first step we encounter imagery and associated vocabulary to describe many important divine agencies and potencies, several of which are embedded in the symbolism of this 21st Key: the Angels of the Shem ha-Mephorash, the Kerubim, the Shekhinah, the Kundalini, the Chakras. The Yetziratic Text and Title of this Key join in conveying an awesome sense of profundity to the sublime frequency of the Universe archetype. Consisting of everything in the Universe of Time and Space, this Key is associated with Saturn, the most distant of the visible planets. Saturn signifies the boundaries of our personal awareness and experience, and as Teacher he brings individuals the understanding of their own spiritual destiny. The Universe is the overseer of the cycles of time and heralds the beginning of a new cycle. On the Path of Emanation, this Key is the final card, the *tau* (ת). Here on the Path of Return, the Universe represents the first stirrings that are felt in needing to enter more deeply into one's consciousness, i.e. bringing into conscious awareness the realm of the subconscious/superconscious; hence a new cycle begins, as its spiralling force, through trials and testings, seeks to bring everything back to its source.

The beautiful figure in the centre of this card is the Egyptian goddess Hathor, and in considering her nature we become more familiar with the archetypal power of this Key. Hathor was not just considered the Great Mother of this world, the personification of

Nature, as in nurturing and creating, in cycles of life, death and rebirth, but was also a cosmic goddess in the form of the Sky Goddess, and Goddess of the Underworld. She dances joyfully upon the black cubical altar of the material universe, from which shines the letter *tau*. *Tau*, meaning 'cross,' symbolizes sacrifice, pictorially shown in Hathor's crossed legs. The Egyptians understood the creative feminine principle within Nature as a sacrificial act: the goddess would lower herself from the House Above to bring to life a new realm below. This is nowhere better illustrated than in the 30 Enochian Aethers, wherein the feminine creative principle descends to the Aether below to maintain the life force and feed it from the waste material of the Aether above. As the final letter of the Hebrew alphabet, and in its interpretation as a cross, the *tau* also corresponds to Yeheshua.

> "I am Alap and I am Tau, The First and The Last,
> The Origin and The Fulfillment."

Rev. 22:13 (Aramaic Bible in Plain English)

Hathor is crowned with the crescent Moon, and above the crescent moon there are seven stars. Traditionally, the Golden Dawn Universe card has a seven-pointed star above the crescent moon. The seven-pointed star links to Venus (The Star card) and Aphrodite. In the *Golden Dawn Temple Tarot*, the seven stars better demonstrate the seven levels of consciousness (corresponding to the seven chakras in the body) that need to be explored and where archetypal frequencies are balanced.

Behind Hathor is the full potential of her creative source – an evolving galaxy, revealing Divinity manifesting through nature. This force also exists within each of us as a coiled serpent imbedded at the base of the spine, known as the kundalini. This latent, sexual force is overlaid by a green veil (which partly covers the hexagram, representing nature's veiling of Spirit), shaped like the Hebrew letter *kaph* which connects the Universe card to the Wheel of Fortune, further emphasizing the cyclic nature of this Key.

The work of the Great Archangels Metatron and Sandalphon, who are connected to the Upper and Lower Shekhinahs, is to reunite both upper and lower aspects within ourselves, as is also revealed in the central hexagram, placed on Hathor's womb in the process of birthing a new level of consciousness.

The Shem ha-Mephorash,[1] the 72-fold Name of God, is composed of wheels of Celtic knotwork to symbolize the movement of Time from one cycle to another. It is placed at the outer edge of the 12 constellations of the Zodiac, revealing the border between the physical universe within Time and Space and the astral, angelic, spiritual realms. This

---

1   See Appendix I

4

border also creates a hint of the Cosmic Egg, with potential of new life. Within the Cosmic Egg, a transformation occurs from physical consciousness into spiritual consciousness, where one's mind links with the One Mind of God.

When we start out on our path into the subconscious realms, we must first face the four Kerubim, depicted in the four corners of this Key. They act as a wall which protects the ego from accidentally passing into the subconscious realms unprepared. The first realm experienced as we leave the physical is the etheric realm, which is still very dense and is depicted in this card as fine lines. The Kerubim, the Strong Ones, are the living powers of the Tetragrammaton, the Unknowable Name of God, *YHVH*. They are depicted as the Kerub of Fire, the Lion, and the sign of Leo; the Kerub of Water, the Eagle and the sign of Scorpio; the Kerub of Air, Adam the Man, and the sign of Aquarius; and the Kerub of Earth, the Bull, and the sign of Taurus. They are the Guardians of the Four Quarters. They are the four living creatures who stand in the midst of and around the throne of God.

The first living creature was like a lion, the second was like an ox,
the third had a face like a man, the fourth was like a flying eagle.
Each of the four living creatures had six wings and was covered with eyes all around,
even under its wings. Day and night they never stop saying:

" 'Holy, holy, holy
is the Lord God Almighty,'
who was, and is, and is to come."

Rev. 4:7,8 (NIV Bible)

Such is the awesome power which protects the soul who chooses to explore the unknown territory of his subconscious, the rewards of which are blessings indeed.

JUDGEMENT
Key 20 (the 31st Path)

Shin - tooth

The Spirit of the Primal Fire

"The Thirty-first Path is the Perpetual Intelligence; and why is it so called? Because it regulates the motions of the Sun and Moon in their proper order, each in an orbit convenient for it."

△ FIRE

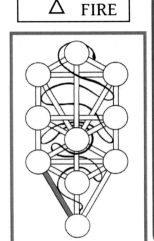

The great Archangel Michael, seen at the top centre of this card, rules the Sun, which can be seen behind him. He blows the shofar, the sound of which awakens the soul to its true calling and activates the spiritual fire within. The solar light splits into seven rays of colour and sound, hinting that there are seven levels to be mastered or balanced before the serpent fire can rise safely. The seven *yods* flowing around the rainbow symbolize the seven spirits around the throne of God. Within the rainbow the Seraphim can be seen as serpents. They bring focus to our true magical path through the purifying fire of kundalini.

The seven rays are connected to consciousness and the energy points in the human body called chakras. Chakras are enlivened by the kundalini fire, which is also termed 'serpent power' or 'serpent fire.' Within these centres energy forms a spiralling movement, as is depicted by the rainbow in this card. Each soul is attuned to one of the rays, indicating the spiritual path that the soul needs to pursue, and each individual responds to this awakening in one of two ways: either the ego responds to the urge to understand oneself more deeply by engaging on a spiritual path, or it resists, daring not to enter the spiritual realm. If the latter, although the ego holds on to the physical world, the individual will feel the need to delve deeply into a study such as history, philosophy, or a science, to shed light upon the innate question: "Who am I?" Such explorations present further opportunities to engage in one's spiritual path, until the resistance is overcome.

A primal force of judgement has now taken place, allowing the serpent fire to begin its journey upwards. This purifying fire can also be described as rapture, which in its essence is pure Love: it would consume us utterly if it were not for the seven rays through which it must ascend. This potential to consume is portrayed by the figure on the left, rising from the earth as Samael, the Angel of Mars (connecting this card to the Tower), depicted in this card as the Egyptian Set and also representing volcanic fire. (In the GD system, Samael is considered demonic.) The rapture is depicted by the right-hand figure(s), Archangel Anael, the Angel of Venus, ruler of astral light. In this card she is depicted as the sisters Isis and Nephthys, the light and dark aspects of astral light, around whom flashes lightning. The Archangel Michael (who is also Osiris in this card), Samael, and the Archangel Anael are connected by a white Fire Triangle, revealing that the three figures symbolize three aspects of Fire: solar, terrestrial, and astral. They also represent the elements Air, Earth, and Water. The element of Fire is expressed by the figure at the base of the picture, rising or resurrecting from the tomb. He is Arel, the ruler of serpent fire, and he is also Horus the Child (Harpocrates). The serpent fire awakening is symbolized by the Caduceus on his back. He raises his arms in the position of the 2=9 Golden Dawn grade of Theoricus, which signifies holding a great weight. He also forms the shape of the Hebrew letter *shin*.

Shin symbolizes the three-fold flame that resides in the secret chamber within the heart, a second chakra hidden within the Heart Chakra, known as the Eighth Ray Chakra.[1] The three-fold flame holds the spark of the Divine Essence, and is the seat of judgement. The central flow of the three-fold flame has within it a beautiful living light of a magenta hue, while entwining the central column are the other primary colours, yellow and cyan. These three coloured flames spiralling together as they are balanced are called the Resurrection Flame, and they are the three colours experienced as the serpent fire rises. As one of the three Mother letters, *shin* takes the primary colour magenta. The energy of magenta helps to bring into focus the main influence of Spiritual Fire, rather than red which holds the energy of terrestrial fire. The letter *shin* is also generated by the lower figures of the card, where the twin nature of Isis and Nephthys evokes the Kabbalistic teaching that while the three-headed *shin* is of this world, the four-headed *shin* is of the World to Come.

"The secret of the *shin* is "the flame [Divine Revelation] bound to the coal [Divine Essence]."…In this world, the changeless is symbolized only by a black, dark coal, not as the revealed light of the flame. Nonetheless the endurance of the flame depends upon the changeless essence of the coal. In the World to Come, the changeless essence will reveal itself within the flame. This revelation of the future is the secret of the fourth head of the *shin*."[2]

1   "Secret Chamber of the Heart." Accessed 10th May, 2014. http://www.aquarianpath.com/secretchamber.php

2   Ginsburg, Rabbi Yitzchach. *The Hebrew Letters: Channels of Creative Consciousness* (Jerusalem, Linda Pinsky Publications, 1990), 310.

THE SUN
Key 19 (the 30th Path)

Resh
- head

⊙ SUN

Lord of the Fire of the World

"The Thirtieth Path is the Collecting Intelligence, and is so called because Astrologers deduce from it the judgment of the Stars, and of the celestial signs, and the perfections of their science, according to the rules of their revolutions."

The Sun, a beautiful star within our galaxy, gives of itself in order to bring life to our planet. Yet behind the Sun is a greater Divine Light, which is the source of all life: in the Sun card, we have attempted to honour both.

Our conscious awareness of Time comes from the movement of the Earth as she journeys around the Sun, from day to night, with the four seasons completing the cycle of the year. This notion of Time and Space helps to fix our consciousness within a three-dimensional framework. Yet, as also shown in the Universe Key, a veil exists between the realm of Time/Space and that which is beyond Time/Space, and this veil prevents us from becoming consciously aware of the hidden Light which feeds the Sun's rays.

Portrayed in this Key is the traditional GD symbolism of the Sun with 12 principal rays representing the 12 signs of the Zodiac – six straight rays symbolizing masculine attributes and six wavy rays symbolizing feminine attributes. The rays are further divided into the decanates of 10 degrees, and quincunxes of 5 degrees, pointing to both the 72-fold Name of God as the Shem ha-Mephorash, and the sequence of Time within Creation, as in the 360 degrees of the astrological wheel.

The Divine Light is revealed as magnetic frequencies, depicting the primordial essence of the four elements. The essence of Fire within the Divine Light is depicted as descending *yods* manifesting from the centre of the Sun, creating a Fire Triangle as they contact the veil or wall beneath, and also revealing a Trinity at work within the Divine Light. The *yods* further demonstrate the broken or volatile nature of the magnetic field of fire/light, hinting why it is that fire burns and gives off light: when the unstable magnetic field of fire comes in contact with another elemental field of magnetism, the former naturally breaks the latter up, thus reuniting that elemental magnetic field with the source of Divine Light from which it originally manifested. This action of returning to the Divine Light explains why the influence of this Key is dominated by innocence and love, qualities pictorially represented by the children.

The wall or veil in the lower half of this Key is made up of 12 downward-pointing triangles, representing the element of Fire. The wall is then further divided into upward-pointing triangles, representing the magnetic field of the element of Air, and below the Air triangles are denser magnetic fields of the elements of Water and Earth. From the bottom of the wall spread the 22 archetypes which again begin to form the elements on a denser level: on the right, Water, on the left, Earth, and in the middle, Air.

The Fire element as light becomes the lower part of the two children, who are beginning to crystallize or become encapsulated in flesh: the children are the physical manifestation of the Divine Will, which has now crystallized around the souls of the children – they are twins, and represent Gemini. On each side of Gemini are the Zodiacal signs of Taurus and Cancer, signifying the additional influence of zodiacal signs in governing the crystallizing of the light into material form. The top halves of the children are fully an image of the cosmic forces moulded around the soul's essence. The soul may now experience the Divine Light materialized as it begins its return journey to the place beyond Time and Space, symbolized by the children holding on to the Caduceus.

The Hebrew letter *resh* is shown in the Sun. *Resh*, meaning 'head,' represents the head and consciousness, showing that light and consciousness are linked. The 19th Key thus shows the importance of focussing on the moment, as consciousness is all about taking in the present moment.

This Key then internalizes the Sun as the creative pulse of our very essence, from which we can and are to return.

THE MOON
Key 18 (the 29th Path)

ℙ	**Qoph** - back of the head

Ruler of Flux and Reflux; Child of the Sons of the Mighty

"The Twenty-ninth Path is the Corporeal Intelligence, so called because it forms every body which is, formed beneath the whole set of worlds and the increment of them."

⊗ PISCES

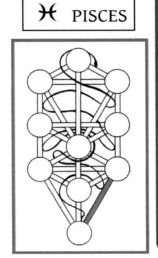

The Moon's silvery light is inherently deceptive, producing dangerous shadows within the landscape and the mind. However, this Key is not illusion in itself, but a way through the mists of self-delusion. On the opposite side of the Tree lies Judgement, where one is awakened. In the Moon Key, the same applies but at a deeper level, where intuition becomes a major faculty through which is perceived the way or path.

The Moon is depicted in its waxing crescent phase and is sided with Chesed, Mercy. From the silver wheel shine 16 principle silver rays or threads which weave throughout the landscape, symbolizing the magnetic influence of the Moon and hinting at the invisible presence of the Moirai (the Fates), who oversaw that the fate assigned to every mortal by eternal laws might take its course. There are also 16 secondary or shorter rays, totalling 32 rays which symbolize the 32 Paths of the Sepher Yetzirah.

In the *Golden Dawn Temple Tarot* Moon card there is a return to a feminine influence, as the Moon has always been connected with the feminine cycles. It is important to understand why the Greek goddess Hecate, one of many Moon goddesses, has been placed in the centre of this Key. Hecate, "Guardian of the Gates," is associated with crossroads and gateways, and she is often depicted in triple form. In her classical portrayal she holds a key, a torch and a serpent, suggesting that she is a kundalini goddess of ancient origins.

Hecate makes the sign of the Water Triangle – the subconscious waters. In psychology, the subconscious is considered the realm of the dragon. If this dragon or subconscious is not checked, it can cause grandiosity, which generates addictions and compulsions, and depression – symptoms associated with Pisces, the astrological sign associated with this Key.

The two towers standing at each side of Hecate represent the limits of conscious awareness and extremes of human experience. Hanging upon them are the Banners of the West and the East, symbolically representing darkness and light – Hecate in between shows that the soul needs to embrace the feminine principle, invoking the qualities of love and mercy. The *yods* represent the four letters of the Divine Name and also the influence of the great Archangels Metatron and Sandalphon, who represent the upper and lower Shekhinahs, and whose work it is to bring them together. Behind Hecate are the Egyptian godforms Thoth, a Moon god, and Hathor, a Moon goddess and the mother of Anubis. Before Hecate is the sea of the collective unconscious, out of which crawls a crayfish, representing the sign of Cancer, and symbolizing the Sun beneath the horizon. It also signifies the awakening soul, waking from its illusory sleep. It is interesting to note that in the Sun Key, the Hebrew letter is *resh*, representing the head, symbolizing consciousness, while the Hebrew letter of the Moon Key is *qoph*, which means 'back of the head' and represents the unconscious. It also represents the faculty of sleep, and can refer to the reptilian part of the brain which links us to our most ancient past and to the instinctual ability to survive.

In the shadows, laying obediently before Hecate, are two dogs, the dual form of the Egyptian Anubis. The dogs can pounce on the soul if they sense fear, or they can act as guardians and pathfinders through the flux and reflux indicated by the winding silver line on the path. The rising path passes through the illusions within religious, cultural and intellectual structures, and even passes through the goddess herself. We cannot see the end of the path, as it extends far beyond the horizon.

THE PEARLESCING
OF PHUL

Elegant, as silver dew
on a delicate weave;

Yet commanding,
Discerning;

With the purest intent.

So attractive,
if alluring,

Then a mirrored pool…

Where magnetic tides that
pull the truth free

Threaten to expose
Deception

As it lays cringing,
Naked on the floor,

'Til merciful waters cover
with warning,

Rolling with power
She breaks the illusion;

Over and over,

Releasing
And cleansing…

Soothing….
Now ebbing…

And in so, pearlescing.

*   *   *   *   *

By Nicola Wendrich, following meditation with Olympic Spirit, Phul.

THE STAR
Key 17 (the 28th Path)

Tzaddi
- fishhook

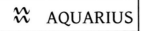

AQUARIUS

Daughter of the Firmament; Dweller between the Waters

"The Twenty-eighth Path is the Natural Intelligence, and is so called because through it is consummated and perfected the nature of every existent being under the orb of the Sun, in perfection."

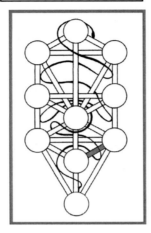

The Star in this image represents the star Sirius of the constellation Canis Major – the brightest star in the night sky. Sirius has a deeply-rooted link with Hermetic Magical Orders, being associated with Thoth-Hermes in Egyptian mythology, the Teacher of Mysteries who came from the stars. Sirius was also worshipped as the goddess Sothis, a goddess of fertility and a guiding light for human destiny, and was associated with Isis and Anubis, when it was sometimes referred to as the Dog Star. Sirius was considered the spiritual Sun behind the physical Sun of our Solar system, and thus the source of our Sun's potency.

The Star emits seven rays, showing that its magical influence can be felt through the seven levels of consciousness. It outshines the surrounding seven planets (which carry their angelic associations, connecting this card to the spiritual realms), making the Star the eighth heavenly body in the image.

> "The number seven denotes the perfection of creation,
> while eight is the entrance into the transcendental." [1]

The figure below the Star is the Supernal Mother, Aima Elohim. She holds two urns which represent Chokmah and Binah, from which pour the sacred Waters of Life. These

1   Aryeh Kaplan, *Sefer Yetzirah: The Book of Creation* (Boston: Red Wheel/Weiser, 1997), 165.

begin as a magnetic light frequency with its source from the star, coalesce into different densities within the living body of nature, and eventually become the Waters of Life which unite as one river below. The pool is shaped like a heart, showing the true nature of this card – a sustaining and replenishing force of love and light, bringing about the healing of a wounded world. On the figure's forehead is another seven-pointed star, symbolising Netzach and connecting the youthful, beautiful woman to the goddess Venus. The rivers of water flowing from the urns delineate the sigil of Aquarius, thus placing Venus within Aquarius. The shining rays of the colour wheel radiating from her sexual centre outwards create fertile ground, showing how the magnetic light frequency works out through the sphere of sensation as a form of sensual magnetism that brings two people together, uniting them for the purpose of procreation. The Hebrew letter *tzaddi* is reflected in the pool below the figure of Venus, and its meaning of a 'fish-hook' can further symbolize the sensual magnetism of womanhood within a social setting. The 17th Key connects Yesod to Netzach, showing that on a deeper level the fish-hook of *tzaddi* symbolizes penetration into the subconscious realms of Yesod, to rediscover such wisdom and knowledge as is veiled by the nature of Netzach, which only reflects the beauty of outward appearances. This Key then connects heightened sexual energy and visualization as a key to meditation and a deeper understanding of oneself.

Both the Tree of Life and the Tree of the Knowledge of Good and Evil are depicted in the background of this card, the latter as a palm tree. The sacred ibis sitting in the palm tree connects with Thoth-Hermes, who was depicted with the head of an ibis. The wisdom of Hermes cannot so much be found in books but is imprinted in the astral realms and may be accessed via meditation. The Golden Dawn keyword for The Star is Meditation, the practice of which takes much patience. With patience comes hope, and hope itself has a magic which is very much linked to this Key.

> But if we hope for what we do not see, we wait for it with patience.
> *(Romans 8:25, English Standard Version)*

The figure of Venus has the appearance of manifesting in space, a deliberate attempt to portray the multi-dimensional aspect to this beautiful and mysterious Key. Her aura suggests the Cosmic Egg, linking this card with the Universe Key, and hinting at that which may be experienced and seen within meditation. In the traditional image of The Star the figure kneels on one knee, demonstrating humility, and although naked remains partially hidden: this crouching Venus relates to the form of the letter *tzaddi*. In the *Golden Dawn Temple Tarot*, she stands upright with raised arms, resembling the final (sofit) form of the letter *tzaddi*. Her outstretched form on tiptoes brings an upwards movement to the card, and shows that what was formerly hidden is now being revealed or coming to light. This implies our modern awakening to extra-terrestrial intelligence, and thus reconnects us to the ancient Hermetic tradition of Sirius.

THE TOWER
Key 16 (the 27th Path)

Peh
- mouth

♂ MARS

Lord of the Hosts of the Mighty

"The Twenty-seventh Path is the Exciting Intelligence, and it is so-called because by it is created the Intellect of all created beings under the highest heaven, and the excitement or motion of them."

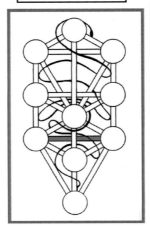

THE TOWER

The Tower is the 27th Path, linking Hod and Netzach, which correspond to the intellectual and emotional bodies. This Path is not easily crossed. The aim here is to renounce the path of the ego and call upon the Higher Self to take charge of one's life. The Tower card may also signify great change in one's physical realm, perhaps involving pain, accident, or loss from circumstances beyond ones control, linking to the Archangel Uriel, symbolized by the unicorn.

The Tower itself is connected to the Tower of Babel of Genesis 11, which literally meant "Gate of God." It was a tower to reach the heavens, built with the intention that men would make a name for themselves – an intention which led God to confuse their language and scatter the people. Attributed to this card is the Hebrew letter *peh*, meaning 'mouth.' The mouth speaks words formed from letters, and the letters of the Hebrew alphabet also represent the archetypal forces of the Major Arcana. The Hebrew alphabet inlaid into the tower structure shows that archetypal frequencies have become out of balance and, being no longer aligned with Divine Will, fail to hold the magnetic frequency required to keep the tower of the ego stable, hence it must fall.

The Flower of Life, depicted within the body of the Mars sigil which dominates the top right-hand corner of the card, represents the matrix from which life first sprang, connecting this ancient geometrical pattern to *Ain Soph*. From this divine matrix, a lightning bolt blasts the crown from the apex of the Tower, which had, up until this point, fortified the ego. The triangle on the symbol of Mars which blasts the Tower symbolizes the triad of Kether, Chokmah, and Binah. The 27th Path of the Tower thus represents unbalanced archetypal forces which are being brought into check by the action of *Ain Soph* working through the Supernals.

Flames explode from three windows of the Tower. The three windows connect to the Solar Plexus Chakra, the Heart Chakra, and the Brow (Third Eye) Chakra. This path is connected to the third chakra, the Solar Plexus Chakra, which directs towards one's true destiny, hitherto veiled by circumstances and programming. The Solar Plexus Chakra – *Manipura* – is located just above the navel. When opened, it releases unnecessary baggage that has hindered the soul's progress. It is associated with the element of Fire and directly affects the mental body. Its purpose is to give mental understanding of the emotions and so, when activated and in balance, will help to control both thought and emotion – Hod and Netzach. *Manipura* means 'resplendent gem or diamond', and denotes the brilliant ball of light that triggers the opening of the Third Eye, initiating the power of transformation. This sudden ability to see reality in a new light is the effect of the Tower, where one's former paradigm is shattered by new insights. This is considered an enlightening, positive, spiritual experience.

Two figures are falling from the tower: one falls on the side of the Tree of Life, suggesting that he will awaken to his spiritual path, but the other falls on the shadowed side of the Tree, towards the Qlippothic shells, implying that he will fall deeper into darkness and emptiness. Yet hope remains, both in the Unicorn of the Stars (which in the Golden Dawn was a metaphor for the soul), and in the rainbow. The rainbow also hints that the destruction and transformation of this Key takes place on seven levels.

There is a cosmic aspect to this Tower Key. In the background two planets collide, creating a vesica which is superimposed over the tower, signifying that a higher power is overcoming a lower one. Although ruled by Mars, which harnesses the energies to cut away aspects in one's life that do not align with Divine Will, there is a strong link between the 16th Key and the astrological phenomenon of one's Saturn Return. The Saturn Return acts as a teacher that redirects one's life towards a closer representation of one's True Will. This can bring the somewhat unsettling experience of existing within two distinct worlds: a higher consciousness engages with the soul causing disassociation with the current status quo, and bringing about a reality check.

THE DEVIL
Key 15 (the 26th Path)

 CAPRICORN

Lord of the Gates of Matter; Child of the Forces of Time

"The Twenty-sixth Path is called the Renovating Intelligence, because the Holy God (blessed be He) renews by it, all the changing things which are renewed by the creation of the world."

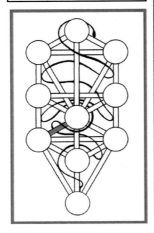

The Devil, in both name and image, presents an emotive arena wherein opinions are as diverse as religious thought. It is important to consider that this Devil is positioned as the 26th Path of the Tree of Life between Hod and Tiphareth, not on the Qlippothic Tree where impure forces are to be found. When we read the Yetziratic text above and consider the Titles of this Key, we can see that powerful natural forces under God's command are at work on this Path. However, as this Path crosses the Veil of Paroketh, it is within the reach of the astral entities of the Qlippoth. This is shown by the two demons in the lower division of the image. The Veil of Paroketh hangs below Tiphareth, marking a division between the triad of Chesed, Geburah, and Tiphareth and the lower Sephiroth, or between the mental body and the astral and physical bodies.

Eliphas Levi's image of Baphomet was used in the creation of the Golden Dawn's 15th Key. Within the *Golden Dawn Temple Tarot*, this figure is depicted with a phallus, representing the pro-creative force of Nature – a force we all naturally experience. Around the phallus is coiled a serpent, representing a seed of consciousness which awakens the Third Eye. The Hebrew letter associated with the 15th Key is *ayin* meaning 'eye,' indicating that this vital component of sexual energy, when recognized, becomes a powerful spiritual force.

However, the inverted pentagram on the Devil's head warns of concentrating the focal point (*ayin*) on material matters: tied to the altar, by choice, are two demons, their addiction to earthly desires demonstrating the limitations of our material world, which can produce symptoms of depression, stagnation, delusions, and fear. Misused sexual energy brings negative traits such as obsessive desire, lust, and bondage to the material world. The reversed pentagram can then be interpreted as bringing clarity into an area of illusion in that it reveals our fears and reveals our material bondage.

The Banner of the West in the background, denoting light shining through darkness, indicates that this Key carries within it occult power and protection against malignant forces. Furthermore, the pentagram in the top centre of the card shines with the supreme knowledge of the True Will and its destiny, invisibly guiding and drawing the conscious awareness inward and upward, as the kundalini serpent demonstrates, making us aware of the true essence of our earthly nature, which is imbued with love.

Another aspect to the Devil archetype is as a Shamanic symbol of our primeval survival instinct, which, when actively invoked as a totem animal, can guide us through the astral realms, in particular the lower astral where the elements are still defined and recognizable as Fire, Air, Water, and Earth. The earth can be seen as mountains; water is beautifully pliable, and one can move through it easily and without the need to breathe. Air is experienced as wind, and fire as a transformative element. As totem animals move through the different elemental realms, their forms or bodies change to harmonize with the elemental realm being traversed. This attunement with the elements can be seen within the figure of the Devil who holds four lower elements symbolically within his being: in his hands are the elements of Fire (the torch) and Water (the cup); his bat-like wings symbolize the element of Air, and his feet and hairy legs represent Earth. His head represents Capricorn, denoting the heights we can travel within these elemental realms. His claws hold the elemental pentagrams within Nature and within the individual upon the cubical altar of the material universe. It is the work of a magician to separate the elements, study and purify them, then bring them back together, crowned with Spirit.

TEMPERANCE
Key 14 (the 25th Path)

Samekh - prop

♐ SAGITTARIUS

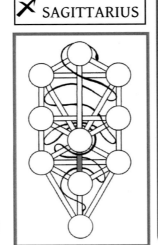

Daughter of the Reconcilers; Bringer-forth of Life

"The Twenty-fifth Path is the Intelligence of Probation, or is Tentative, and is so-called because it is the primary temptation, by which the Creator (blessed be He) trieth all righteous persons."

The Path of Temperance on the Middle Pillar links Yesod, the Foundation, to Tiphareth, the seat of the Higher Self, and also lines up with the Paths of the Universe and the High Priestess. Just as the Path of the Universe passes through the wall of the four Kerubim, and the Path of the High Priestess passes over the Abyss of Da'ath, Temperance passes through the Veil of Paroketh, which prevents the Qlippothic realms from rising as far as Tiphareth. The Hebrew letter that accompanies this card is *samekh*, meaning 'prop.' In the interpretation of *samekh* we find the symbolism of a spiritual valve which protects against overwhelming pressures of Divine Light that could cause physical damage, if not filtered. Temperance thus generates a safe environment for spiritual and alchemical work which aims to enhance higher states of consciousness through the balancing of the elements.

In the ritual version of this Key, the figure of Temperance has upon her forehead a Solar Disc from which emanates five rays, symbolizing the four elements and Spirit, and also the Supernals and the Sephiroth of Chesed and Geburah. From two vials she pours the Fire of Geburah upon the Waters of Hod, represented by the eagle, and the Waters of Chesed to temper the Fires of Netzach, represented by the lion. The elements of Water and Fire are thus reconciled in Yesodic Air as steam which also rises from the cauldron, creating the wings of an angel, and suggesting astral flight. The cauldron, linked to rebirth, symbolizes the work of an Adept to balance and purify the four elements and Spirit. The fire below

it suggests the kundalini fire, now rising upon the Middle Pillar. The chains linking the lion and eagle to her waist represent the Paths and signs of Capricorn and Scorpio (The Devil and Death) whom Temperance (Sagittarius) stands between.

The second Temperance card has a much lighter, more spiritual aspect to it. It is as if once the alchemical influence of Temperance has produced the purifying effect of steam, the elements of Fire and Water can be generated in a more magical and creative way, ultimately becoming a rainbow – the seven levels of light promising God's protection on all levels. The rainbow echoes the Sagittariun influence of the Key, and the bow and arrow were also associated with Sirius in ancient Chinese, Mesopotamian, and Babylonian astrology.

The Temperance figure stands with one foot in water and the other on dry land. In the background we see green pasture, symbolizing new life. Her wings are made of water and rise into flames of fire. She holds urns representing Hod and Netzach: the essence of life passes out of one and enters the other, creating a loop which surrounds the womb of the figure. The life-giving essence has been impregnated with light, giving a hint of a rainbow, symbolizing conception. She wears a square, golden breastplate which hints at the transformation of base material into gold. On her forehead is a Sun sigil touched by one beam of light which descends from the Hebrew letter *samekh* in the rainbow, showing the prop to be a valve which allows Divine Light to descend and to act as a transformer of consciousness. It also shows that the energy has been balanced and stabilised, as only one beam descends and ascends: the rising kundalini fire eventually collapses into a silver line which connects Kether to Malkuth, creating a new connection with the Divine Will. This silver line represents the line that must not be crossed, i.e. transgression of the Divine Law, as the Yetziratic Text reveals. Obedience to Divine Law keeps the balance of the Middle Pillar and prevents a pull into the material world, or of excess and extremes.

The two elements of Fire and Water so prominent in the Temperance cards are connected to the Hebrew Mother letters *shin* and *mem*, and the Third Eye and Solar Plexus Chakras. The Solar Plexus Chakra initiates the opening of the Third Eye. Together, these two images symbolize the inner alchemy of the Temperance image, the complex nature of which may indicate that this spiritual process is the continuation of work from past lives.

DEATH
Key 13 (the 24th Path)

Nun
- fish

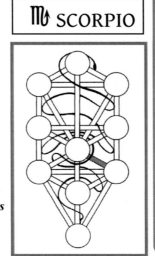

♏ SCORPIO

The Child of the Great Transformers; Lord of the Gates of Death

"The Twenty-fourth Path is the Imaginative Intelligence, and it is so-called because it gives a likeness to all the similitudes, which are created in like manner similar to its harmonious elegancies."

Ꭵ   DEATH   ♏

Death is without doubt a truth that we all have to face. It is never far away, since every cell dies and is born anew in order that the envelope which we call a body, housing our soul, is maintained, allowing the soul to experience for a brief time the laws of the material universe.

Death is part of the human experience which is often feared – the fear of letting go, held within the archetype of the opposite Path on the Tree, The Devil. Yet death works on many levels to bring transformation, including within our spiritual work – rekindling the silent inner voice of our own Higher Selves, once so ruthlessly vanquished by the outer ego. As long as the soul projects outwardly into Time and Space, with a desire to experience, it will always come face to face with Death. Through focussing our conscious point outwardly, we invite Death's transformative force into our life: renewed life rises to the call of the Higher Self. The archetypal structures of Death break down the outgrown ego, which in this image is strewn across the field of play like the dismembered limbs of king or pauper alike. The broken pillars show that the Inner and Outer Orders are also subject to Death.

The Hebrew letter *nun* lies silently, like a shadow amongst the debris. *Nun* means 'fish' which paradoxically is a symbol of the life force: in the image, the fish rises upwards with spermatozoa, representing the masculine influence, whilst above, the serpent, carried by an eagle, represents the feminine influence. These create a magnetic pull which draws ever-higher into the transformative phoenix. At the top we can see a ringed ellipse, which suggests the uniting of the Higher Self with the lower, in the final act of transformation. The 13th Key also reveals three stages of the soul's transformational journey through life. The scorpion represents the emotional and sexual level of the soul's experience. The eagle represents the intellectual and cultural experiences of the soul. The phoenix expresses spiritual awareness as the soul journeys through life. It is a symbol of rebirth from the ashes of the past, and it also represents the victory of life over death, thus immortality. In this respect, we can also acknowledge a connection with the fish of *nun* to Yeshua.

When the perishable has been clothed with the imperishable, and the mortal with immortality, then the saying that is written will come true:
"Death has been swallowed up in victory." "Where, O death, is your victory?
Where, O death, is your sting?" The sting of death is sin, and the power of sin is the law.
But thanks be to God! He gives us the victory through our Lord Jesus Christ.

I Cor. 15: 54-57 (NIV)

Through experiencing the archetypal forces within our life's journey, the elemental forces within us become balanced. The conscious point begins to focus inwardly, and, as we become more balanced, our Heart Chakra becomes activated. It is here that time begins to lose its hold, and fear transforms into love. The Heart Chakra is the point from which we leave our body after death. It is where the soul is assessed in ascertaining its next level of existence.

Studies in the subject of the afterlife have suggested that once the soul has been assessed, it is taken to a type of school on the inner levels. The human mind can only comprehend so much, but after the body has been discarded, everything that the soul had experienced may be taken to its fullest potential. If, after death, the soul experiences trauma, it is taken to a type of hospital where it can have time to recover. The soul is then placed into a level of the inner realms where it is best suited according to its light frequency vibration, and its Utopian idea of the ideal on Earth. The soul that is fixed on a particular aspect of living (obsession or addiction) is placed in a loop of an experience on Earth played over and over again, until the soul breaks through the particular illusion/obsession. From these levels, the soul will return to Earth for another incarnation, which is hinted at with the sperm rising upwards on the right-hand side of the image. But at some point the soul enters a great light like a sun, from which it will not return except by choice, until the time comes when death exists no longer.

...Behold, the tabernacle of God is with men, and he will dwell with them,
and they shall be his people... and there shall be no more death, neither sorrow,
nor crying, neither shall there be any more pain: for the former things are passed away.

Revelation 21:3,4 (NKJ)

THE HANGED MAN

Key 12 (the 23rd Path)

Mem
- Water

△ WATER

Spirit of the Mighty Waters

"The Twenty-third Path is the Stable Intelligence, and it is so called because it has the virtue of consistency among all numerations."

The 23rd Path between Hod and Geburah holds a certain mystery. On one hand it is an image of punishment or enforced sacrifice, yet on the other it is an image of enlightenment and of the Adept: this Key represents a period of sacrifice of the self which has its roots in the deeper realization that Love is the underlining force in the Universe.

Geburah acts as the level of consciousness needed to quieten the Hod consciousness, allowing for magical silence to oversee and guide the lower awareness. This idea is further emphasized by the leopard-skin worn by the Hanged Man; whilst acknowledging his animal self, it can be seen slowly falling off, showing that the Hanged Man symbolizes a process of attainment rather than its conclusion. The 12th Key represents a certain level of arcane knowledge, inner peace, patience, and the sensitivity to understand that some things are destined, some are mentally created, and some require physical effort; sometimes a problem can be solved by taking a reversed action, and sometimes action must be suspended.

Attributed to this Key is the element of Water and the Hebrew Mother letter *mem*, whose shape suggests a womb with an opening at the bottom for conception and the passage of birth. It doesn't take much imagination to see in the form of the letter *mem* the Egyptian goddess Nuit. So we can find in this key a powerful feminine current of bringing forth new life, and yet the new life is veiled by the dark recesses of the cave from which a giant hangs by his left leg. The cave symbolizes the passageway into the Earth, suggesting the progression from the conscious mind to the subconscious mind, or a deeper awareness of Mind within the astral realm – the Spirit of the Mighty Waters.

The Hanged Man has his head underwater, his hair spreading out as tentacles exploring, like a child looking for its mother. He is listening to the inner voice of intuition guiding, and he is becoming aware of deeper feelings of love – he has become active within the realm of Mind, the penetration of which brings about a second birth. His legs form the *tau* cross and his arms a triangle, symbolizing the power of the Spirit of Life rising above the Triangle of Water.

> "Most assuredly, I say to you, unless one is born of water and the Spirit,
>   he cannot enter the kingdom of God."
>
> *John 3:5 (NKJ)*

He is held by a golden thread, suspended from the barque of Isis, hinting at Osiris slain and risen. From the 5=6 ritual of the Grade of Adeptus Minor, we read:

> "Poverty torture and death have ye passed through; they have been but the
>   purification of the Gold."[1]

This brings us to the link between the Hanged Man and the Vault of the Adepti. The symbols within the Vault hold the complete Western Mystery Tradition. The Vault acts as a tomb which symbolizes entering the earth, further acting as a mystical womb of a second birth. Herein lies a hint: from this point, the expansion of our conscious awareness does not take an upward course (which the Tree of Life glyph may have seemed to suggest), but rather an inward penetration into the very Soul of the Earth herself, the Anima Mundi, or World Soul. The expressions Higher and Lower, Inner and Outer, demonstrate the limitations of our lexicon in describing such an expansion of spiritual awareness within a material reality.

Consciousness connecting to the Soul of the Earth holds the mystery of this Key.

---

1   Israel Regardie, *The Golden Dawn* (Woodbury, MN: Llewellyn, 1989), 36.

JUSTICE
Key 11 (the 22nd Path)

 **Lamed** - ox goad

Ω LIBRA

Daughter of the Lord of Truth; The Holder of the Balances

"The Twenty-second Path is the Faithful Intelligence, and is so called because by it spiritual virtues are increased, and all dwellers on earth are nearly under its shadow."

Justice holds the scales of balance. There are two types of Justice – at the human level, when one breaks a law, there is a justice system in place to pronounce judgement on us according to human perception. There is also a higher or invisible justice that is beyond human perception, holding judgement over us with much deeper insight into our psychological and spiritual make-up. The former judgement has consequences in this life. The latter judgement has much longer and deeper consequences – it is known as 'karma,' meaning 'work' or 'deed,' and it represents the principle of causality. Karma expresses an individual's sum actions, which determines their future existence.

Justice herself embodies the Egyptian goddess Ma'at, the personification of truth and balance, bringing order to the universe. The Ancient Egyptians believed that the harmony of the universe was linked to moral social behaviour. No one was above the Law of Ma'at: even the Pharaoh bowed to her rule. She was symbolized as or depicted with a single feather, which was used to weigh the *ib* (heart). It was thought that the weighing of the heart with a single feather of the goddess Ma'at was sufficient to judge whether a soul was worthy of entering *Aaru* ('the Field of Reeds'), a heavenly paradise ruled by Osiris. Osiris, who is pictured within the hexagram above Justice, holding two ankhs which symbolize the continuation of life, pronounced final judgement over the *ib*.

The Golden Dawn Neophyte Hall is the scene within the image of this Key. Justice represents the Hegemon, who has her station in the centre of the Neophyte Hall. The scales of Ma'at hold a feather, but, rather than a heart, on the other scale is a Candidate, blindfolded, and ready to enter the Hall. The centre of the scales is formed by the Hebrew letter *lamed*, the letter associated with this Key. *Lamed* is found within the centre of the Hebrew alphabet, just as this Key lies at the centre of the Major Arcana. Justice holds its influence within all the 22 Major Arcana through the underlining universal force of Love – a Love which magnetically attracts opposites, harmonizes and corrects imbalance and discord, and heals the pain of the experience of such. The balancing of archetypal forces produces a breaking down of the illusions, obsessions, and addictions to which the soul had become enslaved. As the Daughter of the Lord of Truth, her Sword connects with Geburah and cuts away unwanted focus on the material world. Once achieved, a spiritual flow is produced which can rise safely upwards, awakening the different levels of consciousness into the awareness of Universal Love.

The letter *lamed*, the meaning of which can be to goad or to prod (an ox) with a staff is also the tallest letter of the Hebrew alphabet. The staff is a symbol of authority, and Justice gives the authority to proceed upon the spiritual path, by weighing the lightness of the heart. Thus The Fool (*aleph* – 'ox') has an important role within the Key of Justice, not only as a love energy, but also as a spiritual influence or force to return to the source. Justice can only work her judgement if the soul has the desire to make the journey. The love that is at the centre of the heart allows the conscious point to be united with the Higher Self or Genius, which is not so much found in a heaven above, but deep within the Earth herself. The green robe of Justice and the dominant green colour of the card help to connect with Nature through the association with Venus, ruler of Libra and Netzach.

The fox is a symbol of wisdom, cunning and agility, and any negative associations are here subdued beneath the authority of Truth. Its place in this Key is to show the importance of discernment and focus on the path ahead. This Path is a spiritual journey where Justice turns the wheel of fate in favour of new beginnings into deeper levels of consciousness, where Love becomes the Law. To be drawn either to the right Pillar of Mercy, or the left Pillar of Severity, which are seen dominating, could lose the concentration that holds the goal in sight – the fulfilment of one's True Will – thus the constant symbolism of a central point of balance must not be overlooked with this archetypal influence of the Key. It is in the state of imbalance either toward mercy or severity that Justice is activated to regain the central ground.

WHEEL OF FORTUNE
Key 10 <small>(the 21st Path)</small>

Kaph
- fist;
palm of hand

2 JUPITER

The Lord of the Forces of Life

"The Twenty-first Path is the Intelligence of Conciliation, and is so called because it receives the divine influence which flows into it from its benediction upon all and each existence."

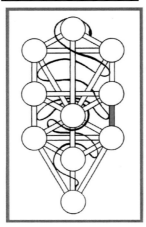

The 21st Path is placed on the right-hand side Pillar of Mercy, between the Sephiroth Netzach and Chesed. Chesed holds the reflection of the soul's true work. As it flows down to Netzach it attempts to manifest through the creative imagination, causing the soul to experience the pull of magnetic attraction and repulsion.

The Wheel of Fortune is an ancient symbol revealing the movements of the celestial spheres and their effects on our lives. Within an individual, these celestial forces can be felt as archetypes. Archetypes hold the magnetic subconscious frequencies which attract and repel outer realities into what the individual soul needs to experience, and therefore, a constant flow or movement of the Wheel brings valuable knowledge of the level of consciousness held by the soul.

The Wheel resembles an astrological chart, split into 12 segments by 12 spokes, which link to a central golden disk. The ancients placed the Sun in the centre of the Wheel, and its spokes were a division of the celestial heavens. In a modern astrological chart, the golden disk would represent the Anima Mundi, the World Soul, which has a sun-like quality. It can also represent our own centre of being, and therefore the Heart Chakra. The colours of the 12 segments are those of the Paths on the Tree of Life connected to the signs of the Zodiac within the range of Queen Scale, placing the Wheel in Briah, the World of Creation and thus indicating a birthing or bringing into existence.

The golden disk is held in place by the Hebrew letter *kaph*, giving an impression of fate or karma, as if a great hand places the soul within a certain frequency of experience. As we traditionally bless with the 'palm of the hand,' this further gives the impression of God's hand over us in blessing. The idea of a higher power manifesting as blessings in our lives is very much felt within the symbolism of the Wheel of Fortune. Jupiter is attributed to the Key, associated with greater prosperity, material and otherwise. The Wheel of Fortune implies change, new experiences, growth and reward.

Around the Wheel of Fortune can be seen many spirals, representing wheels within wheels, or different levels of consciousness being affected by its revolving motion. Within the outer circumference of the Wheel we see the repeating emblem of the triskele, which is pre-Celtic in origin and is in our modern times interpreted in many ways, one of which is birth, death, and re-birth. This spiral movement is consciousness evolving. The outer edge of the wheel is moved by fate and the celestial forces, but within the centre we begin to control our own destinies – from the outer rim, where fear is experienced, to an inward movement toward the centre, into deeper awarenesse of love.

The Wheel of Fortune also alludes to the Round Table of King Arthur where there are no hierarchical structures, yet each soul has to be weighed in accordance with its deeds. In the Egyptian Book of the Dead, Cynocephalus, the dog-headed ape, or baboon, was linked to the god Thoth in the weighing of the heart. The Sphinx above can be seen controlling the wheel, even though she does not touch it. The Sphinx can be found in the mythical story of Oedipus and the Sphinx of Thebes: Oedipus represents the idea of a flawed nature or lower self within humanity, and the search to regain control of one's fate under the weight of karmic debt. The Sphinx was described as having a woman's head and a lion's body. Within the Golden Dawn symbolisms, she also has the hind legs of a bull and the wings of an eagle, connecting the Sphinx to the four Kerubim and the Living Creatures within the wheels of Ezekiel's vision. The Sphinx represents the Higher Self and the synthesis of the elemental forces brought into balance, revealing Spirit dwelling in the centre as a unified field of consciousness.

Both dark and light, severity and mercy are experienced on this Path for the evolution and transmutation of consciousness, but the issue of karma has to be addressed before the soul can become free of the ever-turning Wheel of Fortune that constantly challenges the soul to seek deeper meaning to its existence.

THE HERMIT
Key 9 (the 20th Path)

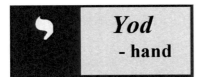

׳	*Yod* - hand

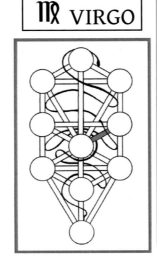

♍ VIRGO

The Magus of the Voice of Light; The Prophet of the Gods

"The Twentieth Path is the Intelligence of Will, and is so called because it is the means of preparation of all and each created being, and by this intelligence the existence of the Primordial Wisdom becomes known."

THE HERMIT ♍

The 20th Path lies between Tiphareth and Chesed. Chesed holds the true blue-print of the soul. As it pours down to Netzach it enters a strong magnetism which distracts the soul from its true purpose. But as it flows down the 20th Path into Tiphareth, the soul awakens to its True Will by linking Spirit into the conscious awareness of the individual.

The Hermit conjures up an image of an elderly man who has retreated from the world of commerce, perhaps because of some accident of fate which revealed the illusionary nature of the world. In times past, this could be achieved by retreating to a desert life, living in a cave and practising prayer and meditation. The modern mystic who desires to retreat is as likely to join some magical order or religious retreat, or will find a way to live more simply so that contemplation on the nature of God/the Goddess and the nature of one's True Will can become one's uninterrupted focus. The archetypal influence of the Hermit is first felt as a disruption in one's life, or a separation from the mainstream which is partly forced and partly chosen, depending on the strength of the ego and the individual's perception of an inner call. There is a link with the archetype of The Fool, as the soul responds to the light of the Hermit. This light has always been there as a guide but now the awareness of it awakens the soul to its True Will and therefore the ego's constructs must be left behind, as they are limited in offering but a shallow existence, which eventually produces feelings of emptiness and pain. Now that the soul has perceived the light of the Hermit, there is hope of future love and serenity.

The *Golden Dawn Temple Tarot* Key of the Hermit shows him illuminating the path in the foreground, as if to coax us through a portal of self-discovery. The three vials filled with blood and water remind us to remain silent.[1] The light that shines from his lamp is the light of Kether, shining through Tiphareth onto Malkuth. It is the hidden knowledge used to lead the Candidate on his journey from darkness into the realm of the perfect Light behind all things. His staff represents his authority to lead the way. It is coloured magenta, yellow and blue, relating to the three Mother Letters of the Hebrew alphabet, *shin*, *aleph*, and *mem*, also representing the archetypes of Judgement, The Fool and the Hanged Man, symbolizing the qualities needed to remain on the path. This is the wand of the Kerux: the Caduceus Wand as it is shown on the Hermit's chest. The twin serpents encircling the wand represent consciousness rising, awakening the chakras as it reaches certain levels of awareness. They are balanced forces of astral light working through the darkness.

The Hermit is closely related to the Magician, as Mercury rules and is exalted in Virgo, the sign which is associated with this Key. The difference between them is that the Magician's quick Mercurial mind can juggle and manipulate the elements to his/her will. The Mercury of the Hermit, embedded in the earthly Virgo, gives the ability to inwardly project deeply into an element, revealing the Divine Light behind all things.

The Hebrew letter *yod* placed just above the forehead can bring more clarity to this Key. It represents a small dot, symbolizing the Divine source of all – the source of creative energy which the light of the Hermit brings into focus. *Yod*, meaning 'hand,' can be translated as the Hand of God. God Omnipresent must be our starting point when considering the Hermit. With the *yod* being on his forehead, he has been anointed with his work to guide all who have heard the inner calling and have responded to the divine light of guidance. The light shines down on a lonely path, unique to each individual – the path of the True Will. Whatever magical tradition or structures the soul is guided into, they are only tools to lead one deeper into oneself. This is a path that the soul must tread alone.

The Hermit is a serious figure. His light is all that one needs to see. All else is but a shadow, fraught with danger – the danger of forgetfulness, the forgetfulness of who we are. The ultimate mystery is the Self. We are occult – our true heritage and nature unknown to us. But through the knowledge that the light of the Hermit reveals, a new strength is born.

---

1   From the Golden Dawn Neophyte Ceremony

STRENGTH
Key 8 (the 19th Path)

Teth
- serpent

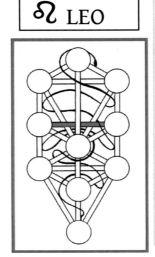
⅋ LEO

Daughter of the Flaming Sword; Leader of the Lion

"The Nineteenth Path is the Intelligence of all the activities of the spiritual beings, and is so called because of the affluence diffused by it from the most high blessing and most exalted sublime glory."

STRENGTH

Strength is one of the three horizontal Paths on the Tree of Life glyph. This 19th Path between Geburah and Chesed lies upon the Path of the Lightning Flash or Flaming Sword, infusing the Eighth Key with sublime glory of the Most High. The Lightning Flash is a conscious magnetic force that binds the Divine Light into the Four Worlds and brings into existence the Solar Light manifesting in our beautiful galaxy.

This card has a lower and a higher frequency to it. The lower is emphasized by the Hebrew letter *teth*, meaning 'serpent'. There are many meanings to the serpent – in most cases it suggests consciousness, but it can also represent a seed, further suggesting inception of Higher Consciousness. The kundalini is also represented by the serpent at the base of the card, a sexual force which transforms consciousness and brings about a rebirth on new levels of awareness. The serpent is coloured blue – the blue of water (the creative magnetism). The serpent is moving on red earth, as Adam was made from red clay, but:

"Only the Spirit, if it breathe upon the clay, can create Man."[1]

The red lion symbolizes the shadow self which holds all the negative and suppressed issues that the personality wishes to hide. As the shadow self projects archetypal influences, fear and hate are generated so that the soul is forced to confront this suppressed side of

---

1   Antoine de Saint-Exupéry, *Airman's Odyssey*, (Florida, Harcourt, 1942), 206.

itself. This restricts the link with the Higher Self. The shadow self must be faced on this Path, and be accepted into the gestalt (not eliminated), dispersing fear of rejection, and transforming hate into love.

In alchemy the red lion is the strongest force, but in this Key, the woman, Venus (green lion), begins to overwhelm the stronger force with love, further illustrated by the green grass (symbolic of life), overcoming the harsh desert sands. The desert sands in the background allude to Da'ath, over which the High Priestess must pass, leading towards the sun in the sky, symbolizing spiritual elevation. The yellow sky links this Key to the Fool, who follows the Path of love and innocence. Love has many faces, suggested by the figure 8, forever in tension between the two powerful forces of Geburah and Chesed, and the five rays radiating from the sun remind us of the strong Geburic influence of this Path.

The sign of Leo rules over this card, the main star of which (Regulus) has the meaning, 'Star of the Prince,' and also, 'Heart of the Lion,' revealing the mystery of this card: Spirit overpowers the strength of a lion through Love.

The higher nature of this card reveals that strength is not found in flesh, but that it is Spirit, the unseen, invisible force behind our visible universe, which holds true strength. The woman dressed in white is an aspect of the Empress and symbolizes purity of Spirit acting over the individual ego, as the Higher Self or Genius. Her connection with the Empress is emphasized by the open green veil revealing her beauty, yet her strength is not in her beauty. As Venus, she can also be seen as the open door of the Vault of the Adepti upon which the Kerubim are positioned. The four roses in her hand symbolize the Kerubim and further point to the four lower chakras which are under her control.

The 19th Path is not an easy Path to travel, but unlike the 27th Path of The Tower, where divine intervention redirects the rebelling ego to its true purpose, here the individual is in union with Spirit and is guided into a refinement of the Divine Law. There is a need for both acceptance and release: the acceptance of all that has been, yet abiding within the truth of who we are unfolding into, and rejecting all that may hinder the Great Work, the Magnum Opus. The Magnum Opus is considered the primal force connecting all living things, and reveals a connection between the human soul, the World Soul, and the Universal Soul (Mind of God). Upon this Path we are led deeper into ourselves, and deeper into the Earth herself, where a fuller connection with the Higher Self is made.

THE CHARIOT
Key 7 (the 18th Path)

Cheth
- fence; enclosure

Child of the Power of the Waters; Lord of the Triumph of Light

"The Eighteenth Path is called the House of Influence (by the greatness of whose abundance the influx of good things upon created beings is increased) and from the midst of the investigation the arcana and hidden senses are drawn forth, which dwell in its shade and which cling to it, from the cause of all causes."

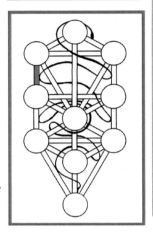

The Chariot of the Sun, as it is sometimes referred, is an apt portrayal of how the light of the Sun is carried by the Moon. As the Moon reflects the Sun's light, so also does the human soul reflect the light of the Earth Soul. The Chariot symbolizes the inward movement or journey to God; it is a journey to a place where the soul can receive rest.

Our spiritual journey does not take us to some starry heaven outside of ourselves, but deep within our own gestalt, connecting us further to the Greater Mother within the Earth. The 18th Path between Geburah and Binah takes us through the veil of the Abyss, which separates the Supernals from the seven lower Sephiroth. In Tiphareth we begin our journey into the Earth, symbolized by the Vault of the Adepti. The level of Geburah and Chesed is where we connect to the Higher Self, but it is in the Supernals that we enter the realm of the Earth Soul (the *Anima Mundi*), perceived as a beautiful Sun shining through the Earth, its life-giving rays of a magnetic light frequency. The Chariot thus leads us to the secret of rebirth: Binah, the Greater Mother, opens her yoni (the magical symbol of Binah) which opens out to a mirror universe, symbolized by Chokmah. We are then drawn further towards the centre of this mirror universe within the self, symbolized by Kether.

The Chariot acts as the throne for the Shekhinah, which has the potential to unite the

Kingdom of God with the kingdom of men. This throne relates to the order of Angels Aralim of Binah, which can be translated as 'The Strong or Mighty Ones.' *Aral* means throne; *Aralim*, thrones. They give us the authority to traverse the higher realms of consciousness. The Chariot is also connected to one's True Will, although there may be many attempts to accomplishing one's life work. The wheels of the chariot represent the Wheel of Fortune, Key 10, wherein are depicted the 12 Zodiacal segments, further connecting the Chariot to Chokmah, and the order of Angels called the *Auphanim* meaning 'Wheels.' The wheels suggest a karmic undercurrent that needs to be considered.

The Hebrew letter *cheth*, as 'enclosure' or 'fence' represents the boundary between the Kingdom of God and humanity. This invisible fence is governed by where we project our awareness – either outwards, or inwards towards a spiritual connection. The Chariot can thus be both earth-bound and celestial.

The Charioteer is characterized as the Divine Will driving the conscious point ever-deeper into the knowledge of the self. He is pointing upwards, his wings indicating that he is not of the mortal realms, but represents the Higher Self. His armour and shield hold the protective aspects of Cancer, considered to be the celestial house of the soul. At the solar plexus region of the Charioteer is a cross depicting the four directions, and in between are the colours of the four elements, representing the Kerubim, showing that the chariot can be moved in any direction by Divine Will.

> The appearance of the wheels and their workings was like the colour of beryl [gemstone of Cancer], and all four had the same likeness. The appearance of their workings was as it were a wheel in the middle of a wheel. When they moved they went toward any one of the four directions. They did not turn aside when they went.
>
> *Ezekiel 1:6 (NKJ)*

The two horses reflect the masculine and feminine aspects of God, and represent the forces emitting from the Shekinah: the black horse represents Law and the white horse Love. They are bound together by Will (the Charioteer). The two serpents symbolize sexual energy. When the forces of Love and Law are unbalanced they prevent the eagle (the high aspect of Scorpio) from projecting the sexual energy to the awaiting Supernal Mother. Instead it is projected to the lesser mother (Malkuth), which has the potential to birth a consciousness into a new physical life rather than initiating higher levels of consciousness within an individual. Yet as Child of the Powers of Water and Lord of the Triumph of Light, on all seven levels of consciousness within the kingdom of human awareness, the keen sight of the eagle will not fail to guide the Chariot to its eternal home.

THE LOVERS
Key 6 (the 17th Path)

Zayin
- sword;
armour

**Children of the
Voice Divine;
the Oracle of the
Mighty Gods**

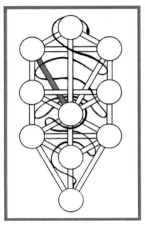

*"The Seventeenth Path is the
Disposing Intelligence which
provides Faith to the Righteous,
and they are clothed with the
Holy Spirit by it, and it is called
the Foundation of Excellence in
the state of higher things."*

THE LOVERS

The Path of The Lovers travels from Tiphareth to Binah, passing over the Abyss. This Key relates to the Orphic Egg in its creative potential of the second birth, which is linked to the human soul, the World Soul, and the Universal Soul. The human soul is the microcosm of the World Soul. The Universe can be likened to a Cosmic Egg from which all existence was birthed.

The human soul has seven levels, or bodies, which can be seen in the background of this Key, reflected onto the horizon. Above, we see a spiralling universe reflected in the clouds, hinting at the portal for celestial forces. The four elements blend together, creating a playground for an evolving soul. The dragon stone stands proud, rising to reach the opening within the spiralling clouds. Inscribed upon the stone are more spirals, hinting at the Wheel of Fortune and the eternal nature of the soul within the cyclic motion of the life and death of the garment she carries in this material dimension.

The 17th Path of the Lovers holds a tension caused by sexual magnetism between terrestrial and celestial forces. The underlining influence is to join opposing forces – such has been termed the Alchemical Wedding – and within the Golden Dawn Lovers card, the story of Andromeda and Perseus is used to describe this influence. Andromeda represents the soul chained to a dream, and Perseus represents the Higher Self attempting to free the soul from its chains. The serpent represents terrestrial consciousness and the desire to explore its beautiful layers. The serpent holds Andromeda in an illusionary place and aims to pull her deeper into its coils. But Andromeda looks only at Perseus: she is awakening from deep sleep. Perseus dives down in heroic fashion, a sun-like shield in one arm and a sword in the shape of the Hebrew letter *zain* in the other. The Lightning Flash on his sword hints at the creative pulse within this Key. As the Higher Self moves to slay the magnetic pull on the soul's consciousness, the serpent rises from the ocean of the subconscious. Andromeda is released from the spell-binder and is set free from the chains of rebirth: the serpent no longer controls Andromeda's conscious point.

Andromeda also represents the power of the reflective Moon with its deceptive waters. She is awakening to new life as the Sun's rays (Perseus' shield) shine upon her bound form. The joining of the Sun and Moon produces a seed. The serpent now becomes this seed, holding a certain level of awareness which will impregnate a higher level of consciousness.

The joining of opposing forces is further symbolized by the astrological sign of Gemini, the Twins who are forever bound together as Twin Souls. The planet Mercury rules Gemini, and through the intellectual influence of Mercury are the polarities of masculine and feminine brought together. The work begins in bringing together the astrological influences within one's own natal chart, in which the archetypal influences eventually join into a unified whole. It is clear that this work takes place below the Abyss, as Mercury's influence can only act below the Abyss. The work of joining opposites is fundamental in bringing about the balance required in order for the kundalini to rise safely. Within this work, the decision also has to be made as to whether one will sacrifice oneself to the higher spiritual work rather than to pursue the experiences to be found within the material world.

Above the Abyss, Divine Love alone holds an influence. With the sacrifice made and opposites balanced, the human soul now connects to the World Soul, bringing about a deep connection, not only to the Earth, but to humanity as a whole. From here, an Orphic Egg begins to form around the soul.

THE HIEROPHANT
Key 5 (the 16th Path)

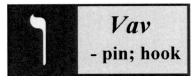

Vav
- pin; hook

Magus of the Eternal Gods

"The Sixteenth Path is the Triumphal or Eternal Intelligence, so-called because it is the pleasure of the Glory, beyond which is no other Glory like to it, and it is called also the Paradise prepared for the Righteous."

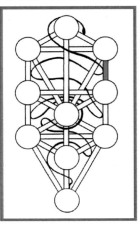

The 16th Path of the Hierophant connects Chesed (Mercy) to Chokmah (Wisdom) and is placed on the upper level of the Pillar of Mercy. It therefore passes over the Abyss. The Hierophant is connected to the sign of Taurus, giving this Key a very stable and sometimes stubborn influence; yet it is also a reflective force, and is a counterpart of the High Priestess. In order to be able to handle and explore highly intensive spiritual energies in the form of archetypes invoked through symbols, it is necessary to have a firm material base within one's home environment. It is also beneficial to join an established and proven magical Order, as such holds the experience to help on many different levels. The Hierophant reflects the laws of the spiritual realms, crystallizing them through symbols and placing them within a tradition. Within the teachings of the Golden Dawn tradition, the Neophyte is gradually introduced to the forces of Creation, which are also held within the self.

Traditionally, the Hierophant was depicted as a Pope, but the *Golden Dawn Temple Tarot* has placed Wynn Westcott, one of the GD founders, as the Hierophant. He holds a warrant for the Isis-Urania Temple. In his right hand he holds the Sceptre of Power which is used to open and close the GD Temple. The sceptre itself symbolizes the Middle Pillar on the Tree of Life. Its primary purpose is to control the elemental forces invoked within the GD ceremonies. His throne is called the Throne of Knowledge: the Hierophant holds the key symbols which allow the student to prepare for his passage over the Abyss. At the base of the throne are five *vavs*, the Hebrew letter associated with the Hierophant, representing nails which hold the tradition of the throne firmly in place. They also link to the Pentagram, a five-pointed star used to banish negativity which eventually enables the Neophyte to withstand and then to work with occult forces. Rabbi Ginsburg describes how, in Hebrew, *vav* is a term of connection –"and."

> "The first vav of the Torah –"In the beginning God created the heavens and [vav] the earth"– serves to join spirit and matter, heaven and the earth, throughout Creation."[1]

Vav is also a divine hook and is used for the hooks which held up the curtains that enclosed the Tabernacle (Exodus 27: 9, 10). In this Key, the curtain, or veil, is held in place by nine hooks, linking with the Hermit (The Magus of the Voice of Light, the Prophet of the Gods). Upon the curtain are placed the symbols of the grading system based on the four elements. The Banner of the East is placed behind the Hierophant in recognition of his role in bringing down the Divine Light in different degrees, so as to be able to explore them. Behind the veil, just visible, a rainbow further hints at the splitting of Divine Light. *Vav* also portrays the *Yashar* ('straight line'), as a beam of light from God to man, seen above the Hierophant. The three crosses on his nemyss represent the descent of Spirit through the spiritual, emotional, and mental planes.

The attribution of Taurus is also associated with sacrifice. The treading of a spiritual path will be tested in adversity so that the soul can be found strong. This struggle comes from not letting go of material concerns: at some point on one's spiritual path, and before one may cross the Abyss, self-sacrifice needs to be consciously made. The stubborn side to the Hierophant energy is also reflected in the inflexibility of a tradition – once firmly established, it is difficult for it to change, perhaps rightly so. Once a magician working within a tradition has firmly established his own True Will, it may be time to move on. The Hierophant does not just imply a teacher who can open up the spiritual path for a student, but he also acts as a priest in the role of marriage. A loving relationship is a powerful influence in bringing stability to one's life. The serpent force or kundalini is connected with the physical pleasure or sensation experienced during love-making, and has a grounding effect. Eventually the soul understands that the sexual energy can also be directed upwards, with the knowledge that love is the only force which can take us safely over the Abyss, as the vision of Saint Francis Xavier Bianchi revealed:

> After this prayer I once found myself inundated with a vivid light; it seemed to me that a veil was lifted up from before my eyes of the spirit, and all the truths of human science, even those I had not studied, became manifest to me by an infused knowledge. This state of intuition lasted for about twenty-four hours, and then, as if the veil had fallen again, I found myself as ignorant as before. At the same time, an interior voice said to me:
> "Such is human knowledge; of what use is it? It is I, it is My love, that must be studied."[2]

---

1 Ginsburgh, *The Hebrew Letters*, 94

2 From *Life of Francis Xavier Bianchi IV*. Quoted in *The Gospel of Jesus: In Search of His Original Teachings*, by John Davidson, (UK: Clear Press Ltd., 2004), 22.

THE EMPEROR
Key 4 (the 15th Path)

Heh - window

ARIES

Son of the Morning; Chief among the Mighty

"The fifteenth Path is the Constituting Intelligence and is so-called because it constitutes the substance of creation in pure darkness, and men have spoken of the contemplations..."

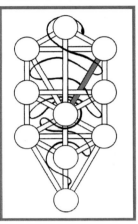

The 4th Key of the Emperor represents the Eternal Self. This is symbolized by the leminiscate – the sign of infinity upon the Emperor's waist. The Emperor also represents the generative male power. The ram under his foot is a solar emblem connecting the Sun in Tiphareth to Chokmah (Wisdom), which has the zodiacal constellations as its astrological ruler. The solar connection to the Emperor is further hinted at with the wand that he holds in his right hand, representing the godform of Amon, who symbolizes the masculine generative power to initiate new life.

Ruled by Aries, this Key is also associated with the ego, the return of the Sun, and new cycles. The eternal Higher Self brings about cyclic change in order to break up our frozen reality, which had been built by the ego's need for security but prevents growth and evolution. The new universe that opens up for the individual is like a flower which has a deep attunement to the True Will of the soul, opening up infinite experiences, thence developing discernment in making the right choices according to one's True Will rather than the inflated whims of the ego.

The Emperor sits on a square throne, relating to the psychological cube of space, which is a metaphor for looking inwardly to deeper dimensions or worlds of consciousness. This connects to Chokmah as an inwardly experienced universe which is constantly changing, giving the archetypal influence of the Emperor a temporal influence.

The Emperor holds in his left hand an orb, upon which is a cross which represents light and life as spoken by Yeshua:

> "I am the light of the world. Whoever follows Me will never walk in darkness, but will have the light of life."
>
> *John, 8: 12, (NKJ)*

The orb and cross also represents the Emperor's dominion over the powerful influence of Mars within this Key. Mars rules Aries and is linked to the kundalini life force coiled at the base of the spine. Its sudden release can bring about the dangerous side effect of infatuation, but under the control of the Higher Self the serpent fire can be projected upwards, opening higher awareness of the spiritual realms. This higher or deeper awareness produces ecstatic expressions of love: The Emperor is balanced on the opposite side of the Tree of Life by the Lovers. This smouldering power just below the surface is symbolized by the volcanoes in the distance.

The orb held by the Emperor also creates a triangle with the outer two orbs on the throne, creating a triangle and cross. The triangle represents the Supernals and is also a reflection of the creative pulse or magnetism within the Divine Light – a Three-fold Law which crystallizes the Divine Light into the Four Worlds of the Kabbalah and brings into existence our beautiful universe.

The Emperor has a unique understanding of righteousness. The archetypal influence of the Emperor is the power to change and confront wrongness with righteousness. If there are any issues with the personality as it prepares to rise over the Abyss, it is here in the Path of the Emperor that they are dealt with. The Emperor is closely connected to the energy of the Vault of the Adepti, in particular its ceiling, the energy of which produces a strong impulse to do the right thing and to confront and challenge that which does not vibrate to Divine Will.

The Hebrew letter *heh* is assigned to this Key. It can be seen framing the Emperor. *Heh,* meaning 'window,' shows that the Emperor sees through the veil of the Abyss into the All-Father Chokmah. The letter *Heh* is used twice to spell out the unpronounceable name of God, *Yod Heh Vav Heh,* holding the masculine and feminine in union. *Yod* represents a seed, and the first *Heh* represents a womb. *Vav* represents the male phallus, and the final *Heh* with a dot within signifies conception and brings into being new life. Within the imagery of this Key, both the the sigil of infinity and the cross of Christ are placed within the *heh*, revealing this Key's deeper meaning as the salvation into eternal life, which reflects God within the heart of man, thus connecting to the Heart Chakra. Through the Heart Chakra the womb of rebirth is opened – such is called Wisdom.

THE EMPRESS
Key 3 (the 14th Path)

Daleth
- door

Daughter of the Mighty Ones

"The Fourteenth Path is the Illuminating Intelligence, and is so-called because it is that brilliant one which is the founder of the concealed and fundamental ideas of holiness and of their stages of preparation."

♀ VENUS

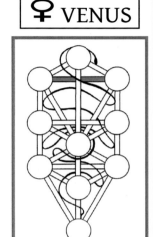

The Empress is Creation on every level, thus there are many aspects to this Key. She is Mother Nature, and as such holds authority over the elemental forces. She also holds authority over the kundalini energy. She veils the Divine Light, yet at the same time acts as a doorway to that same Light, which underpins all matter in the universe. As the Daughter of the Mighty Ones she keeps the balance in conjunction with the Watchtowers, allowing life to fulfil its mission to transform all of Creation to its highest potential. She represents the journey to the Soul of the Earth and also the doorway to the Inner Universe.

The 14th Path of the Empress aligns with the path of the Lightning Flash. The Lightning Flash on the Tree of Life acts as a magnetic or unifying principle and is likened to a downward movement of the serpent force. Although depicted as a sword or lightning flash, its downward motion is slow and pulsates with the rhythm of the cosmic breath – its magnetism holding the Tree of Life together in triangular patterns, first witnessed within *Ain Soph* as the crystallized structure of the Divine Light.

The Empress embodies the unifying principle of opposing masculine and feminine forces. Her power is in sexual magnetism, uniting the mighty Binah and Chokmah, the Archetypal Mother and Father. As an archetype herself, The Empress can be used to direct the sexual energy or serpent force up to the Crown, Kether. Her authority in this area is symbolized by her magenta-coloured gown and the staff in her right hand, surmounted by a white sphere which represents Kether and encompasses the triangle of the Supernals.

The Three Supernals are a representation of the Holy Trinity, and the imagery of this Key is rich in corresponding symbolism: the Divine Name *YHVH* is inscribed upon her golden breastplate, with the central *shin* spelling 'YEHESHUA' over her heart. The dove of the Holy Spirit hovers above her. The golden breastplate reveals that the four elements have been purified and signifies the four risen elemental serpents, demonstrating the authority of the Empress over the elemental forces. Yeheshua has removed karma, allowing the higher consciousness to continue with the Great Work.

The 14th Path is beyond the influence of the Abyss. This Path supports the entire Tree of Life. It is crossed by the Path of the High Priestess, which leads from Tiphareth to Kether: these two Paths generate the glyph of the cross of Christ in the higher echelons of the Tree of Life. The Path of the Empress forms a stabilising horizontal support to the vertical Path of the High Priestess, revealing an earthly stability maintained by the archetype of the Empress which allows for unhindered exploration beyond the open veil of the High Priestess when treading the 13th Path.

The Empress is seated upon a throne which is coloured green with a hint of gold and carved with the paws of a lion. The throne symbolizes the alchemical green lion.

'The Green Lion is the Innermost of everyone.
This work is performed with the Vitriol of Venus.
V.I.T.R.I.O.L. – "Visita Interiora Terrae Rectificando Invenies Occultul Lapidem." –
"Visit the interior of the earth, which by rectifying, you will find the occult stone."
It is necessary to visit our own interior Earth in order to find our blessed stone.'[1]

The Empress is Mother Nature herself. Her green robe links her to the Sephira of Netzach and Venus, the planet of love. She is beautiful, wise, and is the essence of fecundity – fruitful and fertile, as demonstrated by her pregnant form and the cornucopia of the fruit of Venus at her feet. Twin souls within her womb further signify the blessed union of Wisdom and Understanding. In her left hand she holds the ankh, an Egyptian symbol of life, on her lap. The ankh is shaped like the glyph of Venus and is divided by colour into 10 segments representing the Ten Sephiroth of the Tree of Life. Holding the ankh by its lower divisions, her finger points to the opening which overlays her womb. Through this opening can be seen the girdle of Venus, decorated with the symbols of the zodiac. The Empress is pointing towards the doorway which leads to the universe within.

The Hebrew letter associated with the 14th Path is *Daleth*, meaning 'door.' The Empress acts as a doorway into many different levels of consciousness. On a physical level, the

---

1   Samael Aun Weor, *Treatise of Sexual Alchemy* (New York: Glorian Publishing, 2012),13.

sexual union of male and female acts as the doorway to one of the closest physical expressions of a spiritual realm that a person can experience – orgasm. The phallic expression of the serpent enters the Empress and awakens or stimulates the spiritual light hidden by her veil, which then floods into the physical, enlivening every cell with heightened sensitivity, allowing the experience of momentary bliss, illumination, and impregnation.

On another level, the golden beryl stones placed in her diadem highlight the link between The Empress and the Opening of the Third Eye, wherein a rising seed enters the Brow Chakra and opens out into a beautiful flower. This magical process is repeated on many other levels within Nature and oneself, from the seeds of earth's vegetation, the activation of chakras, and the rising of serpents, revealing the Empress to be the archetypal Greater Mother. She wears a brooch with an emerald in the shape of a rosebud – the emerald is a form of beryl, emitting the Green Ray and connecting to the Heart Chakra.

Above her is a green veil, upheld by seven copper rings, further connecting the Empress to Netzach and Venus. The veil represents the visible natural world, symbolized by its pattern of green leaves, and it veils the Divine Light. However, at the sides we see a glimpse of this Light, drawing back into itself the decaying leaves which dissolve once more into the divine matrix. The veil is suspended by the Hebrew letter *daleth*, suggesting that yet another doorway exists whereby one may penetrate nature into its deeper realms: this hints at the door of the Vault of the Adepti, which opens from the Venus Panel. The Vault of the Adepti acts as a womb of the Great Mother and gives birth to Adepts. Within the Vault lies the opportunity to connect with the Soul of the Earth via one's Heart Chakra. A further door is found within the Soul of the Earth which leads towards one's inner universe. The dove reminds us that the key to open these doors is love – the divine Love which overrides one's desire to experience the physical realm, seeking spiritual fulfilment beyond the natural world.

THE HIGH PRIESTESS
Key 2 (the 13th Path)

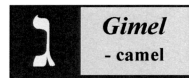

Gimel
- camel

MOON

Priestess of the Silver Star

"The Thirteenth Path is named the Uniting Intelligence and is so-called because it is itself the Essence of Glory; it is the Consummation of the Truth of individual spiritual things."

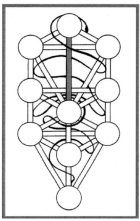

Anyone who walks a spiritual path will at some point need to face the High Priestess, as it is she who guards the gateway to the higher mysteries. The High Priestess is the Divine Feminine, and the working of the High Priestess is to reflect or awaken the awareness of the Divine Light dwelling within all who seek her. The High Priestess dissolves illusions. She ensures that the diverse archetypal forces are in balance and in harmony, and this allows the kundalini or serpent force to rise safely, which brings a deeper connection to higher forms of consciousness.

The 13th Path unites Tiphareth with Kether, forming the upper portion of the Middle Pillar on the Tree of Life which began with the Keys of the Universe and Temperance, connecting with Malkuth and Yesod. This is a holy Path to tread, a Path of Righteousness, and its influence is felt in the lower portion of the Middle Pillar, even as the colour blue becomes more refined from the lowest Path of the Middle Pillar to the topmost. The High Priestess can be seen through the workings of the spiritual fire that is kindled on the 22nd Path of the Universe, as we are awoken to a spiritual reality. As the spiritual fire rises into the 25th Path of Temperance, it begins to purify and increase in intensity, until it rises with such ferocity that it feels as if it will consume us. At this point, the fire collapses into a single line of silver from Malkuth to Kether, vibrating with vigour. As the silver line stills it becomes the pillar upon which the serpent force may rise: this is the Path of the High Priestess.

The Middle Pillar is the balance of the two Pillars of Mercy and Severity. In this image, one Pillar is coloured the magenta of Geburah instead of the traditional black, symbolizing the force of Severity that pulls and buffets the 13th Path. This severity is further highlighted by Diana's Bow leaning against the Pillar. The other Pillar is coloured the blue of Chesed instead of white to symbolize the gift of Mercy, further emphasised by the Hegemon's Wand. Love is the main attribute needed to travel this Path, as love unites all opposites into one harmonious, living pulse of life, guided by the still, silent voice of God.

When treading the Path of the High Priestess, one encounters two main impulses. Both are felt throughout, but the increase in purification as one travels closer to Kether brings a wider parting of the veil, an increase in light, and thus a shift in consciousness, as light and consciousness are linked. The first deals with the self-discipline necessary to traverse the desert-like terrain which crosses over the Abyss. It is likely that the individual treading this path will need to fast in some way, motivated by spiritual desire, and thus quite probably life-changing. The Hebrew letter that is associated with this path is *gimel* (camel) and is worn around the neck of the High Priestess. The camel can travel great distances and can go for long periods without water. Similarly, the Adept who travels this path is filled with light, which sustains and strengthens him spiritually, overriding the impulses of the flesh which can interrupt the long and difficult journey.

Once safely beyond the Abyss and in the realm of the Supernals, the Path of the High Priestess is influenced by those of the Empress, the Magician and The Fool. At this point, the impulse is to mentally let go, and to trust Spirit. The mind needs to be free from physical attachment and focus upon the intuitive faculty for the guidance to cross this Path safely. The Empress promises stability in the physical, because the soul is in harmony with Divine Law. The High Priestess interacting with the Magician breaks the illusion that the physical is dependent upon the physical and the intellectual, and activates the understanding that the soul is under the spiritual rule of the Divine Will. The Fool encourages the surrender to faith and openness of heart and mind which are necessary to receive the wisdom of the 13th Path.

The 13th Path of the High Priestess awakens individuals to the spiritual law, linking them to the Word of God. Older versions of the High Priestess, sometimes called The Papass, held a scroll, the Torah, in her hand. The High Priestess is closely linked to the Shekhinah. The Shekhinah could be considered to be the feminine aspect of God, and is linked to the internal fire of the kundalini. The Shekhinah has an upper and a lower presence; in its upper realm within the Supernals it is experienced as masculine, but in its lower realm it is experienced as feminine and can be seen as serpentine. It is through the written word, the Torah, that the Shekhinah was able to be grounded on Earth, enabling the work of rising the lower Shekhinah back to its divine home. The Torah is holy instruction transmitted uniquely to the heart of each individual rather than an external dogma that has to be blindly followed.

> "I will give my laws in their hearts, and in their souls will I write them..."
>
> *Heb. 10:16 (Jubilee Bible, 2000)*

The High Priestess of the *Golden Dawn Temple Tarot* holds a cup resembling the Cup of the Stolistes, the Purifier. At the rim of the cup are moonstones which symbolize the stimulation of intuition. The moonstone was once called the Traveller's Stone, and was carried as a protective stone on journeys. The cup is also a symbol of spiritual receptivity. The pearl that resides at the stem of the cup relates to the Moon and brings the gift of inner vision. She is also offering us the secret of the Holy Grail: the King and the land are one.

Sheela-na-Gig is a symbol of the consummation of the King and the Land: this figure illustrates the close connection between the High Priestess and the Empress. The archetypal feminine principle behind the High Priestess may take different forms. In recent years, the image of the High Priestess has become more youthful and sensual, alluding to her virginal nature, and in this guise she is the underlining principle of Spirit which gives life to the universe. Sheela-na-Gig on the other hand portrays an old woman which alludes to the ancient nature of this Light. Yet the Light is forever giving of itself and never changing.

The High Priestess personifies the reflective Lunar force, symbolized by the Horned Crescent and Full Moon upon her head. Through the movement and changing phases of the Moon, suppressed issues which block the flow of Divine Light through the body are drawn to the surface of awareness. Issues that have been denied and ignored, hidden from sight, or shrouded in guilt, are gradually pulled from the shadows and given conscious awareness. This magical process may be interpreted as negative by those who resist facing their suppressed fears. On the belt of the High Priestess is written the name GABRIEL. 'Gabriel' means The Strong One of God, also known as Gabriel of Luna. The Archangel Gabriel often acts as a guide through the inner light, also awakening the awareness of deeper levels of existence beyond the physical. She is said to instruct the soul during the nine months of pregnancy.

A veil shaped like a yoni opens behind and around the figure. Unlike the veil of the Empress, the veil of the High Priestess is almost transparent. This veil symbolizes the threshold where the five senses give way to intuition and the inner sight. It seems to hide a great ocean that is in itself a camouflage of the great depths of the unconscious, now becoming conscious. Within the yoni can be seen a silvery glow which has a reflective quality, indicating a mirror effect. When we look deeply into the mysteries we see ourselves looking back at us, and the aphorism "Know Thyself" rises to the surface.

THE MAGICIAN
Key 1 (the 12th Path)

Beth
- house

☿ MERCURY

The Magus of Power

"The Twelfth Path is the Intelligence of Transparency, because it is that species of Magnificence, called CHAZCHAZIT, which is named the place whence issues the vision of those seeing in apparitions. (That is, the prophecies by seers in a vision.)"

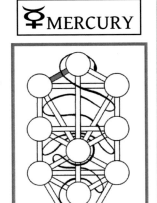

ꓱ THE MAGICIAN ☿

The Magician stands alone yet is surrounded by archetypal forces within the Supernal realm. Without the understanding of these forces, he could not complete his divine mission. The balancing of these archetypal forces enables the kundalini to rise safely, enabling the Magician to see and work within the inner realms, and making the Magician a powerful archetype in his own right.

In this image, an emphasis is placed upon the Magician's will: he has a strong forehead illuminated by light which emanates from the godform Ptah, the Ancient Egyptian god of artists, architects and craftsmen in general. The archetypal influence of the Magician in its purest form is the manifestation of Divine Will, through communication, and via the creative ordering of one's personal universe.

Above the Magician can be seen the Hebrew letter *beth*, meaning 'house,' 'dwelling-place,' or 'internal,' hinting at the deeper levels of consciousness that are being experienced. From *beth* flows the veil of the High Priestess which separates the intellect from the intuitive nature, but which is now wide open. Its yellow and white stripes indicate the nemyss of an Adept; these colours also show the influence of Kether and Mercury, and hint at the Fool's spiritual influence upon this Key. In the background, the Vault door, also open, is connected to the Empress and to the planet Venus, showing that the Magician has reached his understanding through the power of love. It is said that the Vault of the Adepti holds the complete mysteries of the Western Mystery tradition. The

Vault acts as a tomb which symbolizes entering the Earth, within which we are drawn to the unfathomable depths of the Universe. The Vault represents our own spiritual self at the centre of the Universe. The Vault acts as the macrocosm for the Magician, who is the microcosm. Both the Magician and the Vault are houses of the Spirit.

The Magician wears the Rosy Cross Lamen, representing the mystical centre of our inner universe. It also symbolizes the connection between all Adepts as one body in the Great Work. The Rosy Cross Lamen is in many ways a device which opens the heart centre, something only possible when a Magician is in tune with the will of his Higher Self.

The Magician's understanding of the spiritual laws enable him to connect to the matrix from which he brings about changes in accordance with Divine Will. The Magician holds a Lotus Wand, linked to Isis and so further associated with the Shekhinah. The wand indicates his status as Adept. It acts as a lock to the forces within the Magician's will. The coloured bands link into the zodiacal planes within the inner universe of the Magician, and in holding the wand by the white-coloured segment, he suggests that he is invoking or rising up within the spiritual planes.

Above the Lotus Wand is the godform Atum. The name 'Atum' is thought to derive from the word 'tem', meaning 'to complete or finish', and is thought to represent the underlining substance of our world. Atum is also a godform associated with Kether, which shows that the Magician's power does not come from his own will, but rather from drawing the creative will through Kether. Atum was also depicted in serpent form. The Magician wears a serpent belt, the ouroboros, symbolizing eternity, with the name "MICHAEL" in Hebrew overlaid. The name of Archangel Michael suggests that the Magician's lower conscious awareness is being controlled and guided by higher angelic forces. Archangel Michael was believed to hold the keys to the Underworld, suggesting that the archangel is also able to control the kundalini force.

Serpents symbolize different levels of consciousness. The consciousness of Kether holds the Divine Name, *YHVH*, which further holds the creative potential of the four worlds, represented on the altar of the double cube as wand, cup, knife, and pentacle (Fire, Water, Air, and Earth). To each element a serpent is attached, acting as a magnetic crystallizing force to manifest the element of focus from within the Divine Light. The Magician can manipulate the elemental magnetic force to help balance the occult forces within nature, or he can direct the serpent up into the Supernals, rising his personal level of consciousness in an alchemical process of purification, death and rebirth.

The Path of the Magician from Kether to Binah connects the Universal Soul to the Earth Soul. The Empress and the Fool both connect to Chokmah, creating the first triangle in the Tree of Life, called the Supernal Triad. The glyph of the Tree of Life teaches us about the Creative Laws; that of the Tree of the Knowledge of Good and Evil teaches us about the Return. The Threefold Law that constructs the glyph of the Tree has its origins within *Ain Soph*.

The Magician is invoking LVX (LUX – Light). LVX reveals the Threefold Law of *Ain Soph* which splits into *Ain* (No-thing), *Ain Soph* (Limitless Light), and *Ain Soph Aur* (Limitless Light in Extension). The Threefold Law within the negative existence reveals the creation of the Divine Light before it enters the Sephira of Kether. LVX is the formula for the Great Work – to re-enter or penetrate the negative existence where there is no separation from One.

The Magician thus becomes the conduit for *Ain Soph*, as he has learned and mastered the archetypal forces of the Tree of Life and, with the aid of the serpent force, has risen and understood the Tree of the Knowledge of Good and Evil, enabling him to use the occult forces without them controlling him, which would otherwise convert him into a black magician. He has used his intelligence, through the medium of imagination, to project his now divine will, invoking an alchemical process within his own universe, symbolized by the hexagram above the elemental tools. He stands between heaven and earth and moves the elements in new combinations to bring about the balance that allows the Magician to penetrate deep into the Divine Light, returning with prophetic insight.

THE FOOL
Key 0 (the 11th Path)

Aleph
- ox

Spirit of Aether

"The Eleventh Path is the Scintillating Intelligence because it is the essence of that curtain which is placed close to the order of the disposition, and this is a special dignity given to it that it may be able to stand before the Face of the Cause of Causes."

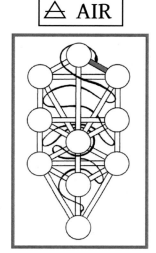

△ AIR

ℵ   THE FOOL   △

The Fool is the initiation of the soul into the truth of itself.

This version of The Fool depicts a boy who has grown through his first cycle of a seven-year period. Some of the Stella Matutina ideas are combined with the Rider-Waite imagery of the Fool: rather than a baby holding a wolf, we have the Fool wearing a wolf-skin, giving the image both a shamanic and an animistic slant. The wolf-skin is invisibly connected to the serpent of desire that pulls against a spiritual longing. It represents the flesh or animal self, which is no longer the focal point. The wolf-skin also hints that the Fool has acquired a sixth sense – a natural faculty of the animal kingdom.

The background colour is yellow, representing the element of Air, but more precisely, Ruach (spirit). The connection between air and spirit is encapsulated by the fact that the element of Air is invisible yet is essential for the maintenance of life, beautifully symbolizing the invisible presence of Spirit throughout life in the Universe. The Fool is also associated with the planet Uranus, not used within Golden Dawn symbolism, but acknowledged as the higher octave of Mercury.

The Three Ring-Pass-Nots can be drawn as a sphere – traditionally the top half would be white and the bottom half darker. We have placed this sphere behind the Fool, showing that his destiny lies beyond the Sephira of Kether, to which he reaches – the top-most rose or fruit on the tree (which is depicted here as the Ace of Wands and represents the entire

Tree of Life in Atziluth). The Divine Light within *Ain Soph* emanates from Kether as the World of Atziluth. Atziluth also represents the element of Fire, which returns everything it touches to the Divine Light. As the Fool reaches towards the highest point on the Tree he leans over a precipice, revealing the powerful, ever-present Da'ath (Knowledge). Da'ath is a dangerous place for those Adepts who consider knowledge to be of greater importance than insight and experience, from which wisdom and understanding are gained. The Fool, however, unreservedly lets go of all the academic knowledge he has gained, even though he appreciates that his studies have served him well and helped to guide his soul to this level of awareness. All his learning has been imbued with the Divine Spark which guides him still further, yet his former opinions and understandings are as nothing to him now, standing in the humility of one standing before the Face of the Cause of Causes. The Fool has been graced with the unique awareness of the One – the oneness of all things within a "Great Mind," or "Consciousness," or "Intelligence." There are no words to describe this awareness – it must be experienced, and once experienced, even for a short time, it will become the obsessive motive of a life to regain and remain within this level of awareness. The experience of Kether is actual Union with God. This is where we get the contradiction of Unity, as Crowley put it.[1] The Fool is still carrying his animal self (meaning he is still within a living, breathing body, scarred by the long and arduous journey undertaken to arrive at this level of reality), yet is at the same time separated from it, as separated from the wolf-skin on his back. The animal self constantly pulls at the Fool, ever-seeking his attention: a glimpse of the universal conscious awareness quickly dissipates into self-awareness.

The Fool began his journey locked within Time and Space on the 32nd Path of the Universe, in which Key the Kerubim are depicted guarding the realms between Time/Space and the Place beyond Time. The Kerubim are the living powers of the Divine Name of Kether, *YHVH*. Now, on the 11th Path, the Fool discovers non-time: his conscious point locks into a Universal Consciousness which transcends Time; it is everywhere, all at once, and yet still within the Time/Space framework of the manifested universe. The Archangel Gabriel rules over the Kerubim, connecting us to the 13th Path of the High Priestess who guards the veil into the Universal Sea of Consciousness and initiates the Fool's growing awareness of its unfathomable nature.

The Three Paths that emanate from the Cause of Causes make up the formula of magic: the 11th Path of the Fool reveals that one must raise one's conscious point into Spirit before a magical operation can begin, and raise it to the Cause of Causes to engage in the creative power of one's being. It is only then that the power of the will of the 12th Path of the Magician can be projected unhindered and imprinted into the Shekhinah. The 13th Path of the High Priestess, in accordance with celestial law, through the power of Luna reflects the will or thought imprint into the dense reality of our material universe. The

1   Aleister Crowley, *Book of Thoth* (San Francisco: Weiser Books, 2006), 63.

Fool archetype frees you to BE YOURSELF in the light of the creative will.

Aleph is the Hebrew letter attributed to this card and gives further insight to the archetype of the Fool. It is the first letter, and its image is an ox or a sacrificed ox. *Aleph*, on an earthly level, can be seen as a plough symbolizing penetration of earth, or on a higher level, symbolizing the divine spark descending into the primordial waters and seeding it with potential. The structure of the letter *aleph* is in three parts – there is an upper *yod*, interpreted as *Ain Soph* and a lower *yod* which can be seen as Kether. They are both attached to a central rising line in between which shows the link or unity between a Universe within Time and Space, and a Universe beyond Time, separated by a great rising serpent.

Jesus portrayed Himself as the *Aleph-Tau* in several Scriptures, and also as the Ox of *aleph*, signifying the childlike, Fool-like, simplicity of the state of knowing God through Yeshua/Jesus, and also revealing the karmic burden which is taken from us through His sacrifce.

> At that time Jesus declared, "I thank you, Father, Lord of heaven and earth,
> that you have hidden these things from the wise and understanding
> and revealed them to little children;
> Yes, Father, for such was your gracious will.
> All things have been handed over to me by my Father, and no one knows the Son
> except the Father, and no one knows the Father except the Son
> and anyone to whom the Son chooses to reveal him.
> Come to me, all who labor and are heavy laden,
> and I will give you rest. Take my yoke upon you, and learn from me,
> for I am gentle and lowly in heart, and you will find rest for your souls.
> For my yoke is easy, and my burden is light."
>
> *Matt. 11: 25-30 (English Standard Version)*

AIN SOPH

and the Birth of the
Tree of Life

Ain Soph
and the Birth of the Tree of Life

The Tree of Life glyph is structured to teach us about the law of *Ain Soph*, revealing the birth of the Divine Light which separates into the Four Worlds of the Kabbalah: *Atziluth*, the World of Emanation, *Briah*, the World of Creation, *Yetzirah*, the World of Formation, and *Assiah*, the World of Action. Above the Tree of Life are portrayed three lines, the Ring-Pass-Nots, which are considered impenetrable. These realms are called *Ain* (Nothing), *Ain Soph* (Limitless), and *Ain Soph Aur* (the Limitless Light).

The concept of *Ain Soph* first appears in the writings of Isaac the Blind of France (1160-1235). His real name was Rabbi Yitzach Saggi Nehor ('Saggi Nehor' means 'much light') and despite his blindness he was able to penetrate deep into the "Root of all Roots." His insights transformed the mystical tradition of the Geonic period into how we view the Kabbalah today. Isaac believed that *Ain Soph* is a Mind emanating Divine Thought or Will, and that from this Will emanated the Ten Sephiroth. He taught that living beings are material manifestations of the Sephiroth, and that through our mystic experiences, consciousness evolves, ascending the levels of emanation until it becomes possible to unite with Divine Thought or Will.

Ain Soph was considered the substance of God Himself, imminent within all Creation. The first Christians equated the concept of *Ain Soph* with the Christ as the Sustainer and Preserver of the universe. 16th Century Lurianic doctrine further developed the concept of *Ain Soph* thus: within God, everything already existed. God contracted part of Himself into a monad, which was termed ZIMZUM, meaning contraction, and *Ain* came into being – a point of light within Nothingness. *Ain* began to vibrate, birthing from within itself many more sparks of light. These lights were souls innumerable which spread chaotically throughout the Dark Light within the realm of *Ain Soph*. This chaos became ordered by the Mind of God. The sparks or souls began to pull together in triangular forms.

The research of Gershom Scholem, in his book, 'Kabbalah,' describes this triangular formation as the three lights – the primordial inner light spread throughout the root of all roots.

"…above all emanated powers, there exist in the "root of all roots" three hidden lights which have no beginning, "for they are the name and essence of the root of

all roots and are beyond the grasp of thought." As the "primeval inner light" spreads throughout the hidden root two other lights are kindled...
It is stressed that these three lights constitute one essence and one root which is "infinitely hidden," forming a kind of kabbalistic trinity that precedes the emanation of the ten Sefirot." [1]

The Four Worlds

Kabbalistic teachings quote Isaiah 43:7 as being associated with the division of the Four Worlds:

> "**Everyone who is called** (Atziluth - World of Emanation) **by My name,**
> **And whom I have created** (Briah - World of Creation) **for My glory,**
> **Whom I have formed** (Yetzirah - World of Formation),
> **even whom I have made** (Assiah - World of Action)."
>
> *Isaiah 43:7 (NASB)*

For the aspirant who seeks to understand how the Mind/*Ain Soph* that is considered One without division brings forth the Four Kabbalistic Worlds and gives birth to the Tree of Life, searching the written explanations of those who have grasped the concept can make for a frustrating task. Many years before my initiation into the Golden Dawn, I had an encounter with an elemental being who greatly helped to elucidate these concepts, and who could in fact be considered the author of the explanation given below.

At first, the magnetic pull between these lights was very weak. The points of light or sparks were a great distance apart, with broken magnetic lines weakly connecting and drawing them slowly together. This contraction was the crystallization or creation of Divine Light. It was the birth of the Shekhinah, and, within *Ain Soph*, the World of *Atziluth*, the archetypal aspect of the element of Fire, was produced. As the contraction and crystallization of the divine sparks continued, the broken lines of magnetized thought became stable, and a thin but weak magnetic line formed the World of *Briah*. This magnetic force corresponds to the physical element of Air, making Briah the archetype of Air. As the points of light were drawn even closer and the magnetic force became ever stronger, the World of *Yetzirah* was formed. This magnetic force equates to the physical element of Water: Yetzirah is the archetype of Water. Once the sparks of light became packed together tightly, the World of *Assiah* was formed – the archetype of the element of Earth.

In the Golden Dawn system, Briah is attributed to the denser magnetic field of Water (Yetzirah) while Yetzirah is attributed to Air, swapping the positions of these two elements. Each Kabbalistic world contains all four elements as its frequency slows down (as revealed in the Court Cards), thus in accordance with the increasing density of elements

---

1   Gershom Scholem, *Kabbalah* (Jerusalem: Keter Publishing House Jerusalem Ltd, 1987), 95.

through the crystallizing of the Divine Light within *Ain Soph*, the Golden Dawn works with a higher frequency of Yetzirah (by assigning Air to Yetzirah) and a lower frequency of Briah (by assigning Water to Briah).

One day, during my early study of Kabbalah, I went for a walk in a beautiful valley near where I was living. Deep in thought about the Four Worlds, I saw something on the ground which resembled four circles. Suddenly, a gnome-like, elemental being with an ethereal or non-material form appeared on my shoulder. I was not at all surprised as I knew that he had been with me since childhood, although he seldom made an appearance. With no introduction, he said:

"Look into this rock."

Beside me was a large rock. The gnome said I should use my Third Eye as a microscope. I suddenly found myself seeing into the rock: first I saw its molecular structure, then into the atomic realm, and then deeper into what I presumed to be the world of quarks. He kept repeating that I should penetrate deeper, until I came to a blackness which seemed to go on forever. Still he encouraged me to look deeper, until finally I came out into a beautiful light. I thought I had reached my destination, but he said:

"Now penetrate into the spiritual light until you find its structure."

Eventually I could clearly see the structure within the Divine Light – it was a tightly-packed magnetic structure of crystallized light of a triangular form which connected to balls or globes of light. The gnome said:

"This is the World of Assiah."

He then told me to look into the water of the river on the other side of me. A similar visual experience came about except that the darkness didn't last as long. The magnetic structure of the Divine Light was not so tightly-packed and seemed to be more pliable, but it still kept its triangular shape, although a little more loosely.

"This is the World of Yetzirah," he said.

He then told me to look at the air, and again the same process unfolded, but when I saw the structure of the Divine Light it was very weak in its magnetic structure and the points of light were quite far apart.

"This is the World of Briah," he said.

Lastly he told me to look at the light of the Sun, but not the Sun itself. I found this very difficult, but eventually I penetrated into the sunlight, reached the Divine Light, and eventually its magnetic structure, which was in fact chaotic. The points of light were of immensely long distances apart and the magnetic field was broken. I had been shown the World of Atziluth, and I could then understand why fire burns: if this chaotic magnetic field is placed over any other field it will break it up and return it to the Divine Light. I also found that physical light and the structure of the Divine Light are very similar and difficult to distinguish between.

The crystallization belongs to a serpentine pulse within *Ain Soph* that works its way through the structure within the Divine Light in the form of the Lightning Flash depicted upon the Tree of Life.

In being given this experience, it shows that elemental beings are not just some low level elemental force, but that they have the ability to penetrate *Ain Soph*: they hold the blueprint of all creation in their work of perfecting each individual creation to its highest potential, making them true alchemists.

Within the context of the Four Worlds, it is also interesting to examine other sources, such as the first 13 verses of the book of Genesis, which detail the first three days of Creation:

> In the beginning God created the heavens and the earth. The earth was without form, and void; and darkness was on the face of the deep. And the Spirit of God was hovering over the face of the waters.
>
> Then God said, "Let there be light"; and there was light. And God saw the light, that it was good; and God divided the light from the darkness. God called the light Day, and the darkness He called Night. So the evening and the morning were the first day.
>
> Then God said, "Let there be a firmament in the midst of the waters, and let it divide the waters from the waters." Thus God made the firmament, and divided the waters which were under the firmament from the waters which were above the firmament; and it was so. And God called the firmament Heaven. So the evening and the morning were the second day.
>
> Then God said, "Let the waters under the heavens be gathered together into one place, and let the dry land appear"; and it was so. And God called the dry land Earth, and the gathering together of the waters He called Seas... So the evening and the morning were the third day.
>
> *Genesis 1: 1-13 (NJK Bible)*

In the Discourse of Hermes Trismegistus: Poimandres,[2] we read:

> ...from the light...a holy word mounted upon the (watery) nature, and untempered fire leapt up from the watery nature to the height above. The fire was nimble and piercing and active as well, and because the air was light it followed after spirit and rose up to the fire away from earth and water so that it seemed suspended from the fire. Earth and water stayed behind, mixed with one another, so that (earth) could not be distinguished from water, but they were stirred to hear the spiritual word that moved upon them.

Donald Tyson, editor and annotator of Agrippa's Three Books of Occult Philosophy, paraphrases Plato's explanation (in the *Timaeeus*) of the relationship between the four elements, following the same sequence:[3]

> The world is one and not many because the Creator is one, and the world is his image. That this single world might be visible he framed it of Fire. That it might be tangible he formed it from Earth. But these two elements could not be joined without a medium in the nature of an arithmetical mean. Had the world been planar one mean would have sufficed, but because the world was solid, two means, Water and Air were necessary. Fire is to Air as Air is to Water, and Air is to Water as Water is to Earth.

YHVH and the Four Elements

Golden Dawn teachings assign the Four Letters of the Divine Name, *YHVH (Yod, Heh, Vav, Heh)* to the Four Worlds and to the Four Elements, resulting in a different order of elements. Thus in the *Golden Dawn Temple Tarot:*

> *Yod* equates to Fire and the World of Atziluth,
> *Heh* relates to Water and the World of Briah,
> *Vav* relates to Air and the World of Yetzirah,
> *Heh* final relates to Earth and the World of Assiah.

The Four Elemental Worlds are represented by the four suits of Wands, Cups, Swords, and Pentacles. The Four Letters are also attributed to the Kings (*Yod*), Queens, (*Heh*) Princes (*Vav*) and Princesses (final *Heh*) of the Court Cards, wherein the four elemental worlds relate to the spiritual, emotional, mental, and physical bodies, respectively.

---

2 Brian P. Copenhaver, trans. *Hermetica*. (Cambridge, UK: Cambridge University Press, 1992), 1.
3 Tyson, ed., *Three Books of Occult Philosophy*. (Woodbury, MN: Llewellyn Publications. 2009), 713.

The four suits find compatability or incompatability with each other, which relates to their inclination to either rise or fall. Tyson explains this through quoting Aristotle:[1]

> "The elements may be divided into a number of contrasting pairs. Fire and Air both expand and rise, and are, Aristotle says, "forms of the body moving towards the limit" (ibid.). In contrast, Earth and Water contract and fall, and are "forms of the body which moves towards the centre" (ibid.). Fire and Earth form the pair of extremes, because in the natural order of the elements Fire rises to the top and Earth falls to the bottom. Aristotle says they are the "purest." Water and Air, on the other hand, form the pair of intermediaries and are "more like blends." Also, "the members of either pair are contrary to those of the other, Water being contrary to Fire and Earth to Air" (ibid). That is to say, the powers of Fire, which are hot-dry, are contrary to the powers of Water, which are cold-moist, and so for Air and Earth.

In the Tarot cards:

Wands pull upward towards Spirit.

Pentacles pull downwards towards Earth, creating a tension.

Swords show the upward movement inherent in the attraction of the mind to the higher Mind. They also reveal mental blocks in the upward flow.

Cups show the downward movement of divine energy (Azoth) and also reveal emotional blocks that can hinder this flow.

The upward movement of Wands and Swords is balanced or opposed by the downward movement of Water and Earth. This parallels the compatabilty of the physical elements: Fire with Air, and Water with Earth.

Wands are compatible with Swords.
Cups are compatible with Pentacles.

Wands and Cups are incompatible.
Swords and Pentacles are incompatible.

---

1   Tyson, ed., *Three Books of Occult Philosophy.* (Woodbury, MN: Llewellyn Publications. 2009), 720

The Scale of Ten and the Divine Name of Extension

Aaron Leitch, within his research into The Divine Name of Extension,[1] discovered the link between the depiction of the Divine Name *YHVH* within the pyramid-shaped Scale of Ten (expounded within Agrippa's Three Books of Occult Philosophy) and the number 72 contained withal. Leitch describes how, in the pyramid form of the Divine Name *YHVH* pictured below, this arrangement of the letters demonstrates the expansion of the elemental worlds (from within *Ain Soph*) to generate the world beneath with an inclusive nature of the preceding element – similarly, the Golden Dawn teaches that the Queens contains the influence of the Kings, the Princes hold the influence of both King and Queen, and that the influence of all three are inherent within the nature of the Princesses.

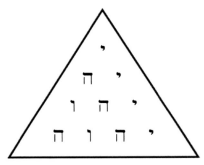

Through the addition of the numerical value of each letter, the sacred number 72 is revealed, bringing further clarity to the title "Divine Name of Extension" in relation to the Shem ha-Mephorash.

Yod (׳)= 10: Heh (ה)= 5: Vav (ו)=6:

Y (׳)= 10

YH (הׁ) = 10 + 5 = 15

YHV (והׁ)= 10 + 5 + 6 = 21

YHVH (הוהׁ)= 10 + 5 + 6 + 5 = 26

10 + 15 + 21 + 26 = 72

The triangular pattern reflects the triangular structure of the crystallization process within *Ain Soph*. The 10 placements relate to the manifestation of the Four Worlds/Elements through the Ten Sephiroth.

---

1   Aaron Leitch, *Shem ha-Mephoresh, The Divine Name of Extension:*
     http://www.hermeticgoldendawn.org/leitch-shemhamephoresh.html

The Ten Sephiroth & the Lightning Flash

The 10 Sephiroth are a direct reflection of the Divine Sparks from *Ain*, and reveal God's presence in His Creation. The Tree of Life depicts this downward movement of Creation as a Lightning Flash, also representing the Sword of the Kerubim which guarded the entrance to Eden. In Tarot terms, the 10 Sephiroth are depicted by the Minor Arcana.

1 = Kether / Aces

2 = Chokmah / Twos

3 = Binah / Threes

4 = Chesed / Fours

5 = Geburah / Fives

6 = Tiphareth / Sixes

7 = Netzach / Sevens

8 = Hod / Eights

9 = Yesod / Nines

10 = Malkuth / Tens

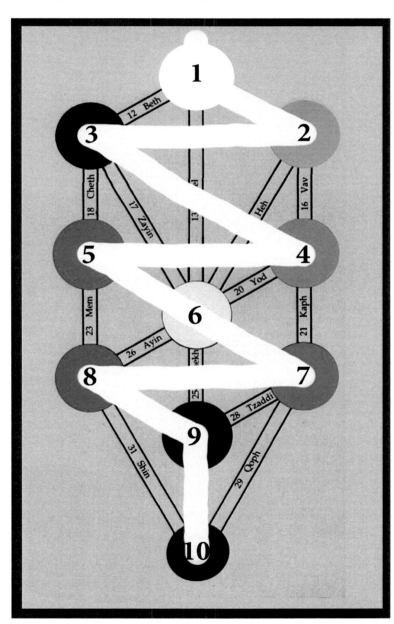

The Shekhinah and the Serpent

Ain Soph is One, beyond Time. There is only Love. From the heart of the Godhead a primordial light shines forth, called the Shekhinah. This Divine Light flowing through Kether repeats the law of three lights as a mirror image of *Ain Soph*, bringing life to the Supernals – Kether, Chokmah and Binah. The Divine Light then splits into an upper and lower Shekhinah. The upper Shekhinah remains in the Supernals. The concept of the three lights in triangular form reappears; upon its descent the Divine Light bringing into being the physical Solar Light of Tiphareth. The lower Shekhinah pulls down and brings into existence the remaining seven Sephiroth of Chesed, Geburah, Tiphareth, Netzach, Hod, Yesod and Malkuth.

The lower Shekhinah drops down below Malkuth and becomes or congeals into the Great Serpent. She crystallizes our material universe, bringing into existence Time and Space, Life and Death. The lower Shekhinah draws down each individual soul, forming a material garment around it with its powerful magnetic force, expressed by the twenty-two paths which pull the Sephiroth together into a tightly-packed unit. But this lower Shekhinah cannot hold the flow of magnetism within Time and Space. Old age is the result of the weakening effect of the magnetic pull of the serpent, and death is the direct result of the magnetic flow diminishing to the point that the soul is once again free of its material restriction.

The 22 Paths equate to the desire of the soul to experience:
The 10 Sephiroth generate the stage upon which the magnetic force is played out.

Let us then take another journey within consciousness as we
open the Sephirothic Gates along the Path of Return...

PART II
The Sephirothic Gates

THE MINOR ARCANA

MALKUTH
The Kingdom

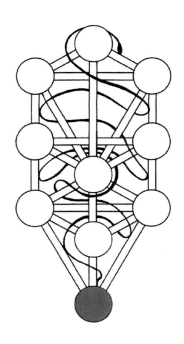

Magical Image:
> **A young woman, crowned
> and throned.**

God Name:
> ***Adonai ha Aretz* -
> Lord of Earth
> *Adonai Malekh* -
> Lord and King**

Archangel:
> ***Sandalphon***

Order of Angels:
> ***Ashim,* Souls of Fire**

Planet:
> **Earth**

Spiritual Experience:
> **Knowledge and Conversation
> of the Holy Guardian Angel**

Titles:
> **The Gate; Gate of Death; Gate of the Shadow of Death; Gate of Tears; Gate of
> Justice; Gate of Prayer; Gate of the Daughter of the Mighty Ones; Gate of the Garden
> of Eden; The Inferior Mother; Malkah, the Queen; Kallah, the Bride; The Virgin.**

*"The Tenth Path is called the Resplendent Intelligence because it is exalted above
every head and sits upon the throne of Binah. It illuminates the splendours of all the Lights,
and causes an influence to emanate from the Prince of Countenances, the Angel of Kether."*

Sepher Yetzirah

Malkuth is Kether manifested within material existence. The Angel of Kether is Metatron,
and he rules over the entire Tree of Life. Sandalphon, the Angel of Malkuth, is his
reflection. She is an aspect of Metatron's work, which is to bring the two aspects of the
Shekhinah together into one within an individual.

Malkuth does not so much represent the physical world but rather a consciousness that
is both individual and yet a spark of the One God. This connection of the individual
soul to its Creator is discovered through the conscious awareness of the present moment
which transcends Time: thus one perceives a non-time reality even while experiencing
the reality within the arena of Time and Space.

Thus Malkuth acts as a feminine principle within God, giving birth into spirit. This rebirth is the Great Work and is a phenomenon which naturally occurs once the magnetic pull of the Great Dragon has been overcome. *Malkuth Shamayim* meaning 'Kingdom of Heaven' is used as a description of peoples who are consciously aware of their connectedness with God.

Many years ago, I asked my guide if I could meet the Angel of Malkuth, Archangel Sandalphon, as I had only read about her but hadn't come across her in meditation. To my surprise, my guide told me that I could not, so I asked if I could meet the angel in the future, and my guide agreed. A few months later, as I sat down to meditate, I was instantly and without warning brought into a square room with no furniture except a central raised structure upon which a beautiful angel stood. There was a dense atmosphere which permeated my psychic senses. She did not speak or move. I started to recite a mantra, OM ZED ZAM which is used to connect with the Master within. She seemed to be uncomfortable with its vibration as if it was too high for her, so I stopped. She was wearing a black cloak, with an inner red lining. The cloak dropped to the floor, sweeping past her wings without obstruction, unveiling her amazingly beautiful naked body. My sexuality began to rise in me. I wanted her and moved towards her. At that moment, the face of Metatron with a fierce expression superimposed itself over her body, causing me to jump back in fright. They disappeared, leaving me confused and shaken.

The odyssey begins with a vision, a quest – but first there is the test. When the visual world has lost its hold on the soul and the ego accepts the higher order, the odyssey may begin, and that journey begins in Malkuth.

TEN OF PENTACLES
Malkuth of Assiah

Esoteric Title:
Lord of Wealth

Divine Name:
Adonai ha-Aretz - **Lord of Earth**

Astrology: **Mercury in Virgo**

Shem ha-Mephorash Angels:
Leviah - **To be Exalted**
Hihaiah - **Refuge**

Sephirothic Colour:
Black rayed Yellow

Card Dynamics:

Assiah, the World of Action and Spatial Awareness, attributed to the element of Earth, sees the manifestation of the Sephira of Malkuth, where Time and Space as the environment for spiritual growth are generated. The Ten of Pentacles is where the dense magnetic field of consciousness brings into manifestation the Divine Plan, crystallizing it into spatial awareness.

Malkuth is linked to Kether, like a mirror reflection of the Divine Will and is therefore the Philosopher's Stone or perfected work, showing that the Ten of Pentacles is perfectly aligned with the Divine Will in transforming lead into gold. In this dense magnetic field, the ego discovers God within the material world and affecting the affairs of men through synchronicities. It is here that a natural law is recognized, and here that the soul experiences good and evil, according to the soul's inclination to experience and explore the life force embedded in the dense field within the Earth element. From here the only way is up, so that the awakening of inner dimensions may bring about spiritual growth.

Rays of light stream down and enliven ten pentacles which stimulate ten white roses, opening to their most beautiful. It is a time of good harvests and growing affluence. The open roses show that everything is flowering into perfection: indeed, the Ten of Pentacles reveals that a perfected world has reached its climax. It represents wealth and

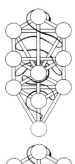

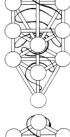

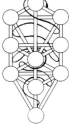

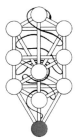

10

PENTACLES

success, often due to an inheritance, which links this card to ancestral knowledge and hereditary gifts in the form of talents, physique, and programmed personality traits, also linking it to ones place of birth, the passage into this world. Because the card is so closely linked to inheritance, it also indicates the temporal nature of worldly success and wealth. This card is linked to the Wheel of Fortune (10) in its most positive aspect.

It is the end of a period of growth and also the starting place for the return journey. Here the soul experiences a battlefield for its salvation - whether the soul becomes entangled within the affairs of the world, pulling it ever-deeper into the material, or whether the soul sees the temporal nature of its environment and begins to look for the doorway into the inner dimensions of the spiritual path that has been prepared for it.

Although attributed to the element of Earth, Malkuth of Assiah has in fact all four elements and spirit mingled together, invoking the pentagram, the perfect man. The pentagram is the tool and the means to open the door into the spiritual realms, and it dispels or banishes negative influences which could prevent the soul from stepping into the light of return.

Astrology:
Mercury, as the ruling planet of Virgo, is very well-placed, enabling one to deal with wealth and a position of responsibility. This placement brings the ability to look very carefully and analytically at any issues that need dealing with, and a practical approach to any problems. Overall, there is an intelligence here that can deal with its affluent environment and flourish within it. However, a preoccupation with detail can bring too much attention into material matters and over-ride the intuitive feelings which may otherwise offer a broader view of the situation.

Archetypal Influences:
The archetypal influence of The Magician (Mercury) and The Hermit (Virgo) shows the ability to create and bring into being the visions that are dominant, but also reveals that the Hermit is awakening the soul to the light that leads one through the labyrinth of the material world. This dense realm of Malkuth of Assiah is the place where information is created through experience and stored in the form of karma. It is

both the playing field of the soul, and the turning point where the soul begins to seek itself. There may be a need to take up meditation or perhaps a martial art that utilises the spiritual forces within the body.

Shem ha-Mephorash:
The two angels associated with this card are Leviah (To be Exalted) and Hihaiah (Refuge), showing that the soul has reached a place of rest in the Lord of Earth.

> Be still, and know that I am God; I will be exalted among the nations,
> I will be exalted in the earth!
> Psalm 46:10,11 (NKJ Bible)

> Trust in Him at all times, you people; Pour out your heart before Him;
> God is a refuge for us.
> Psalm 62:8 (NKJ Bible)

TEN OF SWORDS
Malkuth of Yetzirah

Esoteric Title:
Lord of Ruin

Divine Name:
Adonai ha-Aretz - **Lord of Earth**

Astrology: **Sun in Gemini**

Shem ha-Mephorash Angels:
Damabaial - **Fountain of Wisdom**
Mengel - **Nourishing all**

Sephirothic Colour:
**Citrine, Olive, Russett, Black,
flecked gold**

Card Dynamics:
The world of Yetzirah, the World of Formation, is attributed with the element of Air. Here, combined with Malkuth, the soul is locked in dense forms of consciousness in search of meaning and symbols of its true nature.

Within this magnetic field, the Ten of Swords shows that the mind is at breaking point. It has shut off all links from the higher realms and is struggling to cope with the demands of decision-making without vision or spiritual guidance, bringing the potential for the ruin of plans, or mental breakdown. If the ego denies the intuition and continues on a path that is against the flow of the True Will, the soul may terminate its physical life. There is a finality within this card that can be interpreted as a death or a divorce, but it can also be interpreted as the end-point of a mental struggle or intellectual stronghold, and hence there is hope of a certain freedom with a positive new outlook on the near horizon.

Astrology:
Astrologically, the Sun here represents the soul's realisation that a decision has to be made that brings meaning to one's life. The Sun in Gemini shows a lack of trust in the intuitive faculty, preferring to rely on the intellect. This logical and rational mindset prevents the inner voice from impacting the ego.

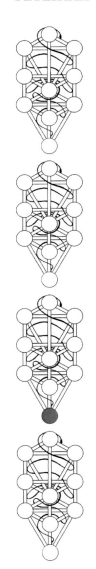

Archetypal Influences:

The archetypal influences of this card are The Sun (Sun) and The Lovers (Gemini). The Sun archetype is often perceived as a child, with an innocent, loving nature. It is considered to be a love energy similar to The Fool, but whereas the Fool is free to roam where he pleases, the Sun is trapped within the walls of its own making. The Lovers show that a decision has to be made – the decision has to come from a higher spiritual power which could free the soul from the magnetic pull of the serpent. The decision then is to let go, so that the Divine can manifest, but this is not an intellectual act of making a decision. The soul itself has been locked up in the intellect and must now let go of the mental faculty so that it can be guided by Spirit rather than the ego. The crossed swords can be seen preventing the soul from making that move. The ego's pride in its own intelligence makes it difficult for the spiritual faith to manifest within the daily routine of the personality.

Shem ha-Mephorash:

The angels connected with this card are Damabaial (Fountain of Wisdom) and Mengel (Nourishing all). These angels reveal that the true nature of this card is a trial to help break the illusion that the ego rules, allowing the birth of the Fool (Air) within, who no longer identifies with intelligence alone. Mengel offers spiritual nourishment to the soul who experiences emptiness when the intellectual constructs fall to ruin. From this place of humility, the soul is rewarded beyond measure in being free at last to witness the true Fountain of Wisdom in the light of Damabaial.

10
SWORDS

TEN OF CUPS
Malkuth of Briah

Esoteric Title:
Lord of Perfected Success

Divine Name:
Adonai ha-Aretz - **Lord of Earth**

Astrology: **Mars in Pisces**

Shem ha-Mephorash Angels:
Aslaiah - **Judging**
Mihel - **Sending forth as a Father**

Sephirothic Colour: **Citrine, Olive, Russett, Black**

Card Dynamics:
In this card, the dense plane of Malkuth is experienced within Briah, the World of Creation, attributed to the element of Water. This generates a realm wherein the True Will acts creatively to manifest the soul's perfect scenario.

The Ten of Cups shows a harmonious environment of emotional stability, wherein the creative force has manifested in abundance. It is a card of good fortune, happiness and harmony, symbolized by the two hands, one above and one below – "As above, so below," – showing that love is the underlining influence, and that the vision of the True Will is being experienced. The image seems to vibrate with fertility. Creativity pours from Kether, causing each cup to overflow with an outpouring of blessings from above. Yet this card holds its own inherent dangers: the emotions may attempt to hold onto this experience of beauty, which, ultimately, is only transitory. This causes a tension which can be channelled into creative avenues.

Astrology:
This tension is also held between the two signs of Mars and Pisces, which placement reveals that the emotional levels need to be channelled into creative or sexual expression: Mars in Pisces can heighten sexual desires to over-ride the logical mind, but if there is no outlet for sexual energy, tension arises which becomes a kind of glue or cement for the

creative pulse to carve out images from the imagination into concrete forms within Malkuth, resulting in an overflowing stream of one's desires becoming manifest.

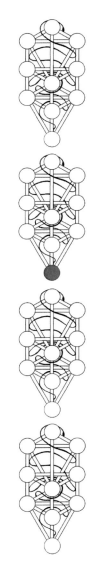

Archetypal Influences:
The Tower (Mars) and The Moon (Pisces) force psychological problems to the surface. The Tower shakes the very foundation of one's reality, and the Moon brings to the surface illusions that still need to be penetrated by the soul. As long as the soul holds onto the vision of the True Will, The Tower pours the fertile seed of life into the cups from the great subconscious sea through the lotus blossoms, and the cups overflow with the Azoth. But as soon as the soul loses sight of the vision and concentrates on the pleasures of its environment, the elixir stops flowing and a lightning flash destroys what seemed perfect to the ego, yet was unproductive to the soul. Such a shift brings the soul back onto the path of Perfected Success and happiness.

Shem ha-Mephorash:
The angels associated with this card are Aslaiah (Judging) and Mihel (Sending forth as a Father), showing that the soul has been judged and rewarded accordingly by the Almighty Father. They remind us that the blessings we receive are to be shared with the world, that our lives may demonstrate the perfect love and grace of the Father within this earthly realm, even as the soul seeks the return to the Oneness of its eternal home.

Within the Golden Dawn's circular astrological arrangement of equating the Decans to the Minor Arcana, the Ten of Cups holds the position of the final Decan of Pisces before the Spring Equinox in Aries. As is explained in Appendix I (Shem ha-Mephorash), this Decan does not fit the sequence of the attribution of Planetary Rulers. The Golden Dawn allocated an additional influence of Mars here, which also rules the proceeding first Decan of Aries. However, the Ten of Cups can equally be considered to receive of the Jupiterian influence which precedes it, thus explaining the tremendous bountiful expression inherent within this card.

10
CUPS

TEN OF WANDS
Malkuth of Atziluth

Esoteric Title:
Lord of Oppression

Divine Name:
Adonai ha-Aretz - **Lord of Earth**

Astrology: **Saturn in Sagittarius**

Shem ha-Mephorash Angels:
Rayayel - **Expectation**
Evamel - **Patience**

Sephirothic Colour: **Yellow**

Card Dynamics:
This card combines the magnetic field of Malkuth – a dense realm of forgetfulness wherein the soul experiences separation from the Divine Light – with the world of Atziluth, attributed to the element of Fire.

Five angelic hands hold two wands each: the five hands emanating from swirling clouds hint at an invisible inverted pentagram, giving the impression of an oppressive atmosphere where the consciousness has become trapped within a material mindset and has become overwhelmed by the physical and mental overload. Yet fire is generated from the friction of the two dominating upright wands in the centre of the card, suggesting a powerful upward kundalini force capable of dissolving the opposition suggested by the eight crossed wands. This powerful surge of energy creates the momentum for the change needed to realign the soul with its True Will.

Atziluth has a fragmenting effect. Its magnetic field breaks up established order and reunites the soul with a glimpse of the Divine Light. On an inner level this is experienced with the rising of the kundalini, or a rising flash which melts away old illusions and gives new directives and insights. If the ego resists this influx of spiritual power it will experience immense pressure or oppression from the surrounding environment which is now no longer in harmony with that which is being birthed: Fire is also the element that brings new life.

Here the soul, finding itself trapped within a prison of its own making, begins to break free. This may be experienced as a need to move to a new environment which is better attuned to the incoming higher frequencies being experienced, and influenced according to how and where the True Will wishes to manifest.

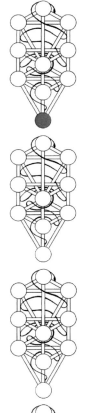

Astrology:
Saturn in Sagittarius suggests a strong focus on intellectual study and a focus on higher education. Saturn can give discipline to the wandering Sagittarius nature, creating a philosophical outlook.

Archetypal Influences:
The archetypal influence of The Universe (Saturn) and Temperance (Sagittarius) shows the movement from a sense of separation from divine influence to a renewed sense of hope through the momentary experience of unity. The Universe reveals that cyclic change is occurring. The influence of Temperance has balanced the elements to such a degree that a burst of kundalini is completely transforming into a new universe or environment, helping the soul into a higher platform from which it can work out its divine objective within what is still an oppressive magnetic field. In the event that the ego struggles to adapt to the new and higher frequency of light, a teacher will appear to help assimilate the transformation, hence the Spiritual Experience of Malkuth: Knowledge and Conversation of the Holy Guardian Angel.

Shem ha-Mephorash:
The angels connected to this card are Rayayel (Expectation) and Evamel (Patience). These loving angels could themselves act as guides, but if the ego fights against the inner voice then a physical guide will appear to help the soul through this transformative period. In either case, the angels serve to encourage the soul with the expectation of relief from the oppressive circumstances, enabling patient endurance within this level of consciousness.

10
WANDS

YESOD
The Foundation

Magical Image:
>   **A beautiful, naked man, very
>   strong**

God Name:
>   *Shaddai el Chai -*
>   **Mighty Living One**

Archangel:
>   *Gabriel*

Order of Angels:
>   *Kerubim,* **The Strong Ones**

Planet:
>   **The Moon**

Spiritual Experience:
>   **Vision of the Machinery of
>   the Universe**

Title:
>   **Treasurehouse of Images**

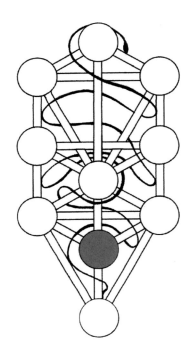

"The Ninth Path is called the Pure Intelligence because it purifies the Emanations. It proves and corrects the designing of their representations, and disposes the unity with which they are designed without diminution or division."

Sepher Yetzirah

The Ninth Sephira, Yesod, is also known as *Tzaddik*, which means "Righteousness." Yesod is generally considered to be the realm of the unconscious. Our modern lexicon has lost the deeper meaning of 'the unconscious,' which has been translated as the realm of the imagination and of dreams, the lower astral realms, and hidden desires. Our modern analytical view has also compartmentalised 'the mind' into different areas – conscious mind, unconscious mind, collective unconscious – but the ancient Hermetic mysteries considered Mind to be a Great Dragon symbolizing a universal life force which encompasses everything. This Dragon was considered to be the light behind the light of the Sun and the foundation of the elements which are moulded through magnetism. This magnetic force is Yesod, and is the reason Yesod is closely connected to sexuality and procreation. To overcome this powerful magnetic force, the conscious point of the soul needs to remain in Love. Love is the fundamental reality of God and manifests righteousness.

The magnetic field of consciousness in Yesod is very pliable, and it is where the conscious point of the soul can imprint its desires. Some desires remain in the magnetic astral field, but others are strong enough to manifest into the physical realms, hence the title, Treasure-house of Images.

The Sephira of Yesod is connected to the sexual organs. Its sexual energy is either projected outwardly towards another person, or inwardly, directed into spiritual exploration which transforms the personality and lifts the soul up into a higher level. Yesod is also connected to the solar plexus. The Middle Pillar on the Tree of Life does not correspond exactly with the chakra system, but Yesod would naturally cover the solar plexus, which is the area from which the Third Eye is awakened. The Spiritual Experience of Yesod is the Vision of the Machinery of the Universe. Sexual energy and divine vision are deeply connected. The opening of the Third Eye is dramatic, as the petals unfold into an enormous flower revealing one's spiritual path. Yesod is thus a foundation on a spiritual level. Such a foundation generates a stable environment, both materially and emotionally, for spiritual work to open up without the danger of it being abandoned due to outer circumstances taking up one's focus and energy.

In the Golden Dawn system, Yesod is attributed to the element of Air, in which the soul gains expression within intellectual pursuits.

NINE OF PENTACLES
Yesod of Assiah

Esoteric Title:
Lord of Material Gain

Divine Name:
Shaddai el Chai - **Mighty Living One**

Astrology: **Venus in Virgo**

Shem ha-Mephorash Angels:
Hazeyal - **Merciful**
Eldiah - **Profitable**

Sephirothic Colour:
Citrine flecked Azure

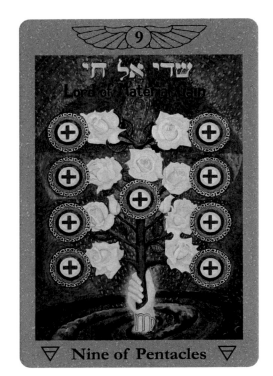

Card Dynamics:
The Nine of Pentacles glows with abundance, success, and potential growth within a chosen field. The glowing angelic hand holds a beautiful rose branch of nine white roses, each touching a pentacle, with two extra buds readying to blossom. The density of the flecked background suggests that the Divine Light is congealing into a blueprint, soon to manifest in Malkuth.

Yesod is a place of forgotten memories, symbols, and unconscious desires which seek to gain expression, but here in the Nine of Pentacles the soul can explore deeper aspects of the subconscious without becoming trapped by temporal lusts. It is a good place to begin the inner search for a deeper meaning to the material gain that seems to manifest as consciousness adjusts to an inner reality. The Moon in Yesod acts as a magnetic force, creating a desire to understand hidden subconscious yearnings, but a soul without a secure foundation finds its hope of following a spiritual path derailed. This foundation may not necessarily be material but could be a belief or philosophy which forms the strong supporting foundation or rock from which to build. In some respects, the angelic hand offers a secure environment, so that the soul's spiritual work can begin in earnest.

The Nine of Pentacles is the final, raw, spiritual energy that has been brought down from the other spheres, ready now to manifest in Malkuth, giving this card a tremendous feeling of abundance and blessing from above. It is often interpreted as an inheritance, not so much from family, but rather the inheritance from work done in the past, even extending to past-life rewards. This card shows that you are being blessed by higher forces and that you are on the right path of self-discovery.

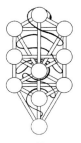

Astrology:
Although, astrologically, Venus in Virgo gives a gentle, unassuming nature, there is a need to overcome sexual inhibitions which have created underlining tensions. A deeper understanding of the sexual aspect of self brings a fuller emotional experience within a loving relationship. Sexual angst needs to be addressed so that the sexual energy inherent in Yesod can flow freely, in preparation for the kundalini energy to rise.

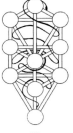

Archetypal Influences:
The archetypal influences within this card are Virgo (the Hermit) and Venus (The Empress). In order to know oneself, it is vital that the soul breaks through illusions concerning sexual intercourse, bringing the need to explore and experience this field more intensively. Archetypally, the Empress, representing material wealth as well as fertile ground and pregnancy, brings the necessary emotional and physical security for the soul to engage in an inner exploration of this vast area of the lower astral, for which the influence of the Hermit in this arena of consciousness is calling.

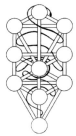

Shem ha-Mephorash:
The two angels associated with this card are Hazeyal (Merciful) and Eldiah (Profitable) showing that mercy has been bestowed upon the individual so that the profitable search for the Higher Self can begin.

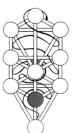

9
PENTACLES

NINE OF SWORDS
Yesod of Yetzirah

Esoteric Title:
Lord of Defeat

Divine Name:
Shaddai el Chai - **Mighty Living One**

Astrology: **Mars in Gemini**

Shem ha-Mephorash Angels:
Nghaneauel - **Rejoicing**
Mochaiel - **Vivifying**

Sephirothic Colour:
Indigo-Purple (Very dark Indigo)

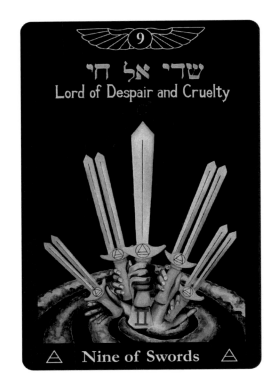

Card Dynamics:
The image of the Nine of Swords has no rose within it, revealing that spiritual direction has been lost or is not perceived due to intellectual activity or pursuits. The swords have a chaotic structure to them, with black zigzag lines emanating from them, symbolizing despair and pain. The hands also look as if they are struggling to keep control, as the central sword brings about a new direction, displacing the other swords.

Swords represent the element of Air, as can be seen on the hilts, and Yesod itself is also attributed to the element of Air within the Golden Dawn grading system, giving this card a focus on intellectual pursuits. The Nine of Swords holds a strong mental activity where the ego attempts to penetrate and understand the deeper mysteries of spirit.

The realization by the ego that the intellect has its limits produces a deep depression, often experienced by artists, and especially writers, who often succumb to this deeply disturbing disease. There is a link between Yesod and Da'ath, Foundation and Knowledge, which is key to Wisdom and Understanding, but which threatens the ego's view of itself as the master of its domain. The revelation that it is controlled by higher forces and ultimately that it must relinquish control to these unperceived forces undermines its perceived existence. This is one of the strongest illusions that needs to be faced and

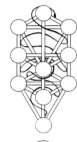

overcome within Yesod. It is in the Nine of Swords that we perceive this illumination and the first struggles of the death of the ego. The ego may attempt to project its problems onto another person rather than facing up to the fact that the cause of the problem lies within.

The Nine of Swords energy is often experienced by women who have been badly treated by their spouses, particularly within the psychological arena, and sometimes is related to severe illness, with the pain and depression accompanying such an ordeal. The conflict within this card is primarily due to the recognition that there is a need to discover the unconscious beginnings and accept the Higher Self. This often surfaces in dreams which seed new ideas and bring vision for the path ahead, although the ego is likely to interpret such as nightmares.

Astrology:
Mars in Gemini further reaffirms the symbolism of this card, connecting it to intellectual challenges, but with a lack of direction due to the loss of the rose, bringing a need for self-discipline.

Archetypal Influences:
As archetypal forces, Mars (the Tower) and Gemini (the Lovers) shows that the ego will experience a loss and breakdown of old ideas of self with the Lovers showing the need to make decisions on a new foundation which accepts higher forces at work within the life of the individual.

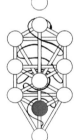

Shem ha-Mephorash:
The angels associated with the card are Nghaneauel (Rejoicing) and Mochaiel (Vivifying), suggesting that the work of this card is to produce a new life or rebirth from the light of a fractured reality. The influence of the Nine of Swords within Yesod is so strong that it can be seen as a kind of death. The illusions inherent within Yesod do not rise beyond Yesod. It is in the Nine of Swords that we break through and leave many disturbing or destructive illusions behind, thus prompting a great rejoicing in the angelic realms.

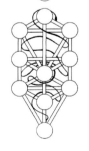

**9
SWORDS**

NINE OF CUPS
Yesod of Briah

Esoteric Title:
Lord of Material Happiness

Divine Name:
Shaddai el Chai - **Mighty Living One**

Astrology: **Jupiter in Pisces**

Shem ha-Mephorash Angels:
Saelaiah - **Mover of All Things**
Naghazaial - **Revealer**

Sephirothic Colour: **Purple**

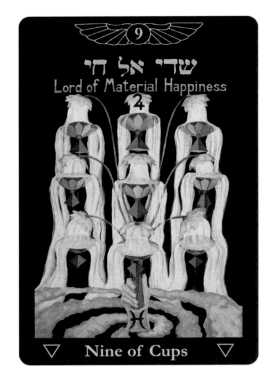

Card Dynamics:
From the nine lotus flowers flow the divine waters of life. The nine cups are seen overflowing with abundant blessings. When there is abundant energy flowing, anything can happen, and everything begins to blossom to its full potential. As such, this card is considered the wish card, as it favours good omens, even when reversed or ill-dignified. The Nine of Cups can also be interpreted as a contract, either in the form of a marriage or in a business sense – in either case heralding both emotional and material happiness.

The Nine of Cups shows that there are no emotional blocks and that the waters of life flow freely, without resistance, proclaiming a time of happiness and fulfilment, where everything is possible. On a deeper level, the solar plexus is stimulated and activated by the influx of the waters of life or Divine Light. The solar plexus is the region from which the Third Eye is awakened.

Astrology:
Jupiter in Pisces shows a strong influence for meditation, also enhancing the heightened faculties of imagination and intuition, through the perceptive insights of the Third Eye. The empathic nature of Jupiter in Pisces draws one to the mystical practices, the creative arts, and the occult.

Archetypal Influences:

Archetypally, Jupiter and Pisces equate to the Wheel of Fortune and The Moon. These two archetypes work towards bringing about the right environment for the spiritual path to be explored. The Wheel of Fortune turns to allow circumstances of financial security and emotional happiness from which the conscious point can begin to explore inwardly. A new path unveils from the deep unconscious (The Moon), which, despite the deceptive light of the Moon, can be safely negotiated due to the awakened inner awareness and heightened vision.

Shem ha-Mephorash:

The two angels associated with this card are Saelaiah (Mover of all Things) and Naghazaial (Revealer). These angels by their very titles represent or govern the soul's initiation into deeper awareness through an influx of Divine Light and the movement of sexual energy via the solar plexus. This energy builds up in force until a ball of light breaks free and ascends in a sporadic fashion until it enters an opening in the forehead, which is linked to the High Priestess. Upon entering, petals begin to open up in layers of such beauty that it can be overwhelming. Once the Third Eye has been opened, the spiritual path is revealed.

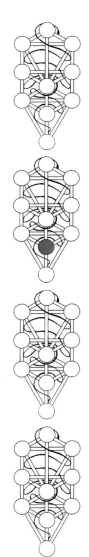

YESOD OF BRIAH

9 CUPS

NINE OF WANDS
Yesod of Atziluth

Esoteric Title:
Lord of Great Strength

Divine Name:
Shaddai el Chai - **Mighty Living
One**

Astrology: **Moon in Sagittarius**

Shem ha-Mephorash Angels:
Irthel - **Deliverer**
Sehaiah - **Taker-away of Evils**

Sephirothic Colour: **Indigo**

Card Dynamics:

An angelic hand bears aloft a large wand through the clouds; four more hands hold it steady but also hold eight other Wands in criss-crossed positions. There is an intensity held within this card, suggesting that a great force has been released – difficult to stop, and dangerous if not guided. The central wand has broken through some major blocks and is now a dominating factor.

The Nine of Wands is the Fire aspect within Yesod, the Foundation, also known as *Tzaddik,* meaning Righteousness. This righteousness is defined in the soul's ability to break through levels of illusion within the subconscious so that the magnetic field can be drawn upward rather than outward within the world. In Yesod lies the battle-ground which allows the soul to understand that it cannot find rest in the outer world, but must turn its attention towards the direction of inner peace. Such can only happen through the balancing of opposites, allowing the kundalini or serpent fire to rise upward, thus transforming the dense magnetic field into a more spiritual frequency.

Outwardly, this awakening of the spiritual fire is observed in conflicting situations whereby former obstacles which had been preventing the movement of a project or plan are suddenly met by the strength and power necessary to push through the difficulty. Artistically, it is a phase of creativity, where the inner spiritual fire needs to be grounded in creative work.

Astrology:

Astrologically, The Moon in Sagittarius gives an optimistic outlook with the determination to square up to challenges. The Moon in Sagittarius highlights the ability to break free of any shackles that prevent the Sagittarius from rising to its full potential, whether intellectual or spiritual. The Moon can sometimes bring the imagination into the realm of magic through the art of visualization.

Archetypal Influences:

The archetypal influences within the card are the High Priestess (Moon) and Temperance (Sagittarius), pinning the energy of this card within the Middle Pillar, revealing the movement of sexual energy upward, and suggesting the opening of the Third Eye as the sexual energy enters a vesica-shaped opening at the centre of the forehead.

Shem ha-Mephorash:

The governing angels of this card are Irthel (Deliverer) and Sehaiah (Taker-away of Evils). They reveal the aspect of God who is able to deliver us from the pull of illusions locked within this Yesodic arena of self-discovery, and free us from that which would negate our True Will.

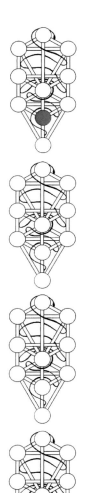

**9
WANDS**

HOD
Glory

Magical Image:
> **A hermaphrodite**

God Name:
> *Elohim Tzabaoth -*
> **Lord of Hosts**

Archangel:
> *Michael*

Order of Angels:
> *Beni Elohim,* **Sons of God**

Planet:
> **Mercury**

Spiritual Experience:
> **Vision of Splendour**

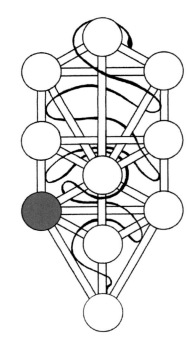

8

**The
Eighth
Sephira**

"The Eighth Path is called the Absolute or Perfect Intelligence because it is the mean of the Primordial, which has no root by which it can cleave or rest, save in the hidden places of Gedulah, from which emanates its proper essence."

Sepher Yetzirah

It is difficult to isolate Hod from Netzach, Geburah and Chesed, as they all express aspects within Tiphareth, the central Sephira on the Tree of Life. Hod, positioned at the base of the left-hand pillar represents the left-hand side of the brain, producing analytical thought and spatial awareness, further producing self-awareness and self-identity. The Sephira of Chesed acts as the higher octave of Hod, as the consciousness at the level of Hod is more directed towards analyzing one's outer environment.

Hod represents the electrical charge or impulse, which stimulates chemical reactions within the brain, represented by Netzach. This shows how closely these two Sephiroth need to work together, in generating certain functions within the brain and body. Hod is also where the memory faculty is located, again often stimulated by feelings and emotions from Netzach.

Hod is also closely connected with communication, whether in speech, writing, computing, or mathematics, and is often seen archetypally as a library. The manipulation of the astral realms by the analytical focus produces effects of magic also associated with this Sephira.

Hod is associated with the planet Mercury, which aptly pins this Sephira into an intellectual and communicative arena. It is a centre for analytical thought where thoughts are projected into new ideas and given energy to manifest into workable designs. Hermes is very much linked to Mercury. Hermes carried a Caduceus wand which points to the Great Work to rise above the mundane and become "more than human." This indicates that the higher learning which is linked to both Hermes and Hod is to help the soul to regain its former glory. Hod translates as 'Glory,' and also as 'Majesty,' 'Brightness,' and 'Beauty.' The Virtue and Vice of Hod are Truth and Falsity.

The Golden Dawn system attributes Hod with the element of Water, as within Hermetic thought, Air (Yesod) is between Water (Hod) and Fire (Netzach), as discussed within the examination of *Ain Soph*.

EIGHT OF PENTACLES

Esoteric Title:
Lord of Prudence

Divine Name:
Elohim Tzabaoth - **Lord of Hosts**

Astrology: **Sun in Virgo**

Shem ha-Mephorash Angels:
Akaiach - **Long-suffering**
Kehetel - **Adorable**

Sephirothic Colour:
Yellow-Brown flecked White

Card Dynamics:

A well-structured form of eight pentacles, four on each side, allows divine forces to move up and down the central column of a rose bush, suggesting strength and stability. Touching the four lower pentacles are four beautiful white roses in full bloom, showing that this card concerns prosperity in the lower material realm. The background has a crystalline pattern which one would expect in the dense magnetic field of earth, showing that new ideas are becoming structured and formulating new growth. In practical matters this level of consciousness is very much to do with tending to one's estate with prudence – the practical maintenance required to ensure future growth and prosperity, and tending that which has been sown. In business it is about using one's skills within one's own business and being of service to a larger community, perhaps in the production of goods which benefit others. The fact that the roses are held at the bottom of the rose bush shows that attention is being given to practical matters on a day-to-day basis rather than one's spiritual needs, which may have been put aside until the harvest has been brought in.

Astrology:

Sun in Virgo highlights the practical nature of this card but also indicates a tension where one gets bogged down with too much detail, bringing anxiety that things are not perfect.

Archetypal Influences:

On an archetypal level the Sun (Sun) and Virgo (Hermit) reveal that there is a strong inclination to get to the bottom of a matter even to the point of needing to explore the underlining structure of reality, whether through science or metaphysical research. The faculty of concentration and one-pointed determination is inherently available and needing to be applied.

Shem ha-Mephorash:

The two angels associated with this card are Akaiach (Long-suffering) and Kehethel (Adorable). These two angels help to maintain the focus by providing the necessary energy for the desire to complete the work that the soul has been allotted within this material realm.

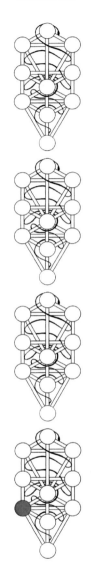

8

PENTACLES

EIGHT OF SWORDS
Hod of Yetzirah

Esoteric Title:
Lord of Shortened Force

Divine Name:
Elohim Tzabaoth - **Lord of Hosts**

Astrology: **Jupiter in Gemini**

Shem ha-Mephorash Angels:
Vemibael - **The Name Which Is Over All**
Lahael - **Supreme Essence**

Sephirothic Colour: **Russet**

Card Dynamics:
Four angelic hands hold eight swords which join as one below a red rose from which shines a cross. The rose radiates love energy and the cross symbolizes spiritual truth. The swords do not penetrate the rose but are just touching it, as if attempting to understand it. Here the intellectual force is being applied to attempt to understand spiritual concepts. However, the mental qualities of Hod are not meant for this type of force. Rather, they are meant for the focus into our outer world as a process for understanding our surroundings. The intellect in Hod is locked in time and space. This shortened intellectual force traps the soul in a mental labyrinth of attempting to understand something which is beyond the mental consciousness of Hod.

The Mercury of Hod brings even more emphasis on understanding truth. But, isolated from Netzach, it will only reach a cold analytical or pragmatic conclusion, which can create a prison of one's own limited perception or outlook.

Astrology:
Jupiter is in its detriment in Gemini. Its expansive nature presents a multitude of ideas in this airy, intellectual realm which can cause one to lose one's sense of proportion. This can create difficulty in making a decision, especially one that is guided from a place beyond the intellect.

Archetypal Influences:

The archetypal influences of the Wheel of Fortune (Jupiter) and the Lovers (Gemini) highlight that a choice has to be made within the context of the truth of a matter. The Wheel of Fortune is turned by divine guidance according to karmic influences, suggesting that even the choice that is made is still under Divine Will, and so this card, with the cross so prominent, shows that even though the soul has not yet understood how to relate to higher matters, it is being divinely guided.

Shem ha-Mephorash:

The angels associated with this card are Vemibael (The Name Which Is Over All) and Lahael (Supreme Essence). They are divinely invoked so the soul may understand the concept of a God or Supreme Essence within and above all things, and desire to penetrate into the unified field of consciousness.

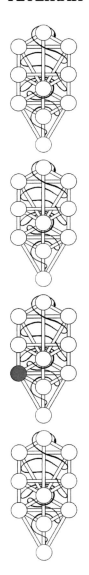

**8
SWORDS**

EIGHT OF CUPS
Hod of Briah

Esoteric Title:
Lord of Abandoned Success

Divine Name:
Elohim Tzabaoth - **Lord of Hosts**

Astrology: **Saturn in Pisces**

Shem ha-Mephorash Angels:
Vavaliah - **King and Ruler**
Ilnaiah - **Abiding Forever**

Sephirothic Colour: **Red-Orange**

Card Dynamics:
An angelic hand rises from swirling clouds holding the stem of two lotus flowers which pour the divine waters of life into the five lower cups. The three upper cups are empty. On a spiritual level this card is showing that the inner vision is unable to penetrate higher abstract concepts due to emotional blocks which need to be worked out, showing that there is a need to withdraw and to meditate or contemplate deeper subconscious issues before any further spiritual work can take place. On a more material aspect, the Eight of Cups is showing that a path or a project that was once thought to have been of purpose or benefit is turning out to have been miscalculated, with the result that energy is now being withdrawn from the project. The concentration upon material matters has, over time, revealed empty cups, bringing the realization that a search for deeper meaning is the true way forward.

Astrology:
Saturn in Pisces shows that there may be a rather depressing outlook in one's life which prevents hope from blossoming. A strong imaginative faculty may be left to delve deeper into depression instead of being directed into creative fields.

Archetypal Influences:
On an archetypal level, The Universe (Saturn) and The Moon (Pisces) herald the end of a cycle, as the former illusion no longer holds. In expectation of this new cycle it is

necessary to seek realignment with one's True Will. Attunement to one's feelings will be beneficial in this regard. The tendency toward depression can be bypassed through focus upon the Light of God.

Shem ha-Mephorash:

The two angels associated with this card are Vavaliah (King and Ruler) and Ilnaiah (Abiding Forever). These two angels bring awareness of the Oneness of everything and the eternity of the soul's journey back to that Oneness. Strength can be drawn from the powerful nature of these angels, to counteract the human tendency to feelings of negativity. They remind us that God is the Lord of the Abandoned Success, and that it has been necessary for illusory forms to be broken.

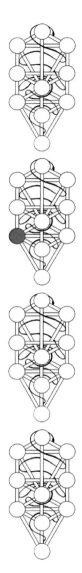

8
CUPS

EIGHT OF WANDS
Hod of Atziluth

Esoteric Title:
Lord of Swiftness

Divine Name:
Elohim Tzabaoth - **Lord of Hosts**

Astrology: **Mercury in Sagittarius**

Shem ha-Mephorash Angels:
Nethhiah - **Enlarger**
Heeiah - **Hearer in Secret**

Sephirothic Colour: **Violet-Purple**

Card Dynamics:
The Eight of Wands is attributed with the element of Fire and gives the visual impression of a swift force. The image on the Eight of Wands is dominated by a circular opening which is formed by the movement of circulating fire, generated by the eight wands above and below, which are held by four angelic hands.

The imagery generates energy, further shown by lightning flashing, and this energy creates an opening or portal. The opening hints at by-passing the normal day-to-day mind, and opening to a higher Mind that is not so linked to the ego but to the Higher Self, connecting with Chesed, the higher octave of Hod. The natural upward force creates a desire for deeper understanding which is only really attainable through a messenger, such as an angel or a spiritual guide, which is the reason that this card traditionally carries the meaning of receiving a message.

Astrology:
Mercury in Sagittarius points to intellectual stimuli, and also hints at the need to travel to far-off places, which in this card can allude to the ability to project astrally or mentally in search of higher knowledge.

Archetypal Influences:

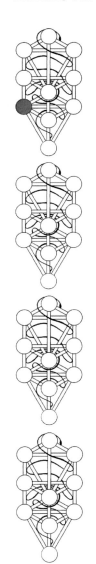

Within this card are the archetypes of the Magician (Mercury) and Temperance (Sagittarius). The Magician, placed here in Hod, at the base of the left-hand path or Pillar of Severity, hints at the need to mentally project the sexual charge to heighten visualization and the use of the imagination. The Magician (Mercury) in Hod makes for a high degree of intellectual force in this card, and whilst Mercury is known for swiftness, a sharp mind alone does not mean that practical solutions can be found. The most efficient passage through a situation or problem may only be found when the intelligent logical framework is open to the unstructured instinctual elements of the environment through which it must move, allowing for a fusion of the qualities of Hod (Mercury) and Netzach (Venus) – Water and Fire. Temperance, on the Middle Pillar, balances the elements of Fire and Water inherent in the Eight of Wands. The mercurial mind of the Magician can logically understand that the balancing of the Sephiroth of Hod and Netzach will realign the soul with the Middle Pillar, adjusting the archetypal energies upward instead of outwards.

Shem ha-Mephorash:

The angels associated with the Eight of Wands are Nethhiah (Enlarger) and Heeiah (Hearer in Secret). These angels show a natural inclination or instinct within this card to enlarge and expand on knowledge, and that such knowledge is not always gleaned from books but through the secret depths of one's being. Their influence is to aid in the accumulation of knowledge of one's environment, and of oneself, and of communicating that knowledge in such a way that it does not threaten another's reality, but helps to enlarge the understanding of our multi-dimensional universe, both within and without.

8
WANDS

NETZACH
Victory

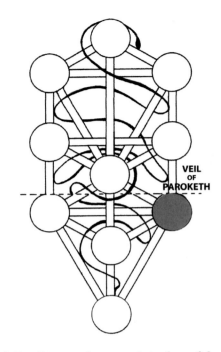

Magical Image:
A beautiful, naked woman
God Name:
YHVH Tzabaoth -
Lord of Armies
Archangel:
Haniel
Order of Angels:
Elohim, **Gods**
Planet:
Venus
Spiritual Experience:
Vision of Beauty Triumphant
Titles:
Firmness. Valour.

"The Seventh Path is called the Occult Intelligence because it is the refulgent splendour of the intellectual virtues which are perceived by the eyes of the intellect and the contemplations of faith."

Sepher Yetzirah

Netzach takes us into the evocative world of Nature Spirits, presided over by the Greek god Pan, who represents the awareness of inner worlds hidden behind the beauty of the green world. Within the green world of Nature is hidden a mysterious, invisible veil which allows us to interact with the elemental and angelic realms, even though they remain invisible to our five senses, which are wired for surviving within the outer manifestation of Nature.

Venus brings a strong sensual attraction. There is a sense here that the feminine principle melts into the seductive arms of Pan – this internal embrace of Nature towards humanity invokes unconditional love, influencing the qualities of instinct and desire. It is here that we find the creative expressions of art, music, dance and poetry.

When Hod and Netzach embrace each other the resulting consciousness produces the confidence and ability to communicate one's True Will and translate it into action. If Hod and Netzach are not properly balanced, there is a risk of losing oneself in sensual pleasures.

Netzach is the conscious realm of sensations, feelings, and emotions. Ruled by Venus, it is dominated by love, and therefore relationships. Through our relationships we discover imperfections of the soul that need to work their way out, and here in Netzach the soul is challenged and tested as to the measure of love inherent within its makeup.

Netzach is situated at the bottom of the right-hand Pillar of Mercy. It is a fiery realm that initiates a new birth. This can sometimes be a violent experience but is ultimately helpful for the soul's emergence into the Divine Light. Devotion and prayer are a way through this complicated and enchanted Sephira.

The Veil of Paroketh acts as a barrier which prevents a strong ego from penetrating the upper spiritual regions beyond the Veil. The ego is dealt a massive blow as it passes from Hod to Netzach through the Key of the Tower, and is further purified through the fiery realms of Netzach before it can pass through the Veil of Paroketh.

SEVEN OF PENTACLES

Esoteric Title:
Lord of Success Unfulfilled

Divine Name:
YHVH Tzabaoth - **Lord of Armies**

Astrology: **Saturn in Taurus**

Shem ha-Mephorash Angels:
Herachael - **Permeating All Things**
Metzrael - **Rising** (sic) **Up the Oppressed**

Sephirothic Colour:
Olive flecked Gold

Card Dynamics:
The Seven of Pentacles seems to radiate the depths of a forest, full of dark places in which one could lose sight of the path, particularly without spiritual guidance. The seven pentacles are prominent in the image, as no open roses are shown, just five rosebuds above the five upper pentacles. The absence of rosebuds on the two lower pentacles demonstrates the unfulfilled success of this arena. Plans could not be realized because the spiritual direction was not understood from the outset. However, the stimulus and hope for future revelation is there, but results are as yet lacking. The fiery nature of Netzach helps to ignite the soul's need to pull free of the sensual magnetism of this Sephira and seek balance so that the vision of its True Will can manifest and take form.

This card also suggests a young person full of hope, ideas, dreams and ambitions, but lacking financial backing. It represents a venture that has started but which as yet does not produce any rewards. However, the rosebuds show that success may yet follow if the dream is not lost.

Astrology:
Saturn in Taurus carries the energy to build structures which last, while promoting a long-term strategy for achieving success. The practical side to this astrological

combination can go against the pleasure-seeking Venus nature of both Taurus and Netzach, but overall there is a strong energy to succeed in material matters.

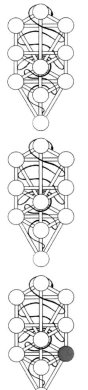

Archetypal Influences:
The archetypal influence of the Universe (Saturn) and the Hierophant (Taurus) shows that the end of a cycle has been reached in the soul's development, and that a new cycle is about to begin. The Hierophant places this new cycle into a firm foundation that has been tried and tested. So although success is still elusive, the new cycle may well bring rewards as yet unenvisaged.

Shem ha-Mephorash:
The two angels of this card are Herachael (Permeating all things) and Metzrael (Rising up the Oppressed). These two angels indicate that the all-pervading Mind within all things is about to click into a higher frequency which will allow the soul, still captivated by material beauty, to rise or adjust its perspective into a more fluent realm of opportunity and understanding.

7

PENTACLES

SEVEN OF SWORDS
Netzach of Yetzirah

Esoteric Title:
Lord of Unstable Effort

Divine Name:
YHVH Tzabaoth - **Lord of Armies**

Astrology: **Moon in Aquarius**

Shem ha-Mephorash Angels:
Kehihael - **Triune**
Mikhael - **Who Is Like Unto Him?**

Sephirothic Colour: **Yellow-Green**

Card Dynamics:
The Seven of Swords has a lively presence. From abundant swirling clouds, three angelic hands emerge, holding seven swords. The rainbow touches the clouds, creating a kind of oval or egg shape which suggests a portal. The central sword is shown with the strong growth of a blossoming rose vine, showing that Spirit is attached to the central sword, which is without doubt the strongest of the seven. The other six swords, three on each side, touch at the top, creating one tip.

The Seven of Swords reveals the struggle from duality into unity. Here the Air element, representing the mind, in itself a magnetic field, begins to unite Hod with Netzach, aligning them within the Middle Pillar around the solar plexus area. The central sword with the rose represents the rising awareness of the soul's True Will. The swords on each side represent other interests that are beginning to align with the True Will but at the same time still cloud its course. In some ways this card represents study that has rekindled the soul's true purpose. Now the soul must let go of unprofitable aspects of the ego's personality which hinder the future unfolding of the soul's true purpose on Earth. There is also an emphasis on the rising of the consciousness, with divine help, on all seven levels. However, a narrow band of intense experiences have brought about an unstable period as the soul and ego realign to a birth of opportunity in a new paradigm – the recognition of the soul's true purpose.

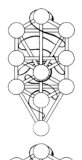

Astrology:

The Moon in Aquarius invokes a strong magnetism and flashes of genius, but attention should be given to one's deep feelings to prevent mental aspirations from concealing the vision of one's True Will.

Archetypal Influences:

The inherent archetypes are the High Priestess (Moon) and the Star (Aquarius). The High Priestess presents us with a formula for the opening of the Third Eye – an essential aspect for a glimpse of one's True Will. The archetype of the Star helps to raise the consciousness above the mundane into a cosmic glimpse of Creation, further magnetising the need for spiritual vision, as consciousness prepares to rise into Tiphareth. Yet the alchemical process of the awakening of the spiritual vision is only possible through the balancing of Hod and Netzach. This is often brought about through exposure of any rift between them, allowing painful conditions to rip apart the mind and emotions, generating an instability within the gestalt (it is significant that the Tower card links Hod with Netzach). The eventual healing of this rift brings the necessary balance for spiritual vision to open.

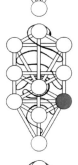

Shem ha-Mephorash:

The angels associated with the Seven of Swords are Kehihael (Triune) and Mikhael (Who is Like Unto Him?) The Triune is a fundamental aspect within the Tree of Life. Hod and Netzach make a triad both with Yesod and with Tiphareth – mirror images on a lower level of the Trinity in Unity of the Godhead. They encourage the soul to focus reverently upon the Godhead – in so doing, stability will arise, whilst that which is unnecessary to the soul's efforts will be unable to cloud the vision.

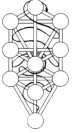

**7
SWORDS**

SEVEN OF CUPS
Netzach of Briah

Esoteric Title:
Lord of Illusionary Success

Divine Name:
YHVH Tzabaoth - **Lord of Armies**

Astrology: **Venus in Scorpio**

Shem ha-Mephorash Angels:
Malahel - **Turning Away from Evil**
Hahaviah - **Goodness in Himself**

Sephirothic Colour: **Green**

Card Dynamics:
The Seven of Cups has a murky undertone, as seen in the background patterns. Seven lotus flowers are fed from one cup at the base and look as if they are lacking substance. No azoth flows from the lotuses, and the cups are also empty. The absence of this elixir reveals a poverty of spirit within this card or level of consciousness.

Even though it may look beautiful in outward appearance, overall the picture portrays a swamp-like landscape where the element of water is plentiful but light sparse. Circumstances are out of balance with spiritual growth and so psychic/spiritual development is needed to obtain true happiness. This Sephira has a difficult energy locked into a sensual arena. It is here that the soul's conscious point struggles with the magnetic pull of the serpent, often associated with water, and as such, this card is often associated with debauchery and the understanding of oneself through sexual and emotional experiences, felt both as great pleasure and great pain:

> "For in a composite body pain and pleasure seethe like juices:
> once immersed in them, the soul drowns."[1]

Such experiences can lead to depression, yet the rainbow suggests that there is hope

---

1   Brian P. Copenhaver, trans., *Hermetica* (Cambridge: Cambridge University Press, 1992), 43.

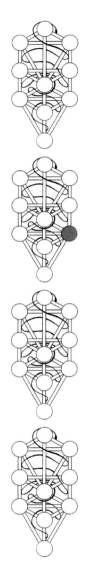

that the soul will struggle free of its sensual chains and begin to understand its immortal nature and inherent creative power.

Astrology:
Venus in Scorpio is very much about sexual desire and strong relationships undermined by possession and jealousy, which can be destructive. On a positive note, this combination brings creativity and energy.

Archetypal Influences:
The archetypal influences are those of the Empress (Venus) and Death (Scorpio). In some ways these two archetypes pin the underlying consciousness of this card. The fertile mother, pregnant and abundant within Nature, is dead within because she has lost her enthusiasm and delight in her natural abilities to nurture. Her consciousness, which, if guided by Spirit, flows within a state of grace, instead trudges through a joyless mire. Unless spiritually-adept, this may not be obvious to others, who see only the illusion of success which she wears as a mantle, beneath which lies her despair. This particular state is often experienced by women at the time of menopause, which, on a physical level, brings the loss of potential new life.

Shem ha-Mephorash:
The angels of this card are Malahel (Turning Away From Evil) and Hahaviah (Goodness in Himself). These two angels by their very titles are given to the soul at this level of consciousness to remind it of the supreme goodness of God and ignite the light of reverence to the source of all. It is the reverence of God within all nature that will help to free the soul from its fixation on pleasures of the outer world and turn it inward to the joy of the Divine Light.

**7
CUPS**

SEVEN OF WANDS
Netzach of Atziluth

Esoteric Title:
Lord of Valour

Divine Name:
YHVH Tzabaoth - **Lord of Armies**

Astrology: **Mars in Leo**

Shem ha-Mephorash Angels:
Mahashiah - **Seeking Safety from Trouble**
Lahahel - **Praiseworthy, Declaring**

Sephirothic Colour: **Amber**

Card Dynamics:
The Seven of Wands is a radiant card, suggesting fiery passion and abundant energy, aided by the King Scale colour of Netzach, Amber. Of the three angelic hands bearing wands, the one emerging from clouds at the base dominates the image with an upright wand.

In the Golden Dawn system, the Seventh Sephira is associated with Fire, and so the Seven of Wands is a strong force to be reckoned with. The main focus is on the Fire element, which cannot be understood properly until the soul detaches itself from the body and enters the realm of Spirit. As long as the conscious point of the soul remains in the element of Fire, its experience will be dominated by unpredictable and to some extent chaotic events. Only when it detaches from the beauty of the outer world and rises above the pull of the flesh will the soul experience the Fire element as a new birth. In some respects this is experienced as purification. This is symbolized by the upward pointing Wand which hints at rising above the sexual magnetism that is also an aspect of this Sephira. This imagery, combined with the rainbow and predominant amber colour, suggests triumph in overcoming the obstacles inherent at this level of consciousness.

Astrology:
The astrological sign of Mars in Leo suggests that there is an emphasis on leadership and an ability to delegate. There is also a love of the arts and a passion for life itself.

Archetypal Influences:

The astrological connection of this card relates to the archetypes of the Tower (Mars) and Strength (Leo), which are the two lower horizontal Paths on the Tree of Life, showing the additional strength in this card. The Tower shows the need to detach from the world and indeed, from one's lower ego. It is from here that the ego breaks away from the qlippothic influence and begins to be influenced by the Spirit, further highlighted in the Strength archetype, which visibly shows how the soul has overcome the lower passions and has risen into a place of innocence. This invokes great courage and strength of character.

Shem ha-Mephorash:

The angels associated with this card are Mahashiah (Seeking Safety from Trouble) and Lahahel (Praiseworthy, Declaring). These two angels further uphold the meaning of the card. Mahashiah offers encouragment in rising the conscious point of the soul above this strong field of magnetism into a safe place and also beyond the troublesome reach of the qlippothic influence. This is not easy to do and is very subtle in its experience and understanding. Lahahel helps to distinguish between two states of consciousness which can only be recognised by the joining of both Hod and Netzach – only when they are united will the recognition of (hence declaration of) this process be possible. The Lord of Valour with whom the soul identifies through rising to the challenge of this Sephira is indeed worthy of praise.

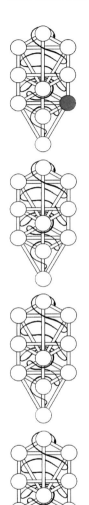

7
WANDS

TIPHARETH
Beauty

Magical Image:
>   **A King. A child. A sacrificed god.**

God Name:
>   *YHVH Eloah ve Da'ath -*
>   **God's Knowledge**

Archangel:
>   *Raphael*

Order of Angels:
>   *Malachim,* **Kings**

Planet:
>   **The Sun**

Spiritual Experience:
>   **Vision of the Harmony of Things. Mysteries of the Crucifixion.**

Titles:
>   *Zoar Anpin,* **The Lesser Countenance.** *Melekh,* **the King.**

"The Sixth Path is called the Mediating Intelligence, because in it are multiplied the influxes of the Emanations; for it causes that influence to flow into all the reservoirs of the blessings with which they themselves are united."

Sepher Yetzirah

Tiphareth is the balancing point on the Tree of Life. This balance is brought about through love – a love that unites the whole tree in beauty and harmony. Tiphareth cannot be fully understood on its own but must be seen as the fundamental truth within the Tree of Life. It represents the love that indwells the human heart, where God is made manifest in the heart of man, and where regeneration or rebirth into the spiritual consciousness is experienced. Tiphareth is therefore the sacred heart of the inner self, connecting to the Divine.

The Spiritual Experience of Tiphareth is the Vision of the Harmony of All Things. This is associated with consciousness which is fully devoted to the Great Work, making Tiphareth a gateway to the Universal Mind as the mirror of the self. The transition into the Tiphareth consciousness brings about a change of the inner body of consciousness. The closer our alignment to the centre of the universe through the power of love, the more our egos release control and contract. Yet the ego must remain strong enough to prevent its total disintegration, as it remains an important aspect of the gestalt. Sacrifice is a fundamental reality in Tiphareth as the outer man/ego gives way to the Inner Being, thus manifesting the True Will within the physical, symbolized in Tiphareth's magical images of a King and a child.

There is only so far one can rise within consciousness – at a certain point it becomes increasingly difficult without the purifying blood of Christ's sacrifice. Tiphareth is where the Mystery of the Crucifixion becomes known. We all carry karmic residue which pulls us down into the physical so that it can be worked out and balanced. Karma has to be brought into harmony with the True Will, and although self-sacrifice is a natural aspect of the Great Work, karma can prevent an individual from participating in the Great Work because he is tied to the experiences which would enable the karma to be balanced out. However, it is possible to shed the karmic residue still remaining: the Mystery of the Crucifixion within Tiphareth shows that a method within the Divine Plan has been given through the sacrificed Christ to lay the karmic burden on the cross. In Christ's sacrifice we find release of that burden, and are freed to enter into a wider consciousness.

Many Adepts see visions or have dreams of the crucifixion after they have been initiated through the Vault of the Adepti. The Vault of the Adepti is made up of seven sides, each holding a colour of the rainbow, symbolizing the seven planets and also hinting at the seven chakras. Each panel has a Tree of Life placed on it, revealing that each chakra holds the Tree of Life within it. The seven sides reveal that there are no opposites within the walls – they are found in the floor and ceiling, which are united by two triangles, one above and one below, producing the hexagram within the centre of the Vault. It is here that we begin to connect with the Heart Chakra within our own centre of being.

The serpent symbolizes localised consciousness within matter and represents the intermediate stage of light transforming around the soul as a body. The influence of the serpent is experienced as desire. The rising of serpents releases the conscious point of the soul from a level of experience of enchantment, but it doesn't necessarily release the soul from the karma that has been accumulated during the period when the soul had been enchanted by material illusions. The Middle Pillar is sometimes referred to as the Pillar of Knowledge, and the Sixes have been called The Serpents. This alludes to the fact that the Sixes can represent becoming entangled in circumstances, as Tiphareth is connected to so many other Paths and Sephiroth: the Sixes reflect the magnetic quality of the Sun's influence in Tiphareth. There is a sense with the Sixes of a tension that pulls upwards towards Spirit and downwards towards the qlippoth, although in Tiphareth the pull of the qlippoth is countered by the Veil of Paroketh.

SIX OF PENTACLES
Tiphareth of Assiah

Esoteric Title:
Lord of Material Success

Divine Name:
YHVH Eloah ve Da'ath -
> **God's Knowledge**

Astrology: **Moon in Taurus**

Shem ha-Mephorash Angels:
Nemamaiah - **Lovable**
Yeile'el - **Hearer of Cries**

Sephirothic Colour: **Gold-Amber**

Card Dynamics:
From swirling clouds an angelic hand holds a rose branch with six beautiful white roses in full bloom, touching six pentacles over which lay six white rose buds, hinting at further increase. In the background is a diamond shape, showing the divine abundance and potential latent in this card. There is a feeling in this card that whatever is being touched upon will turn into gold. The unopened rosebuds reveal a karmic reservoir of material success still to be poured on to those who through hard work and good management have gathered many good harvests.

This card is not just about material success, but also about its distribution, particularly in the form of charitable tithing. In so doing, it is acknowledged that one's success is a divine gift, and that such gifts should not be hoarded but shared, producing gratitude and humility of the heart for all concerned.

Astrology:
The Moon in Taurus is attributed to this card and exerts a powerful influence, as the Moon is exalted in Taurus. This combination stimulates an instinctive pull for material security, even luxury, and emotional happiness. It also produces the strength of character which can spring into action when such security is in any way threatened, although the Taurean influence could induce a possessive and stubborn attitude: the negative side to

the Six of Pentacles is that of greed and arrogance, separating oneself from the plight of one's fellowman.

Archetypal Influences:

On an archetypal level, the High Priestess (the Moon) and the Hierophant (Taurus) combine in the powerful combination of drawing down the Divine Light from Kether into Tiphareth, and then realizing the Divine Will in practical ways, grounding it in traditions of the Great Work. This combination shows that there is a spiritual influence behind the earthly success – the Lord of Material Success manifesting a spiritual understanding, and the teaching of such.

Shem ha-Mephorash:

Nemamaiah (Lovable) shows that an open heart of love and generosity is a strong feature of the Six of Pentacles. The angel Yeile'el (Hearer of Cries) shows that the prayers of those in need will be heard by a merciful heart.

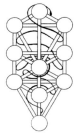

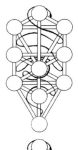

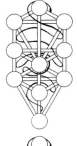

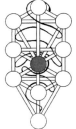

6

PENTACLES

SIX OF SWORDS
Tiphareth of Yetzirah

Esoteric Title:
Lord of Earned Success

Divine Name:
YHVH Eloah ve Da'ath -
  God's Knowledge

Astrology: **Mercury in Aquarius**

Shem ha-Mephorash Angels:
Rehael - **Swift to Condone**
Yeizael - **Making Joyful as Wine**

Sephirothic Colour: **Salmon**

Card Dynamics:
Two swords, each with three blades, cross. The shining rose in the middle where the swords meet represents a new level of consciousness or a flash of new insight. Its balanced position upon the swords affords a calm concentration to study the science behind such. This card gives impulse towards the drawing away from outmoded habits or archetypal structures into more peaceful times so that higher levels of consciousness may be assimilated.

There is also a sense in this card of a celebration of a graduation or completion of a project, with acclaim. The salmon colour in the background generates a quiet, nurturing, stable atmosphere of friendship and love, creating an ideal environment to pause and reflect upon that which has been accomplished, celebrating the earned success with good-natured company.

Astrology:
Mercury in Aquarius offers a very creative energy with the ability to think quickly, bringing about new ideas and promoting originality in any project. This combination holds a quality of communicating either through an orator or a writer. It also represents travel or news from afar.

Archetypal Influences:

At an archetypal level, the Magician (Mercury) and the Star (Aquarius) reveal an underlining force to explore deeper levels of mind. The Star shines a light of hope onto the creative potential which still awaits the soul upon this journey into deeper levels of consciousness.

Shem ha-Mephorash:

These angels remind us that the virtue of Tiphareth is Devotion to the Great Work. Rehael (Swift to Condone) brings encouragement, guidance, and reward in ready accompaniment to one's sincere efforts in working towards the raising of consciousness. Yeizael (Making Joyful as Wine) is met in the truly joyful angelic celebration of one's dedication to the spiritual work which brings the ever-deepening awareness of one's True Will.

> Go thy way, eat thy bread with joy, and drink thy wine
> with a merry heart; for God now accepteth thy works.
> Ecclesiastes 9:7 (King James Bible)

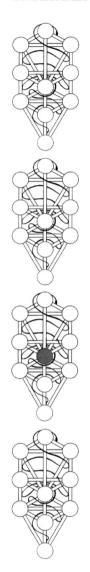

6
SWORDS

SIX OF CUPS
Tiphareth of Briah

Esoteric Title:
Lord of Pleasure

Divine Name:
YHVH Eloah ve Da'ath -
    God's Knowledge

Astrology: **Sun in Scorpio**

Shem ha-Mephorash Angels:
Nelkhal - **Thou Alone**
Yeisel - **Thy Right Hand**

Sephirothic Colour: **Yellow**

Card Dynamics:
One angelic hand rises from swirling clouds holding six lotus stems, from which six pink lotuses bow outwards, passing the waters of life into six cups. The perspective of height and depth in this card is important, as here in Tiphareth one is at the very centre of the Tree of Life, subject to the pull of the lower Sephiroth whilst seeking the higher levels. The cups are not overflowing but are filling up, showing the potential to reach high levels of consciousness, yet the heaviness of the clouds below suggest that past activities and obsessions restrain the consciousness from ascending. There is a need for deep thought and soul-searching to break free of the past, even to the point of entering the serpent's coils to unravel them, somewhat implied in the twisted serpentine form of the lotus stems. The watery background of Briah subtly suggests the form of the Higher Self or an invisible guardian angel who continually keeps watch while the soul works out the karmic residue which holds the consciousness down until perfect balance has been accomplished.

The dominant colour is primary yellow, connecting to the mind, which here needs to deal with memories that must be released and laid to rest. It also links to the energy of the Fool. The colours of the seven rays utilized within the card emit a sense of vitality, balance and openness. The Six of Cups can also represent an egregore of protection within a group who have similar objectives for spiritual attainment, and the pleasure of such companionship.

Astrology:

Astrologically, the Sun in Scorpio carries strong passion and sexual desires, revealing a strong magnetic force that could pull the conscious point towards holding its focus on sexual pleasures. Yet with the Sun amplified in Tiphareth, a joyful, childlike innocence which finds pleasure in the beauty of life itself over-rides this Scorpio tendency. One's heart is better served in utilizing Scorpio's penetrative powers to unravel the serpent's coils.

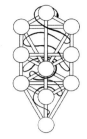

Archetypal Influences:

The archetypal influence is that of the Sun (Sun) and Death (Scorpio), showing that the Six of Cups is an arena of transformation. The magnetic influence of the lower Sephiroth is transmuted into the rising serpent of the caduceus, rising up beyond the light of the Sun into the spiritual and higher levels of awareness, where the pull of Earth no longer rules the ego but gives way to the rule of the Higher Self. Here in Tiphareth, this archetypal combination also alludes to rebirth through Christ's sacrifice and resurrection.

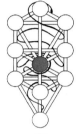

Shem ha-Mephorash:

The angels remind us that in God is the ultimate and true experience of pleasure to be found. Nelkhal (Thou Alone) is indicative of one's absolute commitment and devotion towards God. Yeisel (Thy Right Hand) connects with our reliance upon God for provision and protection.

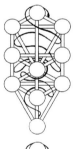

> For thou art great and doest wondrous things;
> Thou alone art God.
>
> Psalm 86:10 (Jubilee Bible 2000)

> My soul clings to Thee;
> Thy right hand upholds me.
>
> Psalm 63:8 (New American Standard Bible)

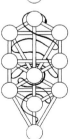

> Thou wilt shew me the path of life:
> In thy presence is fulness of joy;
> At thy right hand there are pleasures for evermore.
>
> Psalm 16:11 (King James Bible)

6
CUPS

SIX OF WANDS
Tiphareth of Atziluth

Esoteric Title:
Lord of Victory

Divine Name:
YHVH Eloah ve Da'ath -
God's Knowledge

Astrology: **Jupiter in Leo**

Shem ha-Mephorash Angels:
Saitiel - **Refuge, Fortress**
Nghelamiah - **Concealed, Saving**

Sephirothic Colour:
Clear Pink Rose

Card Dynamics:
The Six of Wands expresses the upward flow of desire for greater knowledge from a place of perfect balance. The background colour of pink gives this card a sense of peace and strength in love. The two hands clasping three wands each come together at the centre of the card, producing flames of spiritual fire, showing that there is power in the union of opposites. This card heralds both success in a material sense and also a quiet sense of communication with the Higher Self, guiding the success. It shows that a grasp of one's True Will has been understood.

Astrology:
Jupiter in Leo is often associated with intelligence and exuberance. It holds a sense of royalty, which, if negative, can indicate self-delusion or grandioisa which helps to test one's humility and wisdom.

Archetypal Influences:
On an archetypal level, the Wheel of Fortune (Jupiter) and Strength (Leo) indicate that in remaining steadfast in the pursuit of one's True Will, and in committing to one's work with a noble and upright disposition, good fortune and victory will come, bringing respect and recognition.

Shem ha-Mephorash:
Saitiel (Refuge/Fortress) reveals the inner peace that this card promotes. There is a sense of meditation and rest, but with determined penetration into deeper knowledge of oneself. With the Angel Nghelamiah (Concealed/Saving) we see that the purity of this card can be further defined as a redemptive quality where one's inner spiritual life begins to manifest in response to outer circumstances. The two angels help to keep the soul free of entanglements within the serpent's coils, which could otherwise turn into obsessions.

I will say to the LORD, "My refuge and my fortress,
My God, in whom I trust!"

Psalm 91:2 (New American Standard Bible)

It is the glory of God to conceal a thing:
but the glory of kings is to search out a matter.

Proverbs 25:2 (English Revised Version)

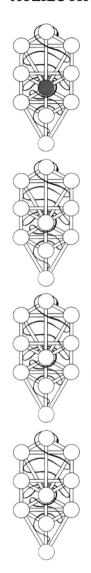

**6
WANDS**

GEBURAH
Severity

Magical Image:
>**A mighty warrior in his chariot.**

God Name:
>*Elohim Gibor* - **God's War; God's Battles**

Archangel:
>*Khamael*

Order of Angels:
>*Seraphim,* **Fiery Serpents**

Planet:
>**Mars**

Spiritual Experience:
>**Vision of Power**

Titles:
>*Pachad, Fear. Din,* **Justice.**

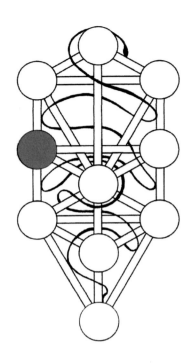

The Fifth Path is called the Radical Intelligence, because it is itself the essence equal to the Unity, uniting itself to the BINAH or Intelligence which emanates from the primordial depths of Wisdom or CHOCHMAH.

Sepher Yetzirah

Scientists are opening up to the idea that parallel worlds exist which have a direct influence upon our own world, yet occultists have always known this. It is in part beautifully shown by the Four Worlds of the Kabbalah. The idea that there are different parallel worlds existing side by side is important in trying to understand the idea that we are moving downwards into the earth, which eventually takes us through into a parallel universe.

I first began to understand this while working through the 30 Aethers of the Enochian system. I discovered that although I was experiencing an upward feeling of rising up, each aether related to a part of the human body, and as I was experiencing rising, my body was telling me that I was descending.

Working with the Tree of Life system of the Hermetic Order of the Golden Dawn has a similar effect, particularly after passing through the Vault in the Adeptus Minor ceremony, when I discovered that I was being drawn down into the Earth. This may sound odd if we associate entering the Earth with the Qlippoth, but it is important to remember that there are different dimensions or worlds: the world of Assiah may border the Qlippoth, but in the world of Yetzirah we enter into the Planetary Body, where we connect with the Higher Self. The process of joining with the Higher Self is a balance between Geburah and Chesed, as the throne of the Higher Self is placed in the palace of Chesed.

The work or influence of Geburah is to cut away anything which may hinder the joining of the lower self with the Higher. We can see why the Hanged Man is so important just below Geburah, as there is a need of sacrifice not just from the lower self but also from the Higher Self, which has moved down to meet the lower self, teaching the ego to remain passive so that the Higher Self can become an active influence within the individual's life and purpose. It is here that the Genius begins to have an impact on the world of Time and Space.

Geburah in Queen Scale takes the colour of the primary which was formerly only available as Red but is today understood as Magenta. Magenta is also associated with the sign of Aries, ruled by Mars, as is Geburah. Thus in Geburah one can find a surge of new vitality and strength to continue the spiritual journey, which can be difficult and exhausting: one deals with a continual flow of new challenges as the consciousness is challenged to rise into new areas of exploration. That which is unnecessary must be cut away here, and sometimes this is drawn out through illness, perhaps necessitating surgery. However, Geburah here also provides a healing energy, giving protection and an extra vitality to heal one's wounds before the next adventure.

FIVE OF PENTACLES
Geburah of Assiah

Esoteric Title:
Lord of Material Trouble

Divine Name:
Elohim Gibor - **God's War;**
               God's Battles

Astrology: **Mercury in Taurus**

Shem ha-Mephorash Angels:
Mibahaih - **Eternal**
Puial - **Supporting All Things**

Sephirothic Colour: **Red flecked black**

Card Dynamics:
An angelic hand reaches out of swirling clouds, holding a withered-looking rose branch which has five beautifully rich pentacles hanging next to four white, decaying roses. The roses suggest that the spiritual focus has been neglected due to material concerns. And yet, in the Five of Pentacles the spiritual idea is still materializing, but with the influence of Geburah being to cut away or shed that which does not fit the blue-print, The Lord of Material Trouble may bring the experience of poverty or illness to the physical vehicle in order to realign the soul to its higher vibration.

The concept of the Higher Self is such a subtle concept that it can be difficult to understand one's deeply-rooted True Will which begins to emerge from the primordial depths. However, when one is living according to this inner direction, the understanding here that a decision must be made which forces one to step away from a physically comfortable situation becomes part of one's education and path. For example, the Five of Pentacles can relate to a decision to live closely to the Earth, or the choice to live with little or no money. There is a sense of hardship in such a situation, and yet a profound and raw connection to the physical world which has a keen spiritual edge. The red flecked black colour of this Sephira is like an animal skin, echoing the sense of proximity to untamed nature and the invocation of one's survival instinct within this card.

The Five of Pentacles may denote a time where experimentation is necessary in order to bring to light new directions or movements for further exploration or development.

Astrology:

The quick mind of Mercury is here focussed within the earthiness of Taurus, so to some degree is frustrated by this strong earthy influence, especially if the environment is choked with material obsessions. Yet once solutions to problems are found and decisions made, a steady, even stubborn, energy will see them through to their outcome.

Archetypal Influences:

The archetypal influence of the Magician (Mercury) and the Hierophant (Taurus) can be just as difficult. The Magician can be helped by the traditional influence of the Hierophant, but at some point the free-flowing Mercury will become stifled by the rigidity of the Hierophant's influence, forcing the Magician to start out on his own.

Shem ha-Mephorash:

The angels of this card are Mibahaih (Eternal) and Puial (Supporting all Things). These two angels help and support the eternal soul on its journey towards the joining of the higher aspect of its nature to the physical realm. This is a difficult transformation, where much has to be left behind as a deeper reality emerges within conscious awareness.

GEBURAH
OF
ASSIAH

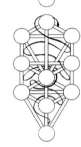
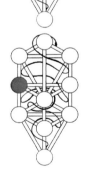

5

PENTACLES

FIVE OF SWORDS
Geburah of Yetzirah

Esoteric Title:
Lord of Defeat

Divine Name:
Elohim Gibor - **God's War;**
                  God's Battles

Astrology: **Venus in Aquarius**

Shem ha-Mephorash Angels:
Anaiel - **Lord of Hosts/Virtues**
Chaamiah - **Hope**

Sephirothic Colour: **Red**

Card Dynamics:
Five swords are held by three angelic hands emerging from swirling clouds. The central sword, pushing aside four smaller swords, represents the penetration of truth, whilst the swords on each side symbolize deception. The rose has been shattered, casting a bloodlike reflection upon the swords. The Five of Swords is a warning of some kind of deception which has entered one's life, perhaps through a close friend, perhaps through a person not yet known, or perhaps self-deception. It could also represent a deceitful relationship or a loss by theft or underhanded action. Circumstances are such that the will must act to break through the barriers to its true course. The red colour of this card shows the action of Mars on the swords as the True Will attempts to break the archetypal structures which no longer support an emerging new paradigm. This new paradigm may not yet be obvious, hence a sense of defeat is experienced as one pushes forward – that which is experienced here does not conform to one's desire, but is a necessary step toward manifesting one's True Will.

Astrology:
Venus in Aquarius is linked to sexual magnetism, which shows that this card is strongly related to sexual relationships, but at the same time remaining unattached and free from entanglements. The Venusian influence, as can be seen by the archetypal and angelic links, is extremely potent in this card, but it faces opposition to the point of destruction from the Sword of Geburah within this red field of Mars.

Archetypal Influences:

The archetypal influence is that of the Empress (Venus) and the Star (Aquarius). This generatres a strongly feminine force, full of life and sexuality, but here in Geburah of Yetzirah this archetypal combination suggests a mental testing akin to that which takes place during the menstrual cycle. One's consolation is in the remembrance that the intensity, pain, and sense of defeat are temporary, and will pass.

Shem ha-Mephorash:

The two angels are Anaiel (Lord of Hosts/Virtues) and Chaamiah (Hope). Anaiel, archangel of Venus, and Chaamiah (Hope) also relate to the Star, further strengthening the idea of a strong feminine influence, but with love as the main virtue. This card represents a difficult phase. The divine Hope carries the reassurance that one shall come through this period into easier times.

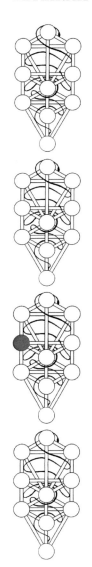

5
SWORDS

FIVE OF CUPS
Geburah of Briah

Esoteric Title:
Lord of Loss in Pleasure

Divine Name:
Elohim Gibor - **God's War;**
God's Battles

Astrology: **Mars in Scorpio**

Shem ha-Mephorash Angels:
Livoih - **Hastening to Hear**
Pheheliah - **Help from Above**

Sephirothic Colour: **Magenta**

Card Dynamics:
The Five Cups are empty of the life-giving waters. The lotus flowers signify a beauty, but lack spiritual depth. The primary colour magenta of this Sephira holds both a pure and powerful love energy, and a strong, sexual energy: this card can indicate that a friend may visit just when you need help or comfort, and it can also indicate a passionate love affair, often one which cannot be fulfilled. But the main influence within this realm of consciousness lies in the fact that without a spiritual awareness, physical pleasure becomes empty and unfulfilling: the continued pursuit of such can lead to experiment-ation into darker areas of gratification, unless a return to a spiritual core is awakened. The idea of turning away from an object of beauty to gather oneself and reconnect with the Divine Light is part of the work of Geburah – testing the soul to its limits so that it understands its own strengths, which lie deep down beyond the sensual flesh and emotional comforts. Such loss brings a feeling of desperation. This level of consciousness brings a temporary loss of light but still holds the tender love needed to continue on one's spiritual path.

Astrology:
Mars in Scorpio brings a strong need for sexual fulfilment, to a point of obsession, and carries with it a secretive and jealous temperament which could destroy any lasting relationships. Here in Geburah, the Lord of Loss in Pleasure removes the object of one's desire from reach, for the sake of spiritual growth.

Archetypal Influences:

The archetypal influences of this card are The Tower (Mars) and Death (Scorpio). Both these transformative archetypes act as catalysts to experiences which allow the soul to become aware that rather than the exhilarating experience of fulfilling one's desires as the main driving force, it is the invisible and all-embracing power of love that dominates the search for fulfilment.

Shem ha-Mephorash:

The angels of this card are Livoih (Hastening to Hear) and Pheheliah (Help from Above). These titles show the underlying movement to reconnect with the spiritual realms and be guided by the True Will. They are a reminder that during such times of desperation, prayers will be heard and responded to swiftly and lovingly.

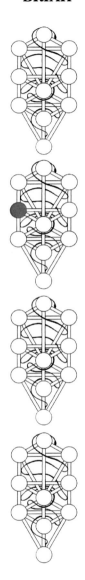

5
CUPS

FIVE OF WANDS
Geburah of Atziluth

Esoteric Title:
Lord of Strife

Divine Name:
Elohim Gibor - **God's War;**
                        God's Battles

Astrology: **Saturn in Leo**

Shem ha-Mephorash Angels:
Vahuaiah - **God the Exalter**
Yelauel - **My Strength**

Sephirothic Colour: **Orange**

Card Dynamics:
Two hands extend from swirling clouds and hold five wands – four crossed, and one within the centre. This card represents the world of Atziluth working out through the conscious level of Geburah. The magnetic frequency of Atziluth is one of breaking up and testing any solid structures. Geburah, governed by the planet Mars, also suggests cutting away unwanted material. This combination produces a powerful force of judgement and readjustment, causing strife as the outer world reflects the changes occurring within the soul. It is therefore an initiatory influence on a spiritual level, which may not be immediately recognized as such, and thus it creates resistance to the flow of change being experienced. Here the Higher Self is felt with power and one experiences the force of the True Will, which breaks apart anything that stands in its way. A strong sexual force is attached to this card, which may suggest illicit affairs or passionate and volatile relationships. With the middle wand so strongly placed, it also suggests a kundalini rise, unblocking any resistance that may hinder its rising.

Astrology:
Saturn gives a strong directional force of the True Will, and thus Saturn in Leo can bring a positive influence of strength and determination to any endeavour, although Saturn's placement in Leo can also generate inhibitions and loss of self-confidence. Strife also occurs within the personality when one perceives the True Will but lacks confidence due to social or domestic restraints.

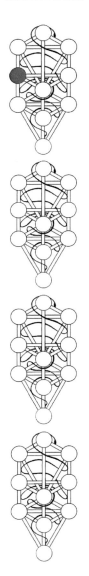

Archetypal Influences:

The archetypal influences are represented by The Universe (Saturn) and Strength (Leo). Working through Geburah in Atziluth, the strong element of Fire suggests a purifying influence that acts on the other three elements, bringing a strong focus on the one unifying force of love, which is the magnetic glue behind all structures. Strife is experienced through the separation of each element to be explored and purified in an initiatory setting. Strength then shows the inner light that drives the movement of change, producing strife modified by love.

Shem ha-Mephorash:

The angels of this card are Vahuaiah (God the Exalter) suggesting the upholding of the Law of God, and Yelauel (My Strength). Through this period of adjustment one may experience friction and lack of understanding within human relationships. However, in focussing steadfastly upon the inner leading of the Higher Self, one will find divine Strength in seeing how God exalts those who remain humble to His Will.

5
WANDS

CHESED
Mercy

Magical Image:
A mighty, crowned and throned king.
God Name:
El - God
Archangel:
Tzadkiel
Order of Angels:
Chasmalim, **Brilliant Ones**
Planet:
Jupiter
Spiritual Experience:
Vision of Love.
Titles:
Gedulah, **Love.**
Majesty. Magnificence.

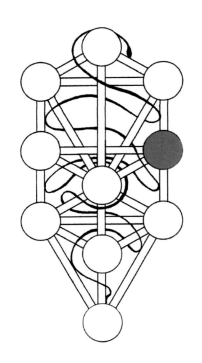

4

The
Fourth
Sephira

"The Fourth Path is called the Cohesive or Receptive Intelligence because it contains all the Holy Powers, and from it emanate all the spiritual virtues with the most exalted essences. They emanate one from another by virtue of the Primordial Emanation, the Highest Crown, Kether."

Sepher Yetzirah

Then God said, Let there be light, and there was light. And God saw the light, that it was good: and God divided the light from the darkness. And God called the light Day and the darkness He called Night. And the evening and the morning were the first day.

Genesis 1: 3-5

On the Path of Emanation, Chesed is considered the first day of Creation and is translated as Mercy, Loving-kindness, or Love. It is the very foundation of the Divine Law which, when translated into the 10 Commandments, provides each soul with an indicator of where one's attention or focus is drawn, helping to realign the soul with Divine Will. The more our thoughts, words, and actions are guided by love, the more we move towards God's love and mercy for us, and the deeper we penetrate our very essence and union with the Soul of the Earth, *Anima Mundi*. It is in Chesed that the human soul connects to the Planetary or World Soul: Chesed could be considered the desire to connect with the Inner Earth and the Greater Mother, Binah, herself.

Both Geburah and Chesed are higher aspects of Tiphareth: the Golden Dawn grading system acknowledges this by their titles, Adeptus Minor (Tiphareth), Adeptus Major (Geburah), and Adeptus Exemptus (Chesed). Geburah cuts away anything that is not needed in the Great Work, and Chesed expands and holds consciousness of the Higher Genius, who is here crowned as king over the individual, and now acts as guide and master over the ego, which remains obedient to his still, silent word.

Chesed is ruled by Jupiter and is beautifully placed to represent the ever-growing and expanding universe, governed by Divine Will and nurtured in love. From Chesed, the Divine Power is distributed throughout the lower Sephiroth, feeding where it is needed.

The power of love and mercy frees the soul of any ties it may hold to the visible creation, bringing it in harmony and balance with the One Who permeates everything. In Chesed we experience peace from fear, and stillness of mind. As our journey upon the Path of Return reaches the consciousness of Chesed, we find that Chesed is light and darkness brought together in love and stillness; not in opposition, but in experience of the depths of God's Love.

FOUR OF PENTACLES
Chesed of Assiah

Esoteric Title:
Lord of Earthly Power

Divine Name: *El* - **God**

Astrology: **Sun in Capricorn**

Shem ha-Mephorash Angels:
Keveqaiah - **To be Rejoiced In**
Mendiel - **Honourable**

Sephirothic Colour:
Deep Azure flecked Yellow

Card Dynamics:
One angelic hand rises from swirling clouds holding a rose branch, with four pentacles making a square surrounded by lush vegetation. In the centre is the most beautiful white rose in full bloom showing that, on the Path of Emanation, Spirit flourishes in this new environment below the Abyss: the Higher Self is held within the material structure that is forming. The speckled background indicates the congealing of the great powers of light into a law on which Creation rests. The rose represents the soul also now being crystallized within matter.

The Four of Pentacles is a reminder of Ezekiel's vision: the four pentacles representing the four Kerubim, which in turn serve the Enochian WatchTowers. These hold order within the elementary powers of the Earth, permitting a beautiful ecosystem which encourages life to thrive and evolve.

Astrology:
The Sun in Capricorn suggests a strong and stable environment for growth and development. The Capricorn/Sun combination brings a youthful and joyful environment allowing for social interaction yet remaining disciplined and focussed.

Archetypal Influences:

Archetypally, The Devil (Capricorn) and The Sun (Sun) make a recipe for success, where the Devil penetrates into material matters and is given the golden light of the Sun to maximize any endeavour with germination and strong growth. But that same light can pronounce the beauty manifesting, invoking desire and passion. There is a danger here of attempting to hold on to the beautiful pentacles, which may symbolize material wealth – such has its own law: if you give, you will receive. Material matters are governed well by the Lord of Earthly Power; however, care must be taken not to lean towards autocracy.

Shem ha-Mephorash:

The Angels of the Shem ha-Mephorash are Keveqaiah (To be Rejoiced In) and Mendiel (Honourable). These two angels show that upon the Path of Return the attainment of this level of consciousness is held in high esteem in its abiding within the Law of God and the rejoicing in His love and presence in a manifesting Creation.

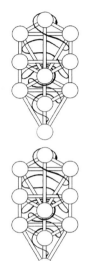

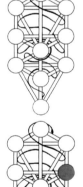

4

PENTACLES

FOUR OF SWORDS
Chesed of Yetzirah

Esoteric Title:
Lord of Rest from Strife

Divine Name: *El* - **God**

Astrology: **Jupiter in Libra**

Shem ha-Mephorash Angels:
Laviah - **Wonderful**
Keliel - **Worthy to be Invoked for Self**

Sephirothic Colour: **Deep Purple**

Card Dynamics:
The Four of Swords exudes stillness. The mind has transcended thought and is experiencing quiet, tranquility and silence. It is a stillness that is pregnant with great awareness, beyond the pull of the chattering thoughts that pull and push the soul in all directions. The soul is preparing to rise over the Abyss and needs to be free.

Two hands rise up from two swirling clouds, holding four swords. The swords cross in the centre, over which is a beautiful, red rose that radiates life. The red rose is connected to Venus, bringing a strong focus on love that overcomes all obstacles. The rose further symbolizes Spirit, bringing a deeper focus on spiritual matters. The conscious mind has become aware of a Great Mind – an Intelligence that has no name but is everywhere in Nature perceived. This is a place of great spiritual attainment. If the soul struggles against this movement into silence, this card can herald a period of enforced confinement where the soul is forced to rest in an attempt to make it aware of the immaculate Intelligence in-dwelling all life in the universe.

Astrology:
Astrologically, Jupiter in Libra brings a warm and friendly energy. This is a beneficial placement for Jupiter: the balanced nature of Libra allows Jupiter to expand without interference, allowing consciousness to meet new horizons, as yet unperceived.

Archetypal Influences:

Archetypally, the Wheel of Fortune (Jupiter) and Justice (Libra) combine to transcend karmic limitations. Consciousness can only rise as far as the karmic debt due, as karma must be neutralized at the same level of consciousness that caused the imbalance within Divine Law.

Shem ha-Mephorash:

Through Yeshua, the angels Laviah (Wonderful) and Keliel (Worthy to be Invoked for Self) help to bring karmic weight down so that the consciousness is not restricted nor pulled back by the need to work out past issues, hence the Lord of Rest from Strife. They carry the Wonderful Name of God, ever-faithful in each soul's quest to "Know Thyself."

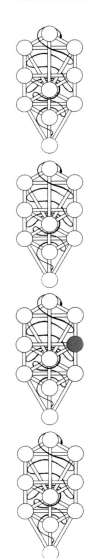

> Open my eyes, that I may behold
> Wonderful things from Thy law.
> Psalm 119:18 (NASB 1977)

> For unto us a child is born, unto us a son is given,
> and the government is placed upon his shoulder,
> and his name shall be called
> The Wonderful One,
> The Counsellor,
> The God,
> The Mighty One,
> The Eternal Father,
> The Prince of Peace.
> Isaiah 9:6 (Jubilee Bible 2000)

4
SWORDS

FOUR OF CUPS
Chesed of Briah

Esoteric Title:
Lord of Blended Pleasure

Divine Name: *El* - **God**

Astrology: **Moon in Cancer**

Shem ha-Mephorash Angels:
Heyaiel - **Lord of the Universe**
Mevamiah - **End of the Universe**

Sephirothic Colour: **Primary Cyan**

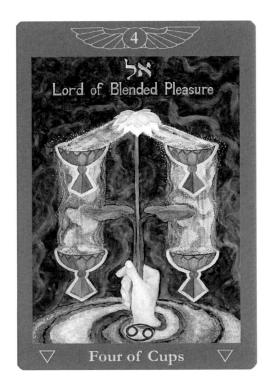

Card Dynamics:
An angelic hand rises from swirling clouds holding a lotus stem which pours the Azoth into two upper cups, which in turn overflow into the two lower cups. Although the life force flowing into the two upper cups is strong, the lower cups do not overflow, showing that it is needed to feed and nurture new life, creating a self-centred and nurturing disposition. Emotionally, this is a time of absolving past hurts, letting go of former expectations and ideals, and focussing in on who we truly are, allowing altruistic love to permeate the new growth. The Four of Cups can also indicate unwanted interference in an emotional area, warranting a time of separation or introspection, but most of all it is about conception of a new life and the readjustment needed to birth that life. The primary cyan blue of the border and the cups amplify the connection with the High Priestess and the still, small voice ever-present in this introspective environment.

Descending the Tree on the Path of Emanation, this new life would concern a forthcoming birth into the physical. The Four of Cups reflects the concept of impregnation coupled with morning sickness, where after becoming impregnated there is a physical reaction to the new life that has been seeded and is now growing within the womb, creating a period of imbalance, and blending the pleasure of this state with often extreme physical discomfort. The early stages of pregnancy are the most difficult in this regard. The conscious point is forced to turn inward to rebalance and connect with the new life developing. That which is being formed may be a new project rather than a child, but the same dynamic applies.

On the ascent, upon the Path of Return, this card is concerned with the soul's birth into Spirit. The Lord of Blended Pleasure demonstrates the blending of an influx of spiritual wisdom from Chokmah of Briah into Chesed of Briah, temporarily disrupting the status quo until this wisdom is assimilated.

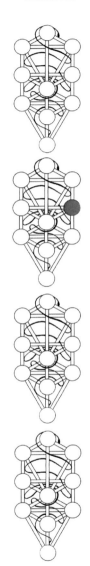

Astrology:
Cancer is considered the archetypal Mother, and the fact that the Moon heightens the Cancerian traits brings here a sensitive, feminine intuition that can be trusted. Cancer rules the stomach area, bringing further attention or focus upon the womb and the digestion, but perhaps the most important influence of the Moon in Cancer is the heightened Cancerian need to withdraw into its shell and meditate on one's inner needs.

Archetypal Influences:
Archetypally, The Chariot (Cancer) and The High Priestess (Moon) combine as a powerful force needed to pass over the Abyss. The Chariot has balanced opposing forces and is guided by the Higher Will. The central Path of the High Priestess traverses the Abyss towards Kether, leading the soul to encounter the archetypal forces of the Mother and Father (Binah and Chokmah). She also brings deeper awareness of the spiritual work of one's True Will.

Shem ha-Mephorash:
The Angels of the Shem ha-Mephorash are Heyaiel (Lord of the Universe) and Mevamiah (End of the Universe). These two angels help to lead the soul deeply into a mirror universe within, which opens up as the soul connects with the Earth Mother.

4
CUPS

FOUR OF WANDS
Chesed of Atziluth

Esoteric Title:
Lord of Perfected Work

Divine Name: *El* - **God**

Astrology: **Venus in Aries**

Shem ha-Mephorash Angels:
Nanael - **Caster-down of the Proud**
Nithael - **Celestial King**

Sephirothic Colour: **Deep Violet**

Card Dynamics:
Chesed of Atziluth is like a seed that has germinated into a beautiful flower which in turn brings about many more seeds. This is the Shangri-La of the Minor Arcana, the Earthly paradise which manifests the presence of the Higher Self, also introducing feelings of love and altruistic benevolence. Here, the human soul connects with the *Anima Mundi* or Soul essence of the Earth, invoking the True Will in its purity, and preparing for the second birth into Spirit.

The violet/purple[1] colour of this Sephira brings a regal richness to the image, suggesting prosperity and success in all endeavours. It also carries a priestly energy; purple being a dominant colour within the consecrated priestly garments, the curtains of the Tabernacle, and the veil separating the Holy Place from the Most Holy Place (Exodus 26-28). Correspondingly, this deep violet reflects the sense of quiet holiness felt at this level of consciousness as the soul is prepared for the crossing of the Abyss into the Supernals.

Astrology:
The combination of Venus in Aries brings passion and the need to embrace and explore love on many different levels. It brings enjoyment of friends and loved ones, social engagements and happy interactions, also initiating new creative enterprises and business ventures.

---

1   See Violet and Purple, Colour Magic of the Golden Dawn, p.224.

Archetypal Influences:
The archetypal influence of The Empress (Venus) and The Emperor (Aries) complements the title Lord of Perfected Work, the Empress being pregnant with twins and the Emperor initiating forces which manifest the highest ideals, thus reflecting the title.

Shem ha-Mephorash:
The angels of this card are Nanael (Caster-down of the Proud) and Nithael (Celestial King). These two angels bring great success to an individual as the True Will is perceived in its purity. Through Nithael do we clelebrate in the Perfected Work of the One God. Any sense of self-adulation here will be dealt with by Nanael, bringing to mind the fate of the earthly King Nebuchadnezzar.

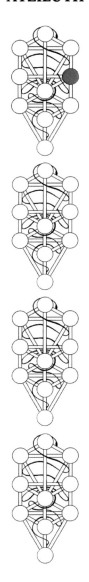

4
WANDS

DA'ATH
Knowledge

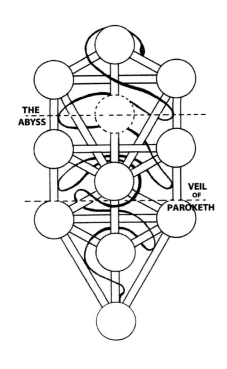

Magical Image:
A head with two faces, looking both ways;
Sheila-na-Gig

God Name:
A conjunction of *YHVH* and
YHVH Elohim

Archangel:
The Archangels of the Cardinal Points

Astrological link: **Sirius**

Spiritual Experience:
Vision across the Abyss

Titles:
The Invisible Sephira. The Hidden or Unrevealed Cosmic Mind.
The Mystical Sephira. The Upper Room.

Da'ath is something of a mystery in that it does not exist as a Sephira: it is depicted neither upon the Tree of Life nor upon the Tree of the Knowledge of Good and Evil, yet it exists as a potential or as an opening. It has been suggested to be the placement of Malkuth before the Fall; an invisible placement halfway between Tiphareth and Kether, lying across the Abyss. Da'ath has also been described as the invisible side of Kether, further connecting it to Malkuth and a state of awareness beyond Kether.

Above Geburah and Chesed lies the Supernal triad of Kether, Binah and Chokmah. These are separated from the lower Sephiroth by a great Abyss which leads to the qlippothic realm, and for exploration of this dark realm it is best to be in the company of an angel of light. Upon the journey into the Abyss, the first visual image one encounters is of a great lake within which are seen lost souls, desperately trying to escape. It is a qlippothic trap: once entered, one cannot leave. Descending into a vertical tunnel, exits can be seen at different points. Travelling further or deeper down, the magnetic pull within the qlippoth becomes stronger, until it becomes the dominating force which would overwhelm. At this point in the exploration, one should take an exit that leads into one of the horizontal tunnels, for to continue downwards would mean never to return. It is at this balancing point that the dark entities can be met: at first they appear as shadows, but this is just a mask which, once removed, reveals undeveloped forms. This shows the nature of the qlippothic realm: it is opposed to creation and evolution, representing an aspect of God that opposes His own Creation. The Abyss is likened to a rip in the fabric of Time. It is guarded by millions of angels, preventing the two realms from ever coming together.

Da'ath is connected to the Abyss, although it is not necessarily the same. Da'ath is more complex in its understanding and can represent a doorway or opening – perhaps a doorway into the qlippoth, but perhaps a doorway into a parallel universe, or a doorway into the Earth. Da'ath is sometimes referred to as an empty room, but the empty room is rather a state of being within Da'ath. The action of Da'ath is an opening, much as the vesica-shaped opening at the forehead allows a seed to awaken the Third Eye, and as such, Da'ath (Knowledge) is very much connected to the Tree of The Knowledge of Good and Evil: the Kabbalistic glyph of the serpent entwined around the Tree represents a masculine seed that fertilizes greater awareness and higher forms of consciousness, also alluding to a second birth.

Da'ath is considered to have two faces – one is a barren landscape wherein Da'ath is an invisible potential, and the other is a doorway. When the archetypal Mother and the archetypal Father (Binah and Chokmah) are brought together in acting through love, the door within the Heart Chakra opens, aligning with the World Soul deep within oneself and within our beautiful planet, Mother Earth. The High Priestess and The Empress represent the two aspects or faces of Da'ath – the former to cross, and the latter to enter.

BINAH
Understanding

Magical Image:
> **A mature woman**

God Name:
> *YHVH Elohim*

Archangel:
> *Tzaphkiel*

Order of Angels:
> *Aralim,* Thrones

Planet:
> **Saturn**

Spiritual Experience:
> **Vision of Sorrow**

Titles:
> *Ama,* **the dark, sterile Mother;** *Aima,* **the bright, fertile Mother.** *Khorsia,* **the Throne.** *Marah,* **the Great Sea.**

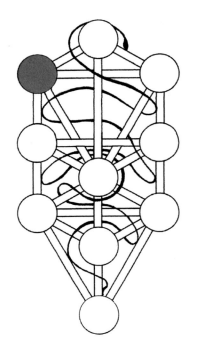

"The Tenth Path is called the Resplendent Intelligence because it is exalted above every head and sits upon the throne of Binah. It illuminates the splendours of all the Lights, and causes an influence to emanate from the Prince of Countenances, the Angel of Kether."

Sepher Yetzirah

Binah is the Greater Mother. She represents the Soul of the Earth, which can only be revealed through Divine Love. Love opens the gates to the innermost essence of our being, which is closely connected to our planet. Binah represents the internal spiritual essence of our planet, the beauty of which manifests outwardly within Creation in all its diversity as the Lesser Mother, Malkuth. This is evident by the angels of Binah, the Aralim (the Strong and Mighty Ones), also called Thrones, who work under the direction of Archangel Tzaphkiel, and watch over the plants, trees and the germination of seeds. Tzaphkiel also protects from the damaging influence of hatred.

Binah is closely connected with the concept of the Shekhinah, the Divine Presence within Creation. The Shekhinah is felt as the feminine influence – God's protective and nurturing influence. The Shekhinah is symbolized as the River of Life, revealed in the Minor Arcana flowing into the Cups, sustaining and nurturing the spiritual life held within Divine Law. There are two sides to Binah: AIMA, the bright fertile mother, represents the active presence of the Shekhinah, while AMA, the dark sterile mother, can represent the withdrawal of the Shekhinah's influence and can be likened to the experience known as the Dark Night of the Soul. The difference between the two is the letter *yod*, which acts as the fertile spark in AIMA (אימא), but is absent in AMA (אמא).

The God-name of Binah is *YHVH Elohim*, which influences the cultivation of civilization, allowing humanity to grow in strength and experience and express itself through love. Within this love is the understanding that all life stems from the Oneness which we call God, and that our environment is not something we can exploit and destroy. Rather we need to partake in the natural cycles of life with an awareness of the need to nurture and protect our environment, as the consciousness of the planet is part of our own.

THREE OF PENTACLES
Binah of Assiah

Esoteric Title:
Lord of Material Works

Divine Name:
YHVH Elohim - **It is, It Was, and it Shall Be**

Astrology: **Mars in Capricorn**

Shem ha-Mephorash Angels:
Yechuiah - **Knower of All Things**
Lehahaiah - **Merciful**

Sephirothic Colour:
Grey flecked Pink

Card Dynamics:
Binah in Assiah is where the True Will takes on its full potential in changing and redirecting outmoded or outdated thought-forms that have prevented a deeper integration within Divine Light. The angelic hand emanating from the clouds holds a rose branch upon whose tip are two rosebuds, revealing the fertile potential of the card. The background is seen as crystallized light which is ready to be transferred into structures of immense beauty, preparing to bring all consciousness back to its source. It is a work in progress and will not end until all is One again. The triangular shape created by the three pentacles relates to the magnetic pull for order and manifestation into the material world. It is a sign of great creative potential and success in one's true desires.

Astrology:
Mars in Capricorn generates a strong drive to succeed in fulfilling one's True Will, with long-lasting determination. With Saturn ruling Binah it may take many years to see results, or may extend beyond the lifetime of the individual who set it in motion, but the influence or consequences will be unstoppable, because each step is carefully laid in the Divine Light's matrix of truth and light.

Archetypal Influences:
Archetypally, the influences of The Tower (Mars) and The Devil (Capricorn) show the overwhelming of the lower world by the higher (or the infiltration of the outer self by that of the inner depths) – The Devil symbolizing the focus on the perceived goal, and the Tower breaking apart anything that stands in its way.

Shem ha-Mephorash:
The angels of this card are Yechuiah (Knower of All Things) and Lehahaiah (Merciful). Their influence works with that of Saturn, slowing the changes that are coming down from on high and creating long-term plans which, whilst keeping the dramatic changes needed to build the vision of the True Will, does so with minimum disruption – that is, with merciful compassion with regard to the limits of our human capacity for dealing with such change.

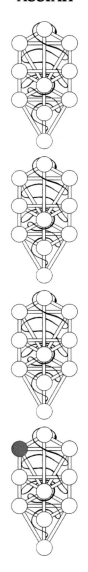

3

PENTACLES

THREE OF SWORDS
Binah of Yetzirah

Esoteric Title:
Lord of Sorrow

Divine Name:
YHVH Elohim - **It is, It Was, and it Shall Be**

Astrology: **Saturn in Libra**

Shem ha-Mephorash Angels:
Harayel - **Aid**
Hoqmiah - **Raise Up, Praying Day and Night** (*sic*)

Sephirothic Colour: **Dark Brown**

Card Dynamics:
Three hands rise out of swirling clouds: each holds a sword which destroys the beautiful, red rose, of which only the falling petals remain. The swords formerly crossed in creative potential are now pushed aside by the relentless drive of the central sword of one's True Will. As we leave the haven of the Four of Swords, a new paradigm begins to emerge above the Abyss, bringing the experience of pain and sorrow.

Binah has a dark side called *Ama*, the Dark, Sterile Mother. Here in Yetzirah, *Ama* is experienced through the pain of the flesh and the emotions as the Shekhinah withdraws its blessing. The Three of Swords is about letting go, either voluntarily or forced through outer circumstances. It is about getting divorced from the material pull and adjusting one's focus within the spiritual reality. Emotional pain caused by the breaking of illusory mental constructs can elevate consciousness to very high levels of awareness in one's search for truth.

Astrology:
Astrologically, there is no better teacher than Saturn – strict in correction if the conscious point cannot fully grasp the new level of reality engaged. Faith in the flesh must now be

exchanged for focus within the spiritual life. Saturn is well-placed in Libra, bringing a sense of justice and the need to remain in balance. It is with this aspect that adjustments are made in one's outer reality to remain in balance with inner workings of the spiritual life, including adjustments in one's partnerships, workplace, living environment, and even one's established approach to communing with the Divine. Sorrow is experienced in that momentarily there is no clear vision of the joy to come, just the pain of loss within the changes taking place.

Archetypal Influences:
The archetypal influence is that of the Universe (Saturn) and Justice (Libra), showing that a cycle has come to an end and a new cycle is beginning with the necessary adjustment to keep in alignment with the True Will.

Shem ha-Mephorash:
The two angels are Harayel (Aid) and Hoqmiah (Raise Up, Praying Day and Night). These two angels together show that while there is a call to let go and rise up into higher areas of knowledge, loving help is at hand. Prayer is the most effective channel to heal the pain caused by loss, with faith promising such clarity and vision as yet not experienced.

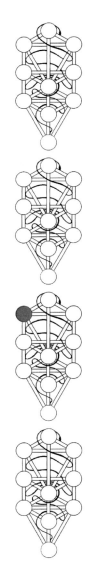

**3
SWORDS**

THREE OF CUPS
Binah of Briah

Esoteric Title:
Lord of Abundance

Divine Name:
YHVH Elohim - **It is, It Was, and it Shall Be**

Astrology: **Mercury in Cancer**

Shem ha-Mephorash Angels:
Rahael - **Beholding All**
Yebamaiah - **Producing All by His Word**

Sephirothic Colour: **Black**

Card Dynamics:
An angelic hand rises out of swirling clouds holding four lotus stems which form a heart. The lotus flowers pour the life-giving waters of the Shekhinah abundantly into three cups which in turn overflow in abundant streams. Binah in Briah, the Field of Form, is pregnant with potential birth and the joy of such. But it can act as a distracting force, as time and energy are needed to nurture the new creation. This card is such that it can project one into fame, which can become a stumbling block to the work of the True Will. The Three of Cups also shows a time of communicating between friends on a social level, meeting new friends and acquaintances, but ultimately it is the celebration of a new life, whether spiritual or physical, and with it comes the need to nurture it, as it will transmute old beliefs and habits and bring us into a deeper realisation of the soul's true nature within the play of life.

Astrology:
Mercury in Cancer generates an excellent imaginative nature, which can be creatively used in magic. Yet it can also be troublesome if allowed to bring worry in small things. Worry can destroy faith; it wastes energy and brings unprofitable thought-forms.

Archetypal Influences:

Archetypally, the Magician (Mercury) and the Chariot (Cancer) exemplify the force of will and its projection under the guidance of the True Will, manifesting the Lord of Abundance, so that the spiritual work can continue without worrying about material concerns.

Shem ha-Mephorash:

The angels of this card are Rahael (Beholding All) and Yebamaiah (Producing All by His Word). These Angels reveal the deep connection within the symbolism of this card with *Ain Soph* (the Word beholding all and producing all).

> In the beginning was the Word, and the Word was with God,
> and the Word was God. He was in the beginning with God.
> All things were made through Him, and without Him
> nothing was made that was made.
>
> John 1:1-3 (NKJ)

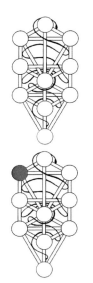

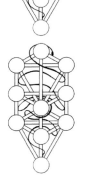

3
CUPS

THREE OF WANDS
Binah of Atziluth

Esoteric Title:
Lord of Established Strength

Divine Name:
YHVH Elohim - **It is, It Was, and It Shall Be**

Astrology: **Sun in Aries**

Shem ha-Mephorash Angels:
Hechaseiah - **Secret and Impenetrable**
Amamiah - **Covered in Darkness**

Sephirothic Colour: **Crimson**

Card Dynamics:
The world of Atziluth represents the magnetic matrix in chaos, within the structure of Divine Light. This Light has not yet formed into its triangular structures, the patterns which define the laws of Creation within three points. Binah in Atziluth is a dynamic force which is difficult to resist. It is a surge of energy that directs an individual, a community, and humanity, towards their true spiritual work. When the human soul has joined with the World Soul it is in harmony with Divine Will to establish Heaven on Earth. Consciousness struggles against structure, yet the Three of Wands shows that order is establishing direction. The ego will attempt to control, but is overwhelmed by the influence of creative energy. It must let go of all perceived ideas, allowing the True Will to fulfil its mission.

Astrology:
The Sun in Aries exemplifies the dynamic influence that brings new life to all aspects of creation. It enlivens new growth on the decomposing remnants of past structures. The Sun in Aries also brings out the unconventional personality, which does not like conformity.

Archetypal Influences:

The archetypal influence of The Sun (Sun) and the Emperor (Aries) is one of great benefit as it helps to protect and enrich ones environment. The Lord of Established Strength is in keeping with the Emperor's stronghold on matters of importance, bringing swift order to any discord which may enter this realm of consciousness.

Shem ha-Mephorash:

The angels Hechaseiah (Secret and Impenetrable) and Amamiah (Covered in Darkness) guard against accidental penetration within this secret place of the Divine Light. If we were able to penetrate matter we would discover great depths of darkness before entering into a glorious Divine Light. Through the empowerment of Love, a penetration into the Soul of the Earth becomes possible, but only with the Higher Self, for it is he who guides us through the darkness, like the Hermit with his guiding light.

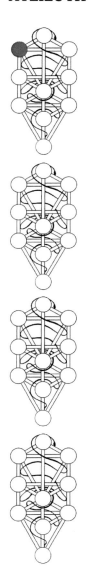

3
WANDS

CHOKMAH
Wisdom

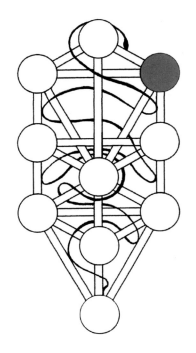

2	The Second Sephira

Magical Image:
  A bearded male figure
God Name:
  Yah - **LORD**
Archangel:
  Ratziel
Order of Angels:
  Auphanim, Wheels
Astrological Connection:
  The Zodiac
Spiritual Experience:
  The Vision of God face to face
Titles:
  Power of Yetzirah; *Ab*; *Abba*; **The Supernal Father; Tetragrammaton; Yod of Tetragrammaton.**

"The Second Path is called the Illuminating Intelligence. It is the Crown of Creation, the Splendour of Unity, equalling it. It is exalted above every head, and is named by Qabalists, the Second Glory."

Chokmah is situated at the top right-hand side of the Tree of Life. The Spiritual Experience of Chokmah is the "Vision of God Face to Face." It represents the Supernal Father, not in gender terms, but in its linear movement of magnetic attraction to the centre of the universe within oneself.

Binah holds the symbol of the Outer Robe of Concealment, which refers to the penetration through the dark layers of the Earth before entering the beautiful light of the Earth Mother, or Soul of the Earth. Chokmah symbolizes the penetration through the Soul of the Earth, into deep space. Remember, we are travelling within ourselves: the vision of the central, spiralling galaxy is the destination and we are pulled towards it like metal filings towards a magnet. Chokmah holds no planetary attribution in the Golden Dawn system but is attributed to the Zodiac, hinting at the journey towards Kether, which is the centre of one's personal universe.

Without Binah, that is, without entering the Soul of the Earth, it would not be possible to penetrate into the Chokmah sphere of space. The Three Supernal Sephiroth – Kether, Chokmah and Binah – are as one. Kether feeds the Soul of the Earth (Binah) with the light of life, as a beam of light (Chokmah). Binah in turn, feeds the innumerable life-forms that she forms within her domain.

TWO OF PENTACLES
Chokmah of Assiah

Esoteric Title:
Lord of Harmonious Change

Divine Name: *Yah - LORD*

Astrology: **Jupiter in Capricorn**

Shem ha-Mephorash Angels:
Lekabel - **Teacher**
Vesheriah - **Upright**

Sephirothic Colour:
White flecked Magenta, Cyan, and Yellow

Card Dynamics:
Chokmah in Assiah is in tension – from here we either descend into the material world or rise into pure Spirit. Here we experience a transition of consciousness or knowing of who we truly are – an overview interpreted as Wisdom.

An angelic hand rises out of swirling clouds holding a serpent which has twisted itself into the figure of the lemniscate, symbolizing infinity. The serpent holds two pentacles, one representing light and the other darkness, hinting at a yin/yang interaction of seemingly opposing forces, although the discs themselves are identical.

The serpent has many symbolisms. Here, it represents consciousness but also a magnetic force which binds matter together. The serpent swallows its own tail, indicating that there are inner and outer layers of consciousness overlapping into infinite layers of movement towards a universal source or point of oneness. Although two discs are held together by the serpent, it is actually one disc in transition from the Soul of the World to a Universal Soul. These are divided by Time and Space, a result of the crystallization of matter by the serpent force within creation.

Astrology:
Jupiter in Capricorn can be experienced as a yin/yang type of energy as it pulls back and forth from introverted to extroverted. This trend is encapsulated within the experience of moving from the safety of the World Soul into the spiritual realms of space, pulling strongly to its centre. Jupiter's expansive nature working with Capricorn's capacity for endurance fosters a favourable environment for the journey into the deeper awareness of inner space.

Archetypal Influences:
Archetypally, The Wheel of Fortune (Jupiter) and The Devil (Capricorn) are a force to be reckoned with. The Wheel of Fortune gives constant movement to our ever-expanding consciousness and The Devil gives the focus to drive the conscious point ever-deeper into the knowledge of the Divine Will.

Shem ha-Mephorash:
The angels of this card are Lekabel (Teacher) and Vesheriah (Upright). The Teacher is the written Law (Torah) which is imprinted in the heart and experienced as the Love of God. This Law is the earthing of the Shekhinah, which is also an aspect of Binah. To be upright in the vision of God face-to-face can only be achieved by a righteous soul anointed by the Holy Spirit.

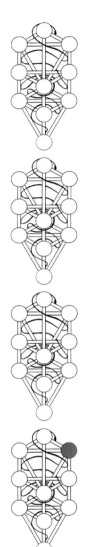

2

PENTACLES

TWO OF SWORDS
Chokmah of Yetzirah

Esoteric Title:
Lord of Peace Restored

Divine Name: *Yah - LORD*

Astrology: **Moon in Libra**

Shem ha-Mephorash Angels:
Lezalel - **Rejoicing Over All Things**
Mevahael - **Guardian and Preserver**

Sephirothic Colour:
Bluish Mother of Pearl

Card Dynamics:
Two angelic hands rise from swirling clouds, each holding a sword: the two swords are crossed, not in conflict but in conciliation, as reflected in the beautiful red rose borne upon them. Balance has been obtained and a new level of consciousness has been established. The rose represents Spirit. Ten white rays symbolizing the purity of the 10 Sephiroth are emitted from a centre which echoes the star of the 17th Key, alluding to the healing and hope inherent in this card.

This card holds the purity and softness of its pale blue-toned mother-of-pearl background and yet carries the energy of a steel–like resolve to remain in balance, particularly following the turmoil of the Three of Swords. Peace Restored is a consequence of renewed focus upon the spiritual dimensions.

In Chokmah of Yetzirah, a portal opens to allow a deeper penetration into inner space: the human soul has joined with the World Soul and is ready to penetrate the centre of the Universe. The meditator or technician of consciousness strives to penetrate ever-more deeply into the realms of the subconscious, seeking the Kingdom of God. The deeper we penetrate, the more we let go of the material world, in the knowledge that the balancing of archetypal forces and the focus upon Divine Will brings its own material rewards.

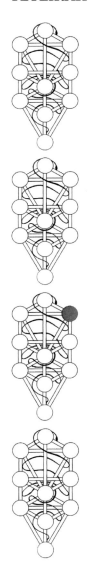

Astrology:
The Moon in Libra brings a natural tendency to seek balance and harmony on all levels. The Moon in Libra is repelled by conflicting and aggressive energies, its inclination being toward peace and a tranquil environment. The Moon in Libra is well-placed for meditation and balancing opposing archetypal forces through study and the interplay of relationships.

Archetypal Influences:
Archetypally, The High Priestess (Moon) and Justice (Libra) bring empathy. Such sensitivity is a natural gift for the soul attuned to the World Soul – a product of the realisation that we are all connected. Justice holds the balance of karmic residue which has been neutralized within Chokmah. Through the power of the crucifixion the conscious point of the soul has been freed to travel into inner space, the High Priestess parting the inner curtain in invitation.

Shem ha-Mephorash:
The two angels are Lezalel (Rejoicing Over All Things) and Mevahael (Guardian and Preserver). The deep level of consciousness experienced within a soul connected to the World Soul brings an empathic sensitivity to all things, and this invokes a joyous wonder of Creation with all its diversity, and of life itself with its manifold expressions and experiences. Herein lays the sacred service of stewarding the Earth in harmony with the Divine – a natural consequence of becoming balanced and attuned in the natural world. Additionally, the deep connection affords the soul an increasingly clearer vision of the True Will while the divine graces of provision and protection minister to one's needs, physical and otherwise.

2 SWORDS

TWO OF CUPS
Chokmah of Briah

Esoteric Title:
Lord of Love

Divine Name: *Yah - LORD*

Astrology: **Venus in Cancer**

Shem ha-Mephorash Angels:
Aiael - **Delight of the Sons of Men**
Chabeiah - **Most Liberal Giver**

Sephirothic Colour:
Pearl Grey

Card Dynamics:

This card portrays a Lotus Wand, resting on a lotus flower which rises from the waters of Briah, the World of Creation. The stem of the Lotus Wand is divided into the 12 segments of the colour wheel, representing the 12 zodiacal signs of Chokmah. The black base symbolizes matter, and the upper white band, Spirit; the ten visible petals of the lotus flower atop the wand represent the purity of the Ten Sephiroth – the Lord of Love manifests in all. From the wand issues a fountain of the living water, the Azoth, which cascades upon the two dolphins, Argent and Or (Silver and Gold), who rise up from the cosmic sea below. The waters take on the essence or colour of the two dolphins and fill to overflowing two cups which are held by angelic hands which emerge from a white centre of swirling clouds.

The dolphin is a highly spiritual symbol of the awareness of and attunement with the Oneness of all things. It represents high intelligence, a high form of consciousness, and emotional release, and is thus well-suited as a symbol in Chokmah of Briah, a place of unconditional love. The expression of such love is a reflection of the powerful universal force whose aim is to bring all life back to the Oneness within the centre of each being and the universe itself.

This Sephira is also an arena for the marriage of opposites, the harmony of masculine and feminine united, the bringing together of two individuals creating one through the magnetic power of love. The experience of sensuality is strangely connected to the spiritual awakening of the soul's awareness of its true nature – that of love – a spark of love connected to God, Who is Love. Thus the Two of Cups is also an expression of this sensual magnetic force which forever tugs at the heart to reunite with its own essence – love.

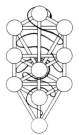

Astrology:
Venus in Cancer holds an experience of love with a protective instinct, understanding and smoothing any interference from the more negative expressions of jealousy and possessiveness, which tend to keep the soul in an emotional flux until true altruistic and universal love is found; such brings a high level of emotional satisfaction.

Archetypal Influences:
Archetypally, Venus represents The Empress, and Cancer, The Chariot. The Empress depicts the fertile mother who has been impregnated with twins. She expresses the abundance of nature through the propagation of the male seed within the female, occurring on a spiritual level as well as physical: sexual union is fundamental to the continuation of life on earth. The Chariot acts as the Higher Will, over-seeing the continuation of life and moving it ever-closer to its Source.

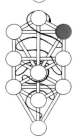

Shem ha-Mephorash:
The angels of this card are Aiael (Delight of the Sons of Men) and Chabeiah (Most Liberal Giver). The ecstatic experience of communion with these angels inspires such a prayer to the Lord of Love as that of St. Francis of Assisi, the duality of which fits well with this card.

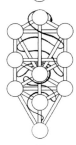

Lord, make me an instrument of your peace,
Where there is hatred, let me sow love;
Where there is injury, pardon;
Where there is doubt, faith;
Where there is despair, hope;
Where there is darkness, light;
Where there is sadness, joy;
O Divine Master, grant that I may not so much seek
To be consoled as to console;
To be understood as to understand;
To be loved as to love.
For it is in giving that we receive;
It is in pardoning that we are pardoned;
And it is in dying that we are born to eternal life.

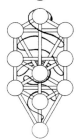

**2
CUPS**

TWO OF WANDS
Chokmah of Atziluth

Esoteric Title:
Lord of Dominion

Divine Name: *Yah - LORD*

Astrology: **Mars in Aries**

Shem ha-Mephorash Angels:
Uhauel- **Great and Lofty**
Daneyal - **Merciful Judge**

Sephirothic Colour: **Soft Blue**

Card Dynamics:
Chokmah in the World of Atziluth focuses on a singularity – the Fountain of Wisdom that lies beyond worldly attachments. The soul here is beyond negative influences as it experiences heightened states of knowing and foresight. The linear magnetic pull towards the centre of the universe also brings the human intelligence in line with the Divine Will, symbolized by the crossed wands held by an angelic hand from which fire explodes into the six directions of space.

Here in Chokmah of Atziluth there is flexibility, but there are also powerful forces of consciousness which elevate the conscious point to a universal awareness joined with self-awareness. There is a desire to merge or become totally immersed within the centre of a spiritual universe within oneself. This creates a Cosmic Egg of protection against higher levels of energy not yet attuned to. The Cosmic Egg has a serpent wrapped around it: the serpent symbolizes Chokmah and the male seed. The Cosmic Egg itself is a symbol of Binah in preparation of the second birth into Spirit.

Astrology:
Mars rules Aries, which brings harmonious energies, full of vitality and strength, to the physical. They are much needed, as the physical vehicle comes under enormous stress when in contact with high levels of consciousness, particularly when weaknesses already exist within the body. Illness can pull the conscious point back into nurturing the body

rather than keeping the inner focus on the prize.

Archetypal Influences:
The archetypal influence is The Tower (Mars) and the Emperor (Aries). Here the Lord of Dominion is exemplified as the Emperor is gifted with higher levels of authority to wield – potentially dangerous amounts of light energy which could be taken away from him if improperly used for selfish ends. Also, the great spiritual forces that influence the Emperor's rule could cause injury if not directed in accordance with Divine Law.

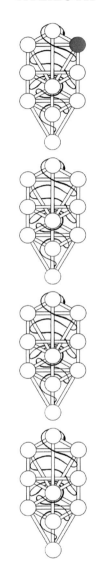

Shem ha-Mephorash:
The angels of this card are Uhauel (Great and Lofty) and Daneyal (Merciful Judge). We are here greeted by two angels which hold one's consciousness within the great and lofty heights of conscious awareness of Spirit, where the soul is immersed in Spirit and needs to remain in harmony with Divine Law. The Pillar of Mercy shows that merciful judgement is pronounced on a person who transgresses the Divine Law, set in the process of Creation itself. Temporary removal from the higher realms is justified in both reminding the ego of that which it has lost, and bringing the humble remembrance that God is ever-present within His Creation, directing all to its highest potential.

2
WANDS

KETHER
The Crown

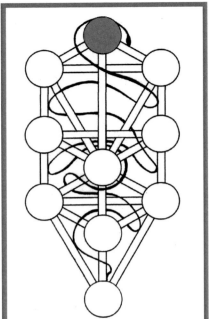

Magical Image:
An ancient, bearded king in profile

God Name:
Eheieh - I AM THAT I AM

Archangel:
Metatron

Order of Angels:
Chaioth he Qadesh, Holy Living Creatures

Spiritual Experience:
Union with God

Titles:
Existence of Existences. Concealed of the Concealed. Ancient of Ancients. Ancient of Days. The Primordial Point. The Most High. The Vast Countenance. Macroprosopos.

1

The First Sephira

"The First Path is Path is called the admirable or Hidden Intelligence because it is the light giving the power of comprehension of the First Principle, which hath no beginning. And it is the Primal Glory, because no created being can attain to its essence."

Kether is the First Emanation on the Tree of Life from *Ain Soph*, holding within itself the Roots of the Four Worlds. The Aces represent the Roots of the Four Elements – *Root of the Powers of Fire, Root of the Powers of Water, Root of the Powers of Air,* and *Root of the Powers of Earth.* Here the Elemental Kings hold their Thrones of authority over the Elemental Serpents in Malkuth.

Archangel Metatron rules over Kether and the Tree of Life itself. Metatron is associated with Thoth-Hermes, and the Egyptian god Ptah. Ptah first appeared from an egg laid by a chaos goose identified as Seb, the Earth god. Ptah then created the primal egg from which all other gods emerged.

Kether is symbolized as a dot or a dot within a circle, although perhaps its most important symbol is that of the flyfot cross, which in itself symbolizes a galaxy whose gravitational attraction holds together millions of stars all of which are within – an inner experience of human consciousness which meets God-consciousness.

If we consider that Binah represents the Inner Earth or Soul of the Earth and Chokmah represents the Zodiac, then Kether represents the centre of the galaxy or the Soul of the Galaxy, which is connected to the Earth Soul and further to the human soul. Because of the immense magnetic attraction, all souls will eventually be drawn back to the source.

Once we are magnetically drawn, we enter the Soul of the Galaxy, which would be damaging for us should we remain for any length of time, as our consciousness cannot adjust so quickly to the new realm of awareness. Thus a protective shell encompasses the human awareness within the Divine. This shell is termed the Cosmic Egg, or Orphic Egg. In alchemy it would be considered the Philosopher's Stone. Within the egg we can grow in safety. The shell of the Cosmic Egg is constructed of the frequencies of the material realms below Kether, to which we are still attached. When we are ready and have grown accustomed to this new realm, the egg breaks open and we experience a second birth into spirit.

It is important to remember that we do nothing in Kether. Kether shows us the way and prepares us for the journey. To use our human will only reels us back to the lower realms. In Kether we are at one with our True Will. Trust is essential.

We now become aware of the interconnectedness of the totality of the Tree of Life and begin to perceive the underlining Unity within *Ain Soph*. With this deeper awareness of reality, Kether becomes the Malkuth for the next stage of the journey, and a new cycle begins. The soul treads the new path from Malkuth with the conscious awareness of the four elements acting in Unity within the gestalt. The ability to exercise the quality of any given element at the prompting of Divine Will becomes the platform from which the soul embarks.

ACE OF PENTACLES
Kether of Assiah

Esoteric Title:
Root of the Powers of Earth

Divine Name:
Eheieh - **I Am That I Am**

Sephirothic Colour:
White flecked Gold

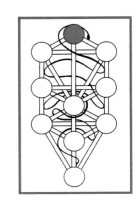

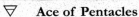
▽   **Ace of Pentacles**   ▽

Card Dynamics:
An angelic hand rises from swirling clouds, holding a rod with three prongs: the central prong holds a beautiful golden pentacle in whose centre is a red cross, representing the four elements in union. From the pentacle shine 12 rays, representing the 12 constellations and their manifestation into Time and Space. The Celtic knotwork, sometimes called the work of angels, represents the spiralling interconnectedness of all things, and the inner and outer worlds. The complex shapes are also a reminder of the matrix within the Divine Light which crystallizes into a myriad of forms within the universe. From this lofty place, new opportunities are initiated which reflect outwardly the inner journey of the Root of the Powers of Earth.

On each side of the pentacle are white roses in varying degrees of bloom which rise up towards a winged disk. The winged disk links to *Ain Soph*. The Ace of Pentacles is the Root of the Powers of Earth, and its roses represent spirit rising up on its everlasting journey. Kether in Assiah is both the crystallization of the Four Worlds of the Kabbalah into light and also the protective shell which shields the conscious point of the soul as it prepares to rise up into the unknown regions of Spirit or the inner depths of the Divine Light.

The golden pentacle of the Tarot was named in the Key of Solomon as the Shekel, representing the riches of the earthly realm. Here, it is placed upon a flowering rose-branch, bringing to mind the flowering Rod of Aaron and linking it to priestly authority. The golden penatacle can thus also be linked with the Disk of Mu which once hung from the Sun Temple in Cusco, but is now hidden in the fourth-dimensional Monastery of the Seven Rays. The Priest of the Sun Temple could initiate changes upon the Earth by sounding certain frequencies on the enormous surface of the disk.

ACE OF SWORDS
Kether of Yetzirah

Esoteric Title:
Root of the Powers of Air

Divine Name:
Eheieh - **I Am That I Am**

Sephirothic Colour:
White Brilliance

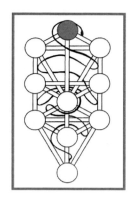

△　　　Ace of Swords　　　△

Card Dynamics:
A sword is held by an angelic hand which emerges from clouds. The sword pierces a crown which represents Kether and the authority to rule over the elemental serpents.

Kether in Yetzirah is aligned with the astral realms – a battle-ground between light and darkness – and the Ace of Swords symbolizes complete authority in the astral realms. The Ace of Swords has an invoking quality and can be likened to a swirling movement, linking the sword to the rising kundalini which has been activated through spiritual work, meditation, and prayer.

Falling about each side of the sword like drops of blood are vavs, six in all, symbolizing Tiphareth and the *Vav* force of the Tetragrammaton. As the serpent force rises upwards it invokes and intensifies the quality of each chakra. When it reaches the Heart Chakra a sword emerges, corresponding to the legend of Excaliber rising from the lake. The sword is given through love and represents pure truth. Nothing false can stand before it. No illusion, falsehood or untruth is able to bear its presence. It is a divine tool that the qlippoth must obey, or else withdraw.

The Ace of Swords represents the True Will in action. Nothing can stand against it, except oneself, through lack of faith and forgetfulness. The path of the True Will is likened to a razor-sharp edge, keeping one's conscious point on the path and continually encouraging us deeper within ourselves. Divine signs and omens are given when needed. From the crown hang a palm leaf and an olive branch – symbols of divine faithfulness and encouragement in the journey of the soul towards the Crown. The symbolism as a whole evokes the path trodden by Yeshua, culminating in His crucifixion: the sword represents the True Will.

"Yet not My will, but Thine be done."　　　(Luke 22:42)

ACE OF CUPS
Kether of Briah

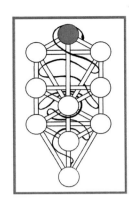

Esoteric Title:
**Root of the
Powers of Water**

Divine Name:
Eheieh - **I Am That I Am**

Sephirothic Colour:
White Brilliance

Card Dynamics:
From swirling clouds emerges an angelic hand, offering a cup. From the cup slither two serpents carrying the crowns of Upper and Lower Egypt, representing the cohesion between opposites, also signified by the Hexagram above. The Cup, in the Key of Solomon, was linked to the Cup of Joseph, who ruled Egypt according to the Pharaoh's decree.

The water that flows from the cup is the Azoth, the First Matter, and is connected to *Ain Soph*. Its Waters split into four rivers, connected to the Four Worlds of the Kabbalah which manifest in Kether. It's spiritual light is the elixir of life; the Azoth is the inner aspect of the Cosmic Egg which slowly transforms and draws the conscious point of the soul into itself.

The image as a whole contains the whole Tree of Life – the ten lotuses representative of the Ten Sephiroth – while the regions above and below the Tree of Life are symbolized in the hand emerging from beyond the clouds, and the lower waters respectively.

The Ace of Cups represents the visible universe as the cup, which holds within itself a divine spark and creative will of all Creation, symbolized in the *heh* above the cup which marks the emergence of the Divine *Heh* force of the Tetragrammaton. The Ace of Cups beckons us to enter within to discover our true nature. The deeper we travel, the more balanced we become, attracting towards us a universal love which brings experiences of great joy and prosperity. As the universal flow of life becomes stronger within us, our future becomes a creative act of Divine Will.

ACE OF WANDS
Kether of Atziluth

Esoteric Title:
Root of the Powers of Fire

Divine Name:
Eheieh - **I Am That I Am**

Sephirothic Colour: **Brilliance**

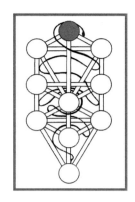

△   Ace of Wands   △

Card Dynamics:
An angelic hand dynamically extends through white clouds. The ring on the middle finger shines brightly and represents the Pole Star, from which the Aces are said to emanate. Around the hand is a Fire Triangle and within its structure can be seen the broken magnetic field of Primal Fire. To place this broken magnetic field onto any other magnetic elemental field it would break it up and return it to the Divine Light.

The three prongs of the wand represent the Three Pillars of the Tree of Life. They are decorated with the Tree of Life Sephiroth, coloured in King Scale. The 22 Yods to the left and right of the wand represent the 22 Paths, and highlight the *Yod* force of the Tetragrammaton. The four sigils on the wand represent the Court Cards. Thus the Ace of Wands represents the complete Tree of Life and sits at its apex.

Kether in Atziluth is an arena of spiritual fire. In its raw form it is attributed to desire, either to experience the material realm or to return to the spiritual home. When we think of a new birth we visualize a birth into the material world, but when we experience the second birth it is into the spiritual realms that we enter, that is, from Kether inwards, and beyond the Ring-Pass-Nots. It is here that the magician can truly manipulate the material world, but only in accordance with Divine Will, as he would have let go of personal will – a natural consequence of the second birth.

The Ace of Wands can thus be seen as a kind of portal to a new dimension of awareness not yet experienced or dreamed of. The Ace of Wands is the awakening into wisdom and understanding of Spirit. It is a high energy symbol and a good omen for success. It is a symbol of Fire on all levels, and is the Root of the Powers of Fire.

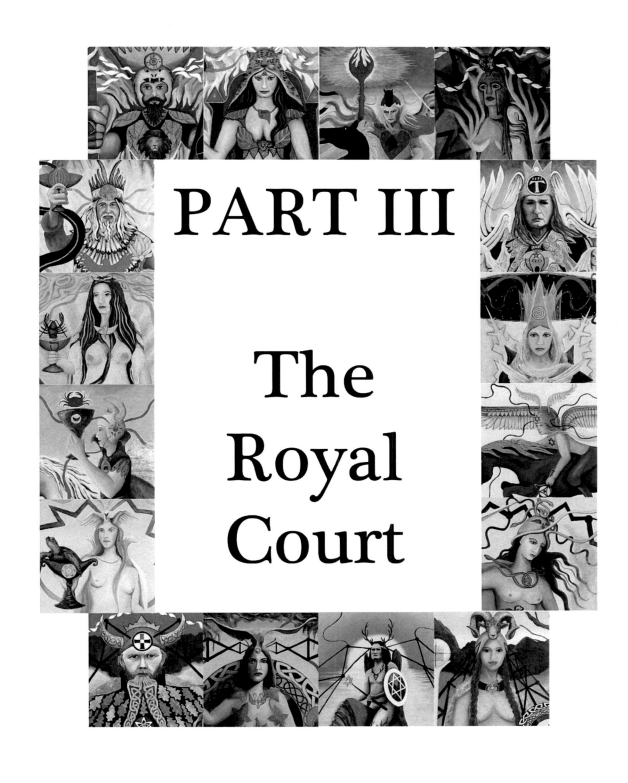

PART III

The Royal Court

Metatron, by Harry Wendrich

The Court Cards

Within *Ain Soph* there is no separation – there is only One – and from within that Oneness emerges the Divine Light, sometimes called Divine Will. As the Divine Light descends it generates the Tree of Life, going through a process of dissolution as it interacts with the Four Worlds of Atziluth, Briah, Yetzirah, and Assiah. This presents us with a four-fold model of the Tree of Life – four Trees, one in each world – wherein the Divine Light (in Kether) crystallizes into solar light (in Tiphareth) and finally into the four elements proper (in Malkuth). Yet this pattern repeats indefinitely, as within each Sephira is a Tree of Life, and within the elements themselves, *Ain Soph* remains the hidden foundation of our material universe.

The four-fold division of each Sephira corresponds to the four elements and to the letters of the Tetragrammaton, *YHVH*, representing the Name of the One God. The Court Cards, sometimes referred to as the Royal Faces, are designed to represent qualities of the Tetragrammaton. They number sixteen in all and are divided into four suits of four. They are represented as:

King = Atziluth = Yod = Fire
Queen = Briah = Heh = Water
Prince = Yetzirah = Vav = Air
Princess = Assiah = Heh final = Earth

As the Divine Light passes through the Court Cards it passes through different degrees of elemental density, gradually lowering in frequency. The Court Cards embody elemental subdivisions, acting as a system of valves which provides a safety mechanism within our experience of the Divine. In other words, the Divine Light is restricted in its manifestation in accordance with our limited comprehension: the Court Cards dilute the Divine Light into experiential frequencies that are safe to experience within our physical reality.

King of Wands/ Fire of Fire	King of Cups/ Fire of Water
King of Swords/ Fire of Air	King of Pentacles/ Fire of Earth
Queen of Wands/ Water of Fire	Queen of Cups/ Water of Water
Queen of Swords/ Water of Air	Queen of Pentacles/ Water of Earth
Prince of Wands/ Air of Fire	Prince of Cups/ Air of Water
Prince of Swords/ Air of Air	Prince of Pentacles/ Air of Earth
Princess of Wands/ Earth of Fire	Princess of Cups/ Earth of Water
Princess of Swords/ Earth of Air	Princess of Pentacles/ Earth of Earth

Court Cards and Humanity

Although the Court Cards may at times represent actual people or act as significators within readings (often corresponding with an individual's age, sex, and astrological profile), they are also indications of experiences that may be dominant at various times for any individual, generated by the interaction of the different elements: every individual can experience the full gamut of experiences depicted by the Court Cards. The elemental combinations manifest the enormity of God's creative expression upon the Earth. The devic realm manifest pure expressions of this vast loving potential. Through these experiential frequencies of Divine Light, humanity is also able to experience what it is to be an expression of God's love, accomplishing God's Will upon the Earth.

Sephirothic Position

The Court Cards are traditionally placed upon the Tree of Life with the Kings in Chokmah, Queens in Binah, Princes in Tiphareth and Princesses in Malkuth, although these positions are not fixed as the King and Prince are interchangeable, hence the differences between Tarot decks. The Court Cards may also be represented within each Sephira, divided into four sections. Their Sephirothic position also connects with the level of soul, as is discussed shortly.

The Elemental Rulers and the Divine Feminine

The Court Cards are connected to the elemental forces of Earth, Air, Water, and Fire, and are experienced within the Golden Dawn gradework corresponding to the lower division of the Tree of Life. However, the influence of the Gnomes, Undines, Sylphs and Salamanders is *not* restricted to the lower division of the Tree of Life. When working within the Sephiroth, it is possible to approach the Elemental Rulers who hold the keys to the Elemental Serpents, connected to the process of kundalini. The ruler of each element (Ghob, Nichsa, Paralda, and Djin) has a throne in Kether from which the serpent force is governed and used as a creative tool for regenerative work. The *Golden Dawn Temple Tarot* introduces this concept into the imagery of the King cards, depicting goddesses beneath their chariots/thrones to show that the Kings have been granted authority over their particular element by the Divine Feminine.

The Representation of the Crystallization of Divine Light within the Court Cards

In the *Golden Dawn Temple Tarot*, the connection between the Court Cards and *Ain Soph* is depicted through incorporating into the imagery lines of different malleability which begin to crystallize into triangular patterns. These lines within the Court Cards symbolize the manifestation of the Four Worlds within *Ain Soph*, reminding us that all the cards are One, as *YHVH*, the Tetragrammaton of the Name of the One God.

Atziluth: Broken white lines in the images represent the chaotic magnetic frequency of the Divine Light equating to the element of Fire within *Ain Soph*.

Briah: Flexible orange lines represent the magnetic frequency of the Divine Light equating to the element of Water within *Ain Soph*.

Yetzirah: Thin, violet, wavy lines represent the magnetic frequency of the Divine Light equating to the element of Air within *Ain Soph*.

Assiah: Thick, black, straight lines represent the magnetic frequency of the Divine Light equating to the element of Earth within *Ain Soph*.

The Royal Court are also used to name the Golden Dawn Colour Scales used to distinguish the Sephiroth and Paths within each of the Four Worlds. These Colour Scales have been used within the colouring of the Major and Minor Arcana of the *Golden Dawn Temple Tarot*, with some modifications according to updated colour theory.[1]

King Scale: all Wands are coloured in the King Scale and hold a masculine, initiatory force.

Queen Scale: all Cups are coloured in Queen Scale and hold a feminine, creative force.

Prince Scale: all Swords are coloured in Prince Scale (a blend of the colours of both King and Queen Scales) and hold a masculine, intellectual force.

Princess Scale: all Pentacles are coloured in the Princess Scale, and hold a feminine, manifesting force.

Attire and Appearance

In the *Book T* descriptions, the Court Cards all have armour attributed to their attire, and the Princesses, who are bare-breasted, allude to the warrior nature of the Amazonian women. The armour is meant to show a struggle between the elements and their manifestation into experience. In the *Golden Dawn Temple Tarot* the armour is in most cases formed from leaves and feathers, suggesting the fragile balance within nature. One notable exception is the Queen of Cups, who is protected by the clear waters of her domain which she wears as a dress, her nakedness symbolizing the emotional realm of love and her reflective force being her armour. The Princes are winged warriors, complementing their element of swiftness, and do not need heavy armour.

---

1   See Colour Theory section, p. 216.

Levels of the Soul

Consciousness is immortal. It cannot be extinguished, only experienced differently, at ever more subtle levels of awareness. The Hermetica states that the "soul is the garment of the mind and spirit the garment of the soul."[2]

The Golden Dawn teaches of three main divisions of the human soul to describe the different levels of consciousness that we experience – the Nephesh, the Ruach and the Neshamah. Within these three overlapping divisions, six sub-divisons, when placed upon the glyph of the Tree of Life, can be associated with the Sephiroth and the Court Cards.

The Nephesh

At the very bottom of the Tree of Life is the Nephesh, covering Yesod and Malkuth. Malkuth itself also contains the G'uph, closely linked to the physical body with inherent physical likenesses, and the subconscious communication between the body and the brain. Above G'uph is the Nephesh situated around both Yesod and Malkuth, thus connected to the G'uph. The Nephesh is considered a primeval instinct within human behaviour. It connects our human soul to the elements and animal vitality, sometimes considered the Shadow Self of the soul. These levels of Soul correspond with the Princesses. The Nephesh can stimulate the Ruach.

The Ruach

The Ruach is centred within Tiphareth, but contains all the Sephiroth from Chesed to Yesod. It acts as the conscious point of the soul, also termed the ego. It is within the realm of the Ruach that the conscious point begins to change its focus from an outward world view to an inner world view. It can also be considered a cultural and intellectual realm of consciousness. This level of soul corresponds to the Princes. The Ruach can stimulate the Neshamah.

The Neshamah

The Neshamah is the highest division of the soul. It contains three aspects of soul, centred in Binah, Chokmah and Kether, and also holds within it the realms of Negative Existence that is, beyond and above the Sephira of Kether. It corresponds with the the soul's highest aspirations.

The aspect of soul within Binah is also termed the Neshamah. At this level, humanity communicates intuitively with the Divine, and thus this level is activated when one begins to communicate with one's Higher Self. This level of soul corresponds with the Queens. Within Chokmah is the Chiah, which holds the memory of being more than human, giving out the yearning for the return to that awareness. Chiah is our True Will, and corresponds to the Kings. In Kether is the highest aspect of the soul, the Yechidah. The Yechidah is the aspect of our soul which is eternal and divine.

---

2   Copenhaver, *Hermetica*. 34.

The Levels of the Soul

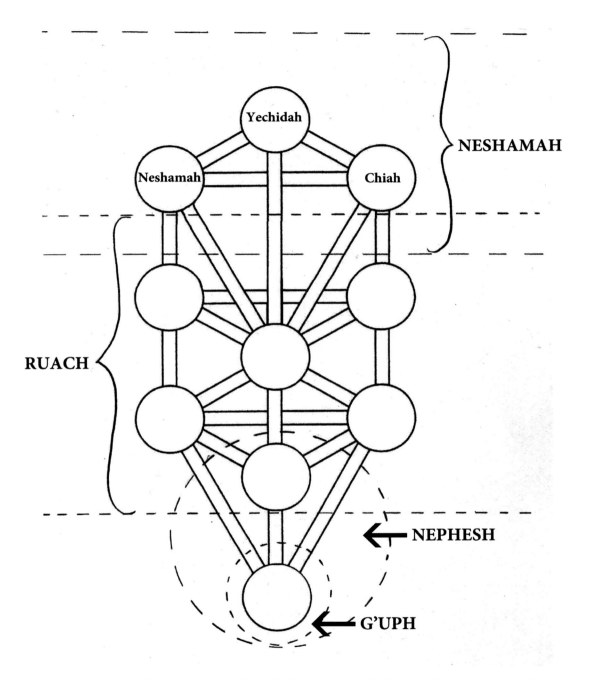

As the higher aspects of soul are stimulated, the Neshamah descends through the levels of soul, bringing conscious awareness of the Higher Self.

KINGS
Chokmah - Wisdom
The YOD Force: Atziluth

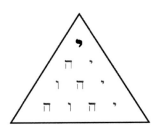

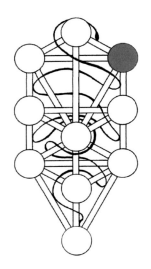

The Four Kings hold the element of Fire, modified by the other elements. They are seated within chariots pulled by the Kerubim and are therefore beyond the influence of the material plane. The chariots represent the Kings' thrones of authority over the elements.

The Four Kings represent the *Yod* force of the Divine Name, *YHVH*. The traditional Golden Dawn interpretation of this force is as being swift and violent in action, but without a lasting effect, rather like the striking action of a match – strong and sudden in appearance but swiftly to pass. This may well be the case when considering the effect of the force that the Kings represent upon the physical realm, as, with its downward movement, Fire symbolizes the very first show of the material realm.

However, it is important to remember that these forces also have an upward movement which has an eternal effect within the realm of Spirit: Fire, being a transformative element, swiftly breaks up the material elements and returns them to the source of the Divine Light, *Ain Soph*, much as the sulphur of a match transforms into light.

If the pure essence of the element of Fire was not modified by the other elements it would dissolve the universe back into chaos, ultimately returning everything into light. Therefore the Kings can be considered an initiatory influence from darkness into light.

The Kings have five aspects to them:

1. The Kabbalistic World within *Ain Soph*, and the influence of the associated forces of the Tetragrammaton.

2. A Watchtower and an Archangel
The Watchtowers are stationed at the four corners of the Earth and govern the elemental forces, balancing their elemental distribution to bring harmony within the world, promoting life, and thus have an important role in establishing the evolution of consciousness on all levels. Each Watchtower is connected to one of the Archangels of the Four Quarters. The Archangels act as intermediaries between human affairs and the environmental conditions created by the great Watchtowers.

> Archangel Michael is connected to the Watchtower of the South, and the Kerub of the element of Fire.
> Archangel Gabriel is connected to the Watchtower of the West and the Kerub of the element of Water.
> Archangel Raphael is connected to the Watchtower of the East and the Kerub of the element of Air.
> Archangel Uriel is connected to the Watchtower of the North and the Kerub of the element of Earth.

3. The Elementals, which work with a particular element to regenerate, maximizing potential. Four Elemental Rulers govern four Elemental Serpents which lie beneath the elemental throne in Malkuth.

> Ruler of the Salamanders: Djin
> Ruler of the Undines: Nichsa
> Ruler of the Sylphs: Paralda
> Ruler of the Gnomes: Ghob

4. The Human Representation – in temperament, astrological affiliation, and physical appearance.

5. The Level of the Soul: Within Chokmah is the Chiah, the seat of our True Will.

All this fits together to make the King an expression of a living being interacting on many different levels.

KING OF WANDS

Titles:
Lord of the Flame and the Lightning
King of the Spirits of Fire
King and Throne of the Salamanders

Astrological Sphere of Influence:
Above 20° Scorpio - 20° Sagittarius

Geomantic Symbol:
Fortuna Major (Leo/the Sun)
"Good for gain where a person has hopes to win."

Watchtower:
The Great Southern Quadrangle of Fire

YOD of YOD
FIRE of FIRE

Card Dynamics:
The King of Wands is portrayed as manifesting from a gaseous flame above the *yod*. Within the flame is also a hint of the kundalini fire. Behind the King is a wall of terrestrial fire. Protruding from his crown are the broken, white lines of the magnetic frequency of *Ain Soph* crystallizing within the Divine Light as the World of Atziluth. The King of Wands is connected to the Watchtower of the South, the sigil of which is placed upon his crown.

The King sits on his throne/chariot which is guarded and pulled by the Kerub of Elemental Fire, symbolized by the Lion. The wheels of his chariot are related to the Wheel of Fortune, symbolizing growth through movement. Beneath the Kerub is the figure of a goddess, showing that the King has been given authority to rule over the Fire element by the feminine principle of the Earth herself. This authority is also carried within his Fire Wand and his ring which has the Pyramid of Fire engraved upon it. He also holds a shield with his sigil engraved upon it.

It is believed that if you invoke a fire salamander there is a strong likelihood of being burned. Although the salamanders tend to be seen as fiery or dancing flames, the King of the Salamanders, Djin, appears in human form. He is pleasant to converse with and does not seem aggressive or impatient as might be expected of a fire elemental. The King of the Salamanders tries to introduce to the conscious focal point of the soul the need to detach itself from the flesh, rising one's conscious focus into spirit: in spirit lies the control of the element of fire.

The King of Wands has a very spiritual influence, and represents a person deeply committed to a spiritual path. His is an initiatory force, and he is able to initiate new ideas and cycles, perhaps just with the right word at the right time, which others receive, act upon, and bring into manifestation.

Fire can be destructive, but it can also initiate new life. In alchemy, the King must die to be reborn, taking us back to the Princess of Pentacles, who is pregnant.

KING OF CUPS

Titles:
The Lord of the Waves and Waters
King of the Hosts of the Sea
King and Throne of the Undines

Astrological Sphere of Influence:
20° Aquarius - 20° Pisces

Geomantic Symbol:
Laetitia (Pisces/Jupiter)
"Good for joy, present or to come."

Watchtower:
The Great Western Quadrangle of Water

KING OF CUPS

YOD OF HEH
FIRE of WATER

Card Dynamics:
The King of Cups is portrayed on his throne/chariot, decorated with the movement of waves. The background consists of flames mingled with a watery background.

From his crown emanates the magnetic frequency within *Ain Soph* of the Kabbalistic World of Briah. The lines are orange in colour and are not broken, but are quite pliable. From them the magnetic frequency of the World of Atziluth emanates as broken chaotic white lines: the World of Atziluth is beginning to transmute into the World of Briah. On his crown is the sigil of the Watchtower of the West.

His chariot is pulled and guarded by the Kerub of Water, the Eagle, and on the eagle's chest can be seen the influence of the *Yod* force. The chariot is coloured silver, connecting to the influence of the Moon on Water, and its wheels are engraved with scorpions.

There is a feeling of a transformative energy within the King of Cups, who is placed within Chokmah where all negative aspects of self have been worked out. This is symbolized by the three great transformative symbols of the scorpion, the eagle, and the serpent, depicted here emerging from a concentration of Water symbols – the chalice, on which is the sigil of the King of Cups, and upon whose finger is a ring also representing a cup.

In the serpent's mouth is the goddess figurine, giving authority to the King over his element of Water via the feminine principle of the Earth herself. The goddess holds the Geomantic sigil of Laetitia, representing joy.

The Ruler of the Undines is Nichsa, but Nichsa is not a King: she reveals herself as Queen in the purity of the essence of Water of the realm of Briah. The Undines are quite fierce in their nature, yet within their watery element is a feeling of security and emotional freedom as they enable the breaking through emotional walls that have been built from past hurts. Here in Chokmah of Atziluth, emotions of jealousy and envy are instantly transformed into generosity and forgiveness, making the King of Cups a joyful figure – loving and altruistic in nature.

He is a force for transformation, on a physical, emotional and spiritual level. The lotus flower held in his left hand shows that the transformation he represents is of the highest nature; his command of the serpent making him triumphant in the breaking of illusions. The deep water below him shows that he is familiar with the astral realm as a practitioner of meditation and contemplation into the deeper meaning of life – the King's inner vision reveals the workings of the subconscious realms, inspiring a boundless flow of creative expression.

KING OF SWORDS

Titles:
Lord of the Winds and Breezes
King of the Spirits of Air
King and Throne of the Sylphs

Astrological Sphere of Influence:
20° Taurus - 20° Gemini

Geomantic Symbol:
Albus (Gemini/Mercury)
"Good for profit and for entering into a place or undertaking."

Watchtower:
The Great Eastern Quadrangle of Air

KING OF SWORDS

YOD of VAV
FIRE of AIR

Card Dynamics:
The King of Swords sits on his throne/chariot from which manifests the Kerub of Air, appearing as a human head with an open mouth, symbolizing the need of Air for maintaining the life force. The chariot is drawn by four arch-faeries, each representing one of the four elements, but under the presidency of the element of Air: the arch-faeries as a whole represent Kerubic Air. The fact that they are visible in this card shows that the King has an awareness of these spiritual beings. They are seen manifesting from within the Earth, symbolized by the goddess figurine who shows that the King has been given authority to rule through the feminine principle of Mother Earth.

This is further emphasized by the sigil of the Watchtower of the East on the King's crown. From his crown emanates the thin purple lines of magnetic force of the World of Yetzirah interacting with the broken white lines of the World of Atziluth within *Ain Soph*. This has the potential for an explosive mix, yet the Watchtower of the East maintains balance and produces a powerful intellectual force. Connected to the Watchtower of the East is the Archangel Raphael who governs the realm of mind and communication on many levels.

The King of Swords has wings, giving him attunement with his element. In his right hand he holds a sword with a sigil of Air on it. The sword is a weapon of Air – it is a symbol of power, and is used to invoke. In his left hand he holds a sickle which is used for cutting away or banishing.

My encounter with the King of the Sylphs, Paralda, was very pleasant. He looked elven and seemed quite grand. During the period of our meetings I began to write articles and papers, some of which related to my experiences with these beautiful beings. It is said that the elementals have no form but are conscious energy vortices. That is true on one level, yet they are also able to communicate with us in a human-type form.

The King of Swords has a high level intellectual capacity that makes him a mentor for the other Kings. He sits between the physical and spiritual realms and is closely linked to the Fool (Air) as he moves from Chokmah into Kether. He is a political figure of high stature, able to envision structures for stable economic and societal environments, with the foresight to project the evolution of ideas. A compelling public speaker, he is able to lead an egregore into the direction that is developing. He is at the very edge of breaking through the illusions of material power, as he is able to see into the spiritual realms and is about to become the Fool who leaves everything behind to gain something only he can see.

KING OF PENTACLES

Titles:
Lord of the Wild and Fertile Land
King of the Spirits of Earth
King and Throne of the Gnomes

Astrological Sphere of Influence:
20° Leo - 20° Virgo

Geomantic Symbol:
Conjunctio
"Good with good, evil with evil. Recovery of things lost."

Watchtower:
The Great Northern Quadrangle of Earth

KING OF PENTACLES

YOD of HEH final
FIRE of EARTH

Card Dynamics:
The King of Pentacles is portrayed sitting upon his golden throne/chariot, which is pulled by a great Bull, the Kerub of the element of Earth. A large Pentacle placed on the Bull's forehead further represents the element of Earth and great wealth. As the red wheels of his chariot turn, the flyfot cross spins in reverse, having the magical effect of destroying all obstacles on the King's path. Beneath the Kerub of Earth is the figure of Sheila-na-Gig, the goddess now inviting us into her domain within the earth. She represents the connection between the King and the land, and his authority as Lord of the Wild and Fertile Land.

On his helmet is the sigil of the Watchtower of the North. Archangel Uriel is connected to the Watchtower of the North and the Kerub of the element of Earth. The Archangels act as intermediaries between human affairs and the environmental conditions created by the great Watchtowers. Some believe that when the world has become unbalanced by the negative influence of human hatred, the four great Archangels will assume the form of the Four Horsemen of the Apocalypse.

From the King's crown emanates strong, straight, black lines, crystallizing into triangular forms within *Ain Soph*, and bringing into existence the World of Assiah. From them emanate the broken, white lines of Atziluth, the combination of which produces a great amount of energy. The King of Pentacles acts as a positive force of the Higher Self on the material plane, his sceptre and orb symbolizing spirit descending into matter and the axiom, "As above, so below." The King of Pentacles transforms the Fire of Atziluth into wealth within the material plane of Assiah. He represents the primal generative force and assertive action. The King's wealth is gained through his prudent understanding and careful use of the Earth's resources. He is patient and laborious, steady and dependable. His long, greying beard shows his wisdom in the affairs of the world.

His understanding of himself is shown by the sigil placed over his heart. His metal armour in the form of ornamental oak leaves shows that in his wisdom he has transformed the raw materials of earth into a protective force that generates a stable environment for the development of community, where children are safe to play and grow, also symbolized by the flowers beneath him.

The King of Pentacles can represent a wealthy and powerful individual, whose material gain can lead to hoarding. Yet this King is often also a pious man, even to the point of religious, and he can be very generous – humbly acknowledging that his wealth and power are gifts from a higher power that is invisible but ever-present. He also possesses a deep passion and sexual vitality, and is brave to the point of ruthless. This strong masculine force can be utilized for good or evil.

The throne of King Ghob, King of the Gnomes, lies within an underground cavern wherein water flows. King Ghob is quick to point out that all four elements are inherent within his kingdom. The gnomes hold the wealth allotted to each individual and release it when appropriate. They are very protective and will shield humankind in times of need. Although the element of Earth is considered the lowest of the elemental realms within the Golden Dawn's grading system, it is important to remember that all elements also exist within *Ain Soph*, and have equal importance, as the words of King Ghob himself elucidate:

> "You can travel very high within the element of Earth."

QUEENS
Binah - Understanding
The HEH Force: Briah

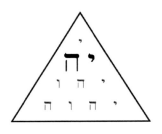

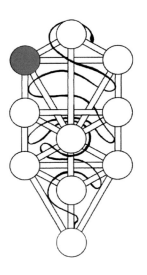

The Queens are seated upon thrones, giving them authority over the element of Water and its elementary modifications.

The Four Queens represent the *Heh* force of the Divine Name *YHVH*. This is a truly feminine force which births the potentiality of the King, the water element bringing a stable environment for the moulding of his will. The field of Water can be interpreted as the unconscious mind, that is, a realm that is not yet conscious within the sensory field of perception, but which has the creative potential to bring about growth and development.

The role of the feminine principle within Creation is illustrated within Dr. Dee and Edward Kelley's Enochian system of 30 Aethers, which are linked to the four elements and light itself. The feminine principle as the goddess holds the aethers in place, each sacrificing her dwelling within her natural domain (with the King) and descending to the aether below where she dwells in a kind of crystalline palace or structure. Each goddess moves down an aether, maintaining its environment for life by converting the waste material from the aether above (her original home) into the life-giving food for that level.

The level of soul represented by the Queens within Binah is the Neshamah, wherein one enters into dialogue with one's Higher Self. Correspondingly, the four Queens also represent the consciousness of the Soul of the Earth (Binah) and the conscious awareness of love on all levels. The Queens operate through the emotional, intuitive body, in response to Love.

QUEEN OF WANDS

HEH of YOD
WATER of FIRE

Titles:
Queen of the Thrones of Flame
Queen of the Salamanders

Astrological Sphere of Influence:
20° Pisces - 20° Aries

Card Dynamics:
The Queen of Wands holds the *Heh* force of the Tetragrammaton *YHVH*, as the *Yod* imprinted with a *Heh* around her neck implies. She sits on her throne around which fierce flames transmute into dense steam. The throne holds the symbolism of both Fire and Water triangles, and upon its armrests the sigil of the Queen of Wands is depicted. Unlike the thrones of the Kings which move by way of the Kerubim, the thrones of the Queens are locked on to the Earth. She is the grounding force for the King, and the representation of the feminine principle which gives the King his authority to rule over the elements/land. The staff in her right hand symbolizes her power to command. The Queen as a representation of the Goddess sacrifices herself to a lower plane or level of rule so as to maintain stability and life.

Her corslet of orange leaves can represent autumn: part of the work of the Salamanders is to return everything back to the source. As the Queen of Salamanders, she judges whether a soul has sacrificed itself to the Divine Will, or whether ego needs to be purged further before it gives in to a higher power. From the winged leopard crowning her head emanate the wavy, orange lines and broken, white lines which symbolize the World of Briah interacting with the World of Atziluth within *Ain Soph* – heat and moisture creating steamy and fertile ground, as a dense jungle maintains abundant, interdependent life-forms, and new growth is fertilized through the heat of decaying undergrowth.

A protective leopard-skin cloak is draped around her, the underside of which holds the deep blue colours of the subconscious waters which are within her domain. She is confident and sexually aware, and her attractive nature is magnetic. She represents the spiritual fire rising fiercely upward, purifying the seven levels of consciousness represented by the rainbow in the background.

The Queen of Wands is self-assured and nurturing. She holds the primeval mother instinct which explodes into action should her young be in danger. Sitting with a cat-like alertness, she has an empathic link with the leopard at her feet, which she keeps in check with a loving hand.

Hers is a strong, steady and adaptable force. She is warm-hearted and generous, her vital energy and natural authority generating growth and success to all that lays within her rule.

QUEEN OF CUPS

HEH OF HEH
WATER of WATER

Titles:
Queen of the Thrones of Water
Queen of the Nymphs and Undines

Astrological Sphere of Influence:
20° Gemini - 20° Cancer

Card Dynamics:
The Queen of Cups here is based on the Queen of the Undines, Nichsa, who appeared to me in meditation wearing a thin film of clear water over her beautiful naked body. Her black hair streamed down to the waters below. In the water she appeared as a mermaid, but as she came onto land she transformed into a graceful, elegant and commanding Queen who sat on a throne of shells within an underwater cavern. Her main aim was to attune me to my emotions, clearing any blockages and allowing my emotions to flow freely in the understanding of who I am. She was the only Queen that I communicated with. All the other elementals were governed by an Elemental King, and although their Queens stood beside them, the Queens remained passive and did not interact with me. Queen Nichsa was the exception, and I did not encounter a King within the realm of the Undines. Queen Nichsa exemplifies the feminine purity of the element of Water.

From the ibis crown of the Queen of Cups can be seen the orange lines of the crystallization within *Ain Soph* of the World of Briah in its purity. The ibis that uphold the throne of the Queen are linked to the Egyptian Moon god Thoth, emphasizing the magical quality of this element which rules the astral realms. The Queen's dream-like reverie is not a daydream but a conscious meditative state, and hers is a powerful force of protection – commanding and perceptive.

The Queen of Cups holds a chalice from which a crayfish emerges – the *Heh* on the chalice a reminder of the *Heh* force of the Tetragrammaton in the element of Water. The crayfish symbolizes Cancer and also connects to the Moon card. The Moon reflects the sun's light and influences the tidal patterns around our beautiful planet. Both the Moon and the water are reflective, and the Queen of Cups holds this powerful reflective force which can be used magically as a protective shield, reflecting any negative influence that may be perceived as harmful back to its source: as it only reflects, there is no karmic residue to work out. Archangel Gabriel may also be invoked for this kind of protective magic.

The Queen of Cups has a gentle and vulnerable nature as her nakedness suggests, and she is extremely sensitive. In a secure environment she may reveal the depths of her intuitive soul, but should she feel in any way threatened her protective shell will shield who she truly is from view and leave her company with a refection of itself. If one senses negativity or a lack of love in some way then it is but a reflection of yourself. Once this is grasped, it is possible to access great depths of self-awareness through interaction with the Queen of Cups archetype.

She may appear impractical but only because she approaches life from an intuitive realm. Structured plans constrict her – she prefers to "go with the flow," naturally moving fluidly in the direction prompted by Spirit, which gives the Queen of Cups an inner knowing, even to the point of prophetic insight. This deep knowing is awakened when the emotions can flow freely without mental blocks. The Queen of Cups is rich in emotional, intuitive and creative expression.

Six lotuses represent Tiphareth as a central point which connects to the Heart Chakra. The lotus that veils her sexual centre hints at the magical nature of sexual energy. The Queen of Cups holds a strong magnetic force which can be invoked to find ones twin soul or ideal partner, as the Queen of Cups also symbolizes one's ideal spouse – her naked form suggesting this aspect of an intimate relationship. Such magnetism has its source within the emotional experience of love.

QUEEN OF SWORDS

HEH OF VAV
WATER of AIR

Titles:
Queen of the Thrones of Air
Queen of the Sylphs

Astrological Sphere of Influence:
20° Virgo - 20° Libra

QUEEN OF SWORDS

Card Dynamics:
The Queen of Swords sits on a beautiful icy throne of crystallized fractal patterns, gleaming silvery in the sunlight of her lofty position above cumulus clouds. The Queen's pale complexion and dour expression suggest a cold and analytical outlook: her emotions have been somewhat crystallized so that they do not interfere with her judgement. Yet her sigil, seen on her crown, belt, and sword hilt, resembles the movement of ripples in a pond from a central point. The Queen herself is penetrating deeper aspects of Mind that transcend logic, suggested by the three-ringed opening within the clouds which reveals the deeper universe. Her perception goes far beyond the analytical mind, into the spiritual realms where few ever reach, and her far-sightedness, clarity, and intuition bring their influence to the lower realms awaiting her guidance.

The Queen of Swords is herself being guided by Higher Forces. Her sword hilt, shaped as a cross, symbolizes sacrifice to a higher ideal and shows that her judgement has its foundation in Yeshua, the Word: the Queen of Swords acts from the realm of *Ain Soph*, the Law of Creation, the Will of which cannot be stood against. This is further illustrated through the wavy, orange lines of Briah interacting with the thin purple lines of Yetzirah as they emanate from her crown and crystallize into patterns of elemental manifestation.

The winged cherub upon her heart demonstrates powerfully that whilst she is capable of penetrating the deceitful mind of man, the heart of this virtuous Queen is ruled by love, and her soul by spirit. The thick, dark, clouds below her throne lighten into a shimmering rainbow within the cold misty air, showing the transformational nature of this Queen, who is capable of transforming the negative attitudes stemming from frozen emotions into love and light.

The winged cherubs also reveal the work of the sylphs in their ability to purify the spirit and transform a heavy heart into a lightness that can be easily moved by Spirit. The sylphs are beautiful and can be seen as fairy-type beings with slender wings. They tend to work in large groups, weaving invisible forces within one's aura. Their subtle presence is hinted at through the orb-like sigils which float weightlessly about the throne. As Queen of the Sylphs, she has a regal demeanour, though is often veiled in privacy. She is graceful and has a dry humour, is strongly independent and highly intelligent. She has confidence and is capable of going it alone, yet she has a strong influence over the King, bringing her unique perspective into the array of thoughts and ideas, and could even be considered psychic. She has the persona of one with a cool exterior yet with a penetrating mind.

Her sword represents the power to take action against anything which stands in her way. Its bloody blade has severed the head held in her left hand, representative of the ego that once thought itself wise among men. Among those who see only the bloodied sword and cool persona she may be considered dangerous, heartless, and even ruthless, but hers is the double-edged Sword of Truth, and among the pure in heart are her virtuous and wise qualities championed.

QUEEN OF PENTACLES

HEH OF HEH final
WATER of EARTH

Titles:
Queen of the Thrones of Earth
Queen of the Gnomes

Astrological Sphere of Influence:
20° Sagittarius - 20° Capricorn

QUEEN OF PENTACLES

Card dynamics:
The Queen of Pentacles represents the *Heh* force of the Tetragrammaton within the element of Earth. The Queens are situated within Binah, the Greater Mother, or Soul of the Earth, and the Queen of Pentacles as the Queen of the Thrones of Earth represents the spiritual and etheric side of our beautiful planet. She sits on her Pentacle throne within a cave. The riches of the Pentacle flow through the watery blue base into the ground, enriching the dry, desert landscape under the Queen's domain, which she can bring to life at her will. This is illustrated by the black lines which emanate from her crown into tightly crystallized patterns of triangular formations from which emanate orange lines that permeate the cave with life, as the World of Assiah interacts with the World of Briah, crystallizing into earth and water from within *Ain Soph*. The stalagmites and stalactites physically reveal water crystallizing into earth. They act as a protective entrance to the cave, and reflect the landforms of the outer world.

The Queen wears a corslet of gilded ivy leaves which barely contain her large breasts, showing her fruitful nature. Ivy grows in a spiral and is a symbol of the Goddess. It also represents fertility and prosperity, and its evergreen nature corresponds with the Queen's Capricornian sphere of influence. Her skirt is of the Malkuth colours, the Lesser Mother, or the Consciousness of the Manifested World. Her personal emblem is the goat which is at her side, representing Capricorn, the Cardinal sign of Earth, a virile and generative power which assures of the great heights to which one can attain within the element of earth, both physically and within the exploration of consciousness. The Queen's sigil, the cube, is seen on her belt and crown, and atop her staff, symbolizing the manifested universe. The golden orb in her left hand represents the inner Earth, perceived as a sun-like disk.

In the physical Earth can spirituality be grounded: in the care and appreciation of the created world can the Creator be honoured. Many are those who hold a sensitivity to the pulse and life of our planet allowing for a deeper experience of what it is to be human, and today do we begin to realize the depths of the spirituality of our ancestors who lived close to the Earth. The combined imagery of the cave with its stalactites and stalagmites, the ivy, and the Capricorn symbolisms generate an atmosphere of the old age of the Earth herself. The cave is a reminder of early peoples who dwelt within the womb of the Earth, wherein the acoustic resonances of the striking of stalactites and stalagmites brought life to forgotten rituals of times past. The cave itself can also represent the passage between the conscious and subconscious worlds. This duality is also revealed in the depiction of the Queen of Pentacles – one side of her face is dark and the other side light, just as the Sephira Binah itself has the two faces of AIMA the Bright and Fertile Mother, and AMA the Dark and Sterile Mother.

The Queen of Pentacles is loving, understanding, intuitive and grounded. Her practical outlook is of great value to the King of Pentacles, and she brings nourishment and assistance to others. She understands that the community that grows around her fertile influence must remain in harmony with its surroundings, as her life permeates all living things.

She is one with the Soul of the Earth and, as the voice of the Earth Mother, she calls to the elemental beings and humanity alike. Under her authority are the Gnomes who are forever working to bring creation to its highest potential or ideal. They continually repair and renew the etheric body within all living beings, which is easily damaged through noise and other pollutants. In healing and repairing the etheric plane, the Gnomes help the consciousness pass beyond the etheric plane into deeper inner realms of astral light.

In a similar way, the Queen of Pentacles assists others. She acts as a representative of the Empress, creating a bountiful and hospitable environment in which all who enter are nourished. She gladly serves the Earth and the creatures thereon, helping others to attain their goals, although her availability, selfless giving, and humble service often go unnoticed or unappreciated, just as the Earth herself gives continually to a humanity who so often plunder without consideration of the consequences.

PRINCES
Tiphareth - Beauty
The VAV Force: Yetzirah

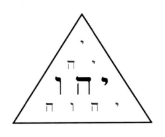

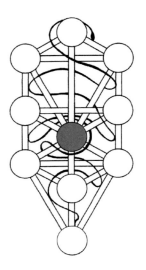

As the *Vav* force and the Element of Air

The four Princes represent the *Vav* force of the Divine Name *YHVH*. They hold the element of Air and its modification by the other elements. The Princes hold the joint qualities of the King and Queen, initiatory and intuitive qualities which the Prince communicates through an intellectual understanding. The interaction of Air with Fire and Water (King and Queen) make the Princes a complex force, not easily controlled, unpredictable, and even dangerous.

The Astral Plane

The lightness felt in the Princes, each of whom has wings, is suggestive of the spiritual/astral realm wherein both angels and demons have their place. The angels, as messengers and guides, help in the process of awakening the consciousness to the Oneness of Creation. The demons, on the other hand, attempt to break the link to the angelic guidance by pulling the soul to transgress the Universal Law of Love, which would result in fragmenting the gestalt into opposing archetypes.

As a force of transition

The Princes are a force of action. They are forever in movement, facilitated by their element of Air, enabling the creative ideas generated and worked out by the King and Queen to realize their final form in the Malkuth of the Princesses. Without the Princes acting to bring into manifestation, ideas would remain ideas, time would pass, and the actualization would not be experienced. The Princes then are an integrated part of the Royal Court - the force of transition between idea and actuality. The Princes are all seated on horseback, and many are the qualities of the horse which resonate with the frequencies held by the Princes, including speed, movement, and endurance. They may be wild and independent or trained and faithful, fearless in battle, hard-working and strong, a social creature of the herd, or a relative loner. The vital yang energy and dynamism of the Prince gets things done. They clear the path and organize the environment so that the next round of ideas can become manifest, and in this way, they ensure growth and productivity on the earth plane. Without their action there would be an excess of yin force, which would generate stillness and stagnation. Eventually, decay sets in to any environment which receives too little of the expression of the Prince.

As people

As people, Princes are young adults, epitomized by young men, full of vigour, with a tendency to move at speed as they get things done. Their increased independence brings the freedom to explore further afield, to travel and thereby absorb a vast range of life's experiences, broadening their horizons and knowledge base, all the while acquiring a new awareness of self. They are the questing knights, setting out upon on what is to be revealed as their spiritual quest – the discovery of their own True Will. With a focus upon the airy faculties of communication and travel, this stage represents the acquisition of much knowledge through study across a broad spectrum of subjects, as in the years of higher education and employment training, but also in the education of life in general. From young adulthood until around the age of thirty (when one's Saturn Return heralds a concentrated direction under the influence of the Higher Self), the experience of the energy of the Princes is at its height. The Saturn Return marks the turning point within the passage of the Prince towards the spiritual maturity which will one day crown him as King.

Level of soul

The Princes are experiencing rapid ongoing development of the levels of soul up to the region of Tiphareth and the Ruach, thus on the physical, emotional and mental levels. This can also be considered a cultural and intellectual realm of consciousness. In the Ruach is the ego housed, yet from hereon (and certainly from the time of one's Saturn Return) the conscious point may begin to alter its focus from an outward world view to an inner world view.

PRINCE OF WANDS

VAV OF YOD
AIR of FIRE

Titles:
Prince of the Chariot of Fire
Prince and Emperor of the Salamanders

Astrological Sphere of Influence:
20° Cancer - 20° Leo

Card Dynamics:
The Prince of Wands is on high alert – he is fully aware, in the moment. He holds aloft the Ace of Wands, which explodes with energy and discharges lightning, setting alight the ground around the black horse which he effortlessly bestrides. The shadow of his horse reveals the *Vav* force of the Tetragrammaton. The horse is fiercely independent: it rears up, ready for action, further empowering and invigorating its rider. The emblem of the horse can also be seen on the Prince's knees and crown, but predominantly as a heart-shaped crest on his elven armour, showing that love is the unrivalled force behind his great dynamism. From his crown emanate the purple, wavy lines of the World of Yetzirah, merging chaotically with the white, broken lines of the World of Atziluth. His sigil upon the Ace of Wands shows that his raw energy can only be controlled by the high forces within Atziluth that are aligned to Divine Will.

This is a high energy, explosive force. The elemental combinations of Air and Fire can create unpredictable lightning bolts and raging infernos fuelled by winds, which can rapidly become out of control – such is the power of the salamanders within Nature. The flames around the horse are like salamanders dancing to the call of the Prince into action. If the energy of this combination can be harnessed, dramatic developments can take place at a rapid pace. This card represents sudden action and movement, even impulsiveness or spontaneity, which, once set in motion, reverberates with power. Such action can be violent and damaging if the ego is not restricted, but is an unparalleled force for bringing into manifestation the impulses and ideas of the King and Queen.

The wings of the Prince transform into fiery serpents, showing that the sexual magnetism pulls in all directions. The life force is at its strongest, and levels of physical activity need to be high in order to transmute this force into positive action. The Prince of Wands gives the impulse to experiment in all things in life. Passions can run wild and unchecked, even to the point of self-destruction, as fire is fuelled by the swiftly-moving air. Self-control then, is a key to utilizing the energy of the Prince of Wands to greatest effect, and creative expressions such as energetic dance, loud, upbeat music, and sports of all kinds, but particularly those with dynamic movement such as martial arts and extreme sports, are natural vehicles for the utilization of this energy, and can have the effect of igniting similar passions in others.

PRINCE OF CUPS

VAV of HEH
AIR of WATER

Titles:
Prince of the Chariot of the Waters
Prince and Emperor of the Nymphs and Undines

Astrological Sphere of Influence:
20° Libra - 20° Scorpio

Card Dynamics:
A rider on a white horse stands majestically within calm blue waters. He is the Prince of Cups, holding high the symbol of his element, the Cup, on which can be seen his sigil. From the cup emerges a glowing crab, representing Cancer, the Cardinal sign of Water. The Moon, ruling Cancer, also moves the deep waters of the emotional and subconscious realms. The Prince of Cups is just beyond the shoreline and the tide is moving inward. He is conscious of his outer environment, but he also stands within his subconscious, connected to the deeper feeling of the oneness of life. The Prince of Cups is focussed on a quest. He knows that the tide is moving towards an understanding of the inner worlds which directly affect the physical realm. Both the horse and the rider look serene, in tune with the moment. His winged helmet emanates the orange lines representing the World of Briah, slowly crystallizing into the world of Yetzirah, within *Ain Soph*; the interaction of the emotional Watery realm with that of the intellectual Airy realm.

The Prince of Cups values self-control over his passions and emotions. He can be secretive and perceptive, yet is nevertheless troubled by his emotions, as like all, he is subject to the purifying fire of the serpent force. Through relationships, the magnetism of the serpent manifests the necessary scenarios which will allow the soul to see itself more clearly and fuel its transformation. Our interactions with other people shine a light upon our truer nature, reflecting that which we suppress and forcing us to deal with our emotional blocks. As the ego struggles to deal with emotional conflict, the persona is used to camouflage one's inner self, in-so-doing constructing a private and safe place from which to analyse and process these new emotional experiences: this reveals both the effect of Air acting upon Water, and the influence of Cancer.

To the world, The Prince of Cups displays the proud and attractive appearance of a peacock, yet his persona can be deceptive – seemingly cool, calm, and perhaps a little mysterious, he is unwilling to reveal, even to himself, what he regards as weaknesses or vulnerabilities in his emotional make-up. The Prince, in his guarded manner, considers his Shadow Self "the dark side," which both fascinates him with temptation and repulses him as he strives to keep control in his personal affairs.

Despite the seeming convenience of the self-generated mists of delusion, care should be taken that the full spectrum of emotional expression doesn't get lost in a fog, as suppressed emotion can lead to grief and depression. The watery emotions need to be expressed somehow through the airy intellect in order to be understood. The art of film and theatre can provide encounters wherein we learn something of the powerful effects of emotion without experiencing first-hand the pain of the actual experiences. Sometimes a physical counsellor becomes available with whom one's private feelings can be shared, although one's Inner Teacher becomes of paramount importance from hereon, as the empathic listener and trusted counsellor who has only the Prince's best interests at heart, and who can help to guide the soul into calmer waters ahead.

His wings resemble fins, reminding us that he is the Prince and Emperor of the Nymphs and Undines. These beautiful creatures are forever attracted to love, producing the magnetism and lightness of spirit that help us to understand our own need to express Universal Love. The combined working of the Spirit of the Moon, casting light upon our deep, secret feelings, with that of the Undines who take on the task of liberating us from emotional blocks, and impressing upon us the importance of faithfulness within a relationship, enable the Prince to reach a level of emotional maturity.

The calm image shows that in finding peace within himself, the Prince is ready to take the journey to the next level of self-knowledge. Through the act of service to the King and Queen, he will one day gain his own kingdom.

PRINCE OF SWORDS

PRINCE OF SWORDS

VAV of VAV
AIR of AIR

Titles:
Prince of the Chariot of the Winds
Prince and Emperor of the Sylphs

Astrological Sphere of Influence:
20° Capricorn - 20° Aquarius

Card Dynamics:
The Prince of Swords symbolizes the *Vav* force of the Tetragrammaton in the element of Air. This is the World of Yetzirah in its purity. His winged helmet emanates the thin purple lines within *Ain Soph* which are beginning to crystallize into the triangular patterns stabilizing the physical experience of the intellect, but not quite grounding it in Earth.

The Prince of Swords with his open wings flies high above the clouds on his magically winged steed. He holds a Sword, the symbol of his element, on which is his sigil. There is a feeling of high altitude and a sense of freedom as the mind moves from one thought to another, creating abstract formulae that few could ever understand. He is highly intelligent yet at the same time totally impractical, unable to manifest any real change on the ground. The concentrated energy of this Prince can result in an individual becoming somewhat divorced from physical reality, with his head "up in the clouds" – so enamoured with the fractal complexity of infinite trains of thought that he can forget to touch base, existing in isolation with his thoughts. As long as the ego is in control, the Prince is trapped within an intellectual world which takes pride in the ability to express ideas in words, and therefore risks holding an aloof attitude, despite his lack of grounding in experience of life outside of its intellectual structures. So high is the value he places upon putting his thoughts into words, he may be unaware of this social handicap. He may be more comfortable as a sole speaker on a platform than in a social group setting, the latter of which holding little purpose for him other than logical debate; thus he fails to recognize the limitations of the intellectual realm. As prone as this element is to unpredictable winds and refreshing light breezes, the stagnation of the doldrums is a reminder that in a fuller range of elemental nuance do we enjoy the subtleties of this element.

Yet the winged rider in his natural element can traverse broad regions and reach great heights within the intellectual realm of ideas, thoughts, and the communication of such. The natural capacity of this element to carry sound waves generates clarity and ease of communication, and the swift transmission of messages in general. The Prince of Swords, with the double influence of Air, may excel in areas of study such as computing, abstract mathematics, or etymology and linguistics. He thinks and works independently, and thus his communication of ideas and discoveries are more comfortably made through the secluded art of writing and, whether factual or fictional, book or blog, the written word can provide an arena for sharing the world of illusions in which his mind is caged without the difficulties that social contact can present.

Despite the symbolism of the sword, The Prince of Swords does not pass judgement lightly. His mind is open to ideas and accepts that across the vast regions of the realm of thought, opinions are many and varied – indeed, he delights in the diversity. Having one's ears open in appreciation of the many different voices of this world (and beyond) is the virtue which can develop this level of consciousness beyond the confines of one's ego. His logical, rational mind makes him a fair witness, but The Sword of Truth must be wielded by one with greater authority than he. For the Prince of Swords, the mastery of the element of Air can only happen when he transcends the levels of mind, allowing the Higher Self to take control. The veil between the mind and the realm of spirit is thin, and the King and Queen await his awakening.

"The word of God is living and active and sharper than any two-edged sword, and piercing as far as the division of soul and spirit, of both joints and marrow, and able to judge the thoughts and intentions of the heart."

(Heb. 4:12)

PRINCE OF PENTACLES

VAV of HEH final
AIR of EARTH

Titles:
The Prince of the Chariot of Earth
Prince and Emperor of the Gnomes

Astrological Sphere of Influence:
20° Aries - 20° Taurus

PRINCE OF PENTACLES

Card Dynamics:
From the banded crown of the Prince of Pentacles emanates the thick black lines of the World of Assiah which quickly crystallize into triangular patterns within *Ain Soph*, creating in this image a type of earth-wings. The thin, wavy lines of Yetziratic Air bring lightness to their density. His green wings and antlers suggest that the Prince of Pentacles is attuned to Nature in its many forms and able to read its signs and omens – the voice of Mother Earth herself. His sigil, the hexagram, can be seen on his shield and in his hexagram wand, showing his place in Tiphareth. He is in complete harmony with the forces of Nature and is an Adept of his magical path.

The quality of Air of Earth draws upon great depths of spirituality from within the natural world. This combination leads an individual to seek a closer spiritual connection within the realms of Nature, whether one decides to live a life as close to the elements as possible, in solitude or within a community of like-minded souls, or simply responds to the call of the Spirit by taking a walk in the woods. Here the mind is freed of itself and becomes the receiver of the sensual world. Thoughts and words are exchanged for the sights, sounds and scents of Nature, impacting the soul directly. One's aura receives powerful cleansing and renewed vitality through direct interaction with the Earth herself, bringing an antidote to the stressful pace of modern life. Prolonged exposure to such an experience opens the heart to a deeper connection to the Earth.

Behind the Prince, the setting sun brings a golden glow to the environment. The horse upon which he sits is at rest and receiving nourishment. The Princes are a force of action, but the action of this Prince is steady and enduring, allowing him to accomplish much on the physical plane. The Prince of Pentacles is strong yet gentle, and dedicated in his work. His honesty, faithfulness, resourcefulness, and readiness to take on responsibility makes him a vital part of the success of a community – he upholds the natural laws which enable peaceful communities to thrive under the rulership of the King and Queen, who rely heavily on their Prince for the wealth of the land to be harvested and stored. The corn in the foreground symbolizes both a harvest and the potential for growth and evolution within the human gestalt.

Whether something is being built up, cleared away, transported, or maintained in some fashion, the Prince of Pentacles is ever-reliable in his practical application and implementation of ideas, maximizing of their potential, and keeping things regulated on the material plane; he carries out both the groundwork and the routine duties which generate the environment for life, in-so-doing bringing increase and sustainability.

We all need to draw upon the energy of the Prince of Pentacles as we go about our daily life, maintaining the physical environment, paying the bills, performing the tasks allotted to us in an efficient manner so that even as the necessary jobs are attended to, the environment is prepared for the spiritual nature of our True Will to occupy the seat of our being. A stable and steadfast attitude held by one with a humble heart enables the enduring energy to work until the necessary jobs are done. The intelligent mind knows that prudence and care about ones tasks ensures minimum waste and thus creates a more profitable and harmonious quality of life in the long-term. As the Prince and Emperor of the Gnomes, he symbolizes the perfected world through evolution via the regeneration of the Earth energies. The gnomes are true alchemists, creating and renewing the physical to its highest potential, as reflection and servant of the spiritual world.

The Prince of Pentacles knows that spirituality is found as equally in earthy and practical tasks as in the depths of the meditative state, to which he is no stranger. He understands that we all have a part to play in the spiritual evolution of humanity and the Earth, and in quiet humility does he play his part.

PRINCESSES
Malkuth - The Kingdom
The HEH final Force: Assiah

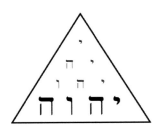

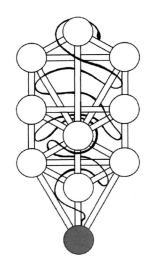

The Princesses present a vast arena of potential interpretation, and their images alone are not able to convey these many nuances in meaning.

The Princesses represent the force of the final *Heh* of the Divine Name *YHVH*. They hold the element of Earth which contains aspects of all the elements as part of its structure, and is further modified by the other three elements as the Princess of each suit implies. This provides a broad platform from which their particular energy may be expressed.

As the manifestation of an idea
The Eternal Light holds the blue-print of all existence within a magnetic structure of Mind as a non-corruptible force. The Princesses can represent the physical manifestation of an idea which is initiated in the realm of the King, is nurtured into form by the Queen, and energized into potentiality by the Prince. The influence of the King, Queen and Prince are therefore felt within the Princesses, who hold the downward manifestation of physical birth. *Book T* describes the force of the Princess as violent and permanent. However, on the Earth plane, where souls find themselves enclosed in a cloak of matter, the final *Heh* cannot permanently hold the eternal nature of the Divine Light within the

outer structure. Time and space corrupt the final process of Creation, which through death returns everything back to the Divine Light.

As a conduit of environmental and elemental forces

The Golden Dawn explains that the Four Princesses are each given the position of rulership of a Quadrant of the celestial heavens around the North Pole because they are best-suited to be the conduit of forces from the Malkuth of one Kabbalistic World into the Kether of the World beneath.

> "Now as Kether of Assiah is to receive from Malkuth of Yetzirah, it is necessary that in and about Kether there should be a force which partaketh of the nature of Malkuth, though more subtle and refined in nature. And therefore it is that the final Heh, or Princess force, have their dominion placed about Kether. They are so placed that they may attract from the Malkuth of the Higher and form the basis of action for the Aces." [1]

The Princesses are thus linked to both Kether and Malkuth. In Kether the Princesses form the thrones of the Aces. The Elemental Kings have their thrones in Kether, and the Princesses have a direct link with the Elemental beings, as it is within Malkuth that our physical experience of the elements is encountered. The *Heh* final force is strongly linked to environmental and elemental forces of nature, and the Four Aces and The Four Princesses also represent the four seasons.

> The Princess and Ace of Wands rule Summer (Cancer, Leo and Virgo)
> The Princess and Ace of Cups rule Autumn (Libra, Scorpio, Sagittarius)
> The Princess and Ace of Swords rule Winter (Capricorn, Aquarius, Pisces)
> The Princess and Ace of Pentacles rule Spring (Aquarius, Taurus, Gemini)

As a connection to the serpent force

The Elemental Kings have thrones in Kether. They also have authority over the serpent force which lies beneath their thrones in Malkuth. The elementals use the serpent force as a regenerative medicine for the rejuvenation and continuation of life on the planet and within humanity. The rising of an elemental serpent into Binah transforms the dense nature of that force into a higher frequency. This serpent of light once again descends beneath the elemental throne in Malkuth, and the elementals manipulate this transmuted force to form a regenerative medicine of a higher frequency. [2]

This gives the Princesses a link to the serpent force which acts both as a corruptible force in Nature and the transformative agent within consciousness, the kundalini.

---

1 Regardie, *The Golden Dawn*, 615, 616.
2 These concepts will be expanded upon in a forthcoming publication by Harry and Nicola Wendrich.

As mighty material powers

The Golden Dawn depicts the Princesses as Amazonian warriors, a legendary nation of warrior women, organized and governed solely by women. However, the final *Heh* force, although an earthy feminine force, does not exist in isolation from the other elements, but rather embodies all four elements.

> The mighty and potent daughter of a King and Queen: a Princess powerful and terrible: a Queen of Queens – an Empress – whose effect combines those of the King, Queen, and Prince, at once violent and permanent; therefore symbolized by a Figure standing firmly by itself, only partially draped, and having but little Armour; yet her power existeth not, save by reason of the others: and then indeed it is mighty and terrible materially, and is the Throne of the Forces of the Spirit. Woe unto whomsoever shall make war upon her, when thus established!

The mighty and terrible material power referred to in *Book T* does not necessarily represent a person, but rather an elemental force. The warrior princess image contradicts the characteristics of the Princesses as individuals, thus we have portrayed their traditional 'armour' in a manner conducive to both their element and their characteristics as people.

As a plane of consciousness

The conscious state of the Princesses is the innocence, purity of heart and sense of wonder that we experience in the early stages of childhood. It relates to the energy of The Fool, and corresponds with the inner child that we seek to find again as adults.

This state of consciousness has a strong link to the natural world and the elemental realms. In a very young child the sense of ego is not fully established, and the entirety of both one's sensory and extra-sensory perception may be considered as being part of one's being. The self extends into the environment, and the Princess (child) is often able to see into the spiritual realms, and communicate with elemental beings and other spiritual beings.

This plane of consciousness holds honesty, humility, and purity, and a sweet nature which emanates a balm of beauty and universal love. There is a continual delight in the created world under an ever-watchful divine presence, which generates perfect praise.

> 'From the lips of children and infants you, Lord, have called forth your praise'
> Matt. 21:16 (NIV)

As an oracle and a muse

The close connection of the Princess to the elemental beings gives them a devic perspective upon life. The Earth and all Nature are considered sacred and awe-inspiring.

---

3   Regardie, *The Golden Dawn*, 544

To contemplate the vast array of natural phenomena is to share a profound moment with the spiritual beings who serve to promote and protect such. In the realm of Earth alone, consider: every rock and crystal, every plant and tree, every creature, every person. How wonderfully then do the elements combine to produce the processes upon the earth, the landforms, the climates, all that our senses perceive, all that is birthed, all that grows, all that decays, all that transforms our awareness, all that touches our experience of life.

The Princesses share the sense of simplicity, service, and love that make for an environmental consciousness. They are very close to the Earth, and suffer with her.

As human experiences
Princesses can represent new stages in life, messages and oracles, opportunities, and new beginnings in general. They can reveal the transitions from one stage of life into another. Their energy is experienced by people of any age who are experiencing an aspect of life for the first time. They also represent the purity of the plane of consciousness described above.

As people
The Princesses are representative of young children through to young adults or adolescents who are still under parental control. Generally, they are still formulating their sense of self and are learning much about the world. The ego begins to establish itself, and within this range of formative years the influence of the Princess extends from the state of childhood innocence, gradually overlapped by knowledge of self and the world. They carry both a state of immaturity and zeal within new territory being explored.

They can also represent a messenger.

As Lunar Phases
The Four Princesses each correspond with a phase of the Moon.

> New Moon – Princess of Pentacles
> First Quarter – Princess of Wands
> Full Moon – Princess of Cups
> Last Quarter – Princess of Swords

As a Level of Soul
The Princesses correspond to the Nephesh and the G'uph, connecting the soul to the elements and representing an animal vitality and primal instincts.

PRINCESS OF WANDS

HEH final of YOD
EARTH of FIRE

Titles:
Princess of the Shining Flame
The Rose of the Palace of Fire
Princess and Empress of the Salamanders

Astrological Sphere of Influence:
Quadrant around Kether
Throne of the Ace of Wands

Card Dynamics:
The Princesses represent the Thrones of the Aces in Kether, also acting as the Thrones of the Elemental Rulers. Yet at the same time the Princesses reside within Malkuth, showing the close relationship between Kether and Malkuth, even as, in this case, Kether of Briah lies over Malkuth of Atziluth.

Within the elemental kingdoms, the Elemental Thrones are situated over the Elemental Serpents. The Tarot Kings are given the authority by the Queens to release the serpent force as an energy of rejuvenation within the elemental kingdoms. The Princes then distribute the serpent force where required. The Princess of Wands wears a serpent bracelet on her arm, symbolizing the use of the serpent force through the throne, in this case, that of the fire serpent.

The Princess of Wands stands with dignity and reverence by her golden fire altar, symbolizing the transformational nature of the fire element. A serpent can be seen at the base of the altar, connecting the transformation with the kundalini. On the altar is a flaming brazier, showing that the purifying flames must rise before the serpent can rise. Rams' heads upon both sides of the altar show that the Princess of Wands represents an initiating energy – a fiery force of revitalization which stimulates a new cycle, quickening that which has been seeded, and firing up the energy centres.

Above the flames can be seen the final *Heh* force of the Tetragrammaton – the Divine Will manifested on Earth. The Golden Dawn's *Book T* depicted the Princesses as Amazonian warrior women, thus associating them with an age group which is sexually active, although Amazonian myths depict sexual union with males as being restricted to annual encounters solely for the purpose of procreation. Thus the Princess of Wands can be an indicator of virginity.

In her left hand the Princess holds a club bearing her sigil, surrounded by terrestrial flames. Within her aura are spiritual flames, and here the salamanders work, manifesting from her aura as a transformative element that purifies and rejuvenates everything with which they come into contact, adjusting the sexual magnetism which perfects the environment within the physical.

From her helmet emanates the pulse of the World of Assiah combined with that of the World of Atziluth within *Ain Soph*. The jagged, black lines and broken, white lines create a cruel force which generates the experience of pain and distress as part of the purifying process. The same combination can also be experienced as extreme passions and an explosive temperament, leading to further conflict and disharmony.

The large tiger in the background and as her emblem shows the power and potential danger of the energy experienced with the Princess of Wands. However, she is also the Rose of the Palace of Fire: the Rose symbolizes Venus and therefore Love, which is the ultimate force of transformation, unifying all of Creation throughout the Universe within the Divine Will.

PRINCESS OF CUPS

HEH final of HEH
EARTH of WATER

Titles:
Princess of the Waters
Lotus of the Palace of the Floods
Princess and Empress of the Undines

Astrological Sphere of Influence:
Quadrant around Kether
Throne of the Ace of Cups

PRINCESS OF CUPS

Card Dynamics:
The Princess of Cups stands amidst the tidal flow of the sea, and within this fluid seascape she solidly faces the vision of her future across the unfathomable reaches of the sea of unconscious waters. In the background is the distant shoreline, but the Princess knows that she has been set aside for the Great Work, and calmly does she await the serendipitous journey before her. The whole image shimmers with the qualities of gentleness, grace, innocence and purity, so characteristic of this state of consciousness.

The emblem of the swan crowns her, from which the black lines of the World of Assiah and the orange lines of the World of Briah within *Ain Soph* issue forth in the combination of Water and Earth. Her garments of swan feathers reflect her devotion to her quest. The swan is a symbol of Venus, and in the figure of the Princess of Cups is the Venusian beauty expressed, together with her muse-like creativity, especially in the arts of music and poetry, and her loyalty to all that she holds dear. The Princess of Cups has a spirit of loving-kindness and compassion which cannot bear the suffering of a fellow-creature. The dolphin in the background echoes a similar humble wisdom of love and peace, sharing its healing vibrations within Creation. In her left hand she holds a lotus flower, revealing her spiritual awareness within the element of Water. She is able to enter the lower astral realms, the dolphin reinforcing her gifted ability of inner vision that brings intuitive and even prophetic insight.

Her form shines with the natural beauty of youthfulness, yet her eyes hold the age of wisdom, symbolized also in the turtle which arises from the chalice bearing her sigil, itself a symbol of the spiritual waters and the fluid nature of the emotions. The turtle represents the ancient wisdom of an old soul. It takes vast journeys within the watery realm yet also learns to adapt to new terrain, as the Princess herself is about to give flight into higher realms of spiritual awareness. Yet as the peaceable turtle possesses a shell of protection, so the gentle and easily wounded heart of the Princess needs shielding from negativity and harmful influences as the tides churn up suppressed emotions and painful memories that have been hidden in the depths. Through the medium of creative expression, such experiences can become assimilated into the emerging new personality, now able to express the deeper feelings of the human heart, whether sublime or offensive. The Undines help in building a new body of light which will enable the move into more spiritual levels of reality.

The Princess of Cups symbolizes a person that needs to find themselves through the art of meditation and contemplation; letting go, if only for a time, of the pull of the material world. Through such, she bears the resultant loneliness of life without a partner, yet at the same time knows that her true partner in life, her twin soul, is out there and will one day walk the same path, as the swan, the symbol of fidelity, reveals the magnetic attraction which will not fail to draw old souls together in love and the Great Work.

PRINCESS OF SWORDS

HEH final of VAU
EARTH of AIR

Titles:
Princess of the Rushing Winds
Lotus of the Palace of Air
Princess and Empress of the Sylphs

Astrological Sphere of Influence:
Quadrant around Kether
Throne of the Ace of Swords

PRINCESS OF SWORDS

Card Dynamics:
As the Throne of the Ace of Swords, The Princess of Swords holds the Air Serpent beneath her. The elemental Air Serpents are slow and lethargic, but once met become volatile and difficult to control until one has attuned to the element of Air with the help of the sylphs. This primeval force of Air locked up under the deep caverns of Earth is symbolized by the Princess' crest of Medusa with hair of serpents, and in her cloak with its serpentine pattern.

From her crown emanate the thin, purple lines of Yetzirah combining with the dark lines of the World of Assiah within *Ain Soph*, which has the effect of bringing a sense of protection within the volatile air element. This can be experienced through the aura contracting while the mind explores and experiments without the interference of the emotions. It can also represent an earthly intellectual arena such as a university, where a student can learn and develop in safety – indeed, this stage represents the acquisition of much knowledge through reading and study across a broad spectrum of subjects, with possible specialization in an area. The Princess of Swords is able to put her knowledge into practical application, but, in her relative immaturity, needs to keep her mind open to fresh understandings through the continued feed of information.

She twists nimbly upon the clouds, showing that she has not yet discovered her true nature but is not frightened of exploring life to the full – in the process, discovering herself. Agile and graceful, she is unencumbered by physical or emotional cravings, but focuses her energy upon uncovering the truth.

The Princesses can represent the different phases of the Moon. The Princess of Swords represents the Last Quarter, which indicates that she cuts away unwanted clutter and emotional baggage. It also makes her a herald of bad news or an archetype of unexpected behaviour, which makes for an interesting friend. In a general sense, the Princess of Swords as a personality has a negative connotation because she is unpredictable, like a young adolescent with exploding hormones. She is headstrong and confrontational yet fragile and fearful of the future, which is out of her reach as she is unknown to herself – her soul yearning for the acceptance which would allow the true love of her nature to manifest.

The Airy part of Earth also sees a link with the dramatic arts, wherein one wears a mask of an archetypal nature, although the danger of such role-playing is that one can lose one's connection to the voice of one's soul. The mask in the case of the Princess of Swords is her helmet, which bears her crest of the head of Medusa – a formidable foe, showing that The Princess of Swords can also be a fierce and intimidating adversary:

"Woe unto whomsoever shall make war upon her, when thus established!"

Her short skirt, patterned with the Malkuth colours, resembles feathers, suggestive of her sprightliness and fluency within her realm. Yet it is also an armoured kilt, as, of all the Princesses, the Princess of Swords best exemplifies the myths of the Amazonian warrior, which bring to mind the forces of feminism, further connecting to movements which bring attention through active protest to other forms of human or planetary rights. The sword in her right hand is called the Sword of Vengeance, which can indicate that a deceitful situation needs to be uncovered.

From the altar arises smoke which acts as a screen from which the true nature of the Princess is hidden – not knowingly, as she is very much a vocal force of honesty and frankness, a skilled arbitrator, eager to share the insights gleaned as a keen observer of life. The Princess of Swords would either in a controlled or a ruthless fashion, slash away all that is unnecessary to seeing the clear picture, but, ironically, she has yet to know the true nature of her soul, and in her immaturity does her strong sense of righteousness pronounce harsh and hasty judgement upon others in situations of which she has neither the breadth of vision nor the humility to understand, risking her becoming hard and embittered. It is in turning her piercing gaze upon herself that she can use her talent to its full potential, cutting away the illusions which have thus far prevented a truer expression of her soul.

PRINCESS OF PENTACLES

HEH final of HEH final
EARTH of EARTH

Titles:
Princess of the Echoing Hills
Rose of the Palace of the Earth
Princess and Empress of the Gnomes

Astrological Sphere of Influence:
Quadrant around Kether
Throne of the Ace of Pentacles

PRINCESS OF PENTACLES

Card Dynamics:

The elemental gradings of the Golden Dawn should never be underestimated: they provide priceless experiences of the inner elemental workings, something that is very difficult to accomplish on one's own merit. In my working through the 1=10 grade of Zelator, there was a real feeling that change was taking place, and my meetings with the Gnomes in meditation was one of the highlights of this work.

As Earth of Earth, the Princess of Pentacles holds something of the energetic frequency of such a journey through the earth element. It must be remembered that the Gnomes, like all the other elementals, work their magic from within *Ain Soph*, here shown in the black lines emanating from the Princess' head-piece – tightly crystallized and grounded within the earth. The Gnomes are not a low-level force but rather have a universal consciousness which is active within our planetary home, and within our own inner communicative power. As Princess and Empress of the Gnomes, her spirituality is experienced within the physical – she is in tune with her body and with Nature, and is able to communicate with the devic realm which sustains her environment. She knows the abundance of Nature and the health of her body are her true wealth, yet the energy of the land is in turn represented by money, and so the Princess of Pentacles can represent the investment of wealth into the land, her pregnant form suggesting the beginning of a new venture which will expand and bring prosperity in the future.

Hers is a very stable energy, and represents the manifested energy of the Queen of

Pentacles - the Princess of Pentacles acting as the Lesser Mother, representing the outer manifested world in all its beauty. On her staff she holds the cube of the Queen of Pentacles but within a sphere, and split into four, showing that the realm of the Princess is the outer world wherein all four elements are experienced. The white staff represents spirit upholding the physical world. Both her staff and the Pentacle that she holds in her left hand symbolize authority over the material world. The Pentacle links to the Ace of Pentacles, and the Throne which rules over the Earth Serpent, linking the Princess to Kether. From the earth beneath her feet are the twelve white rays which emanate from the Ace, a reminder she stands on the Earth within the astrological sphere of the Heavens, showing that while this frequency of Earth of Earth brings the state of being fully grounded and fully aware in the moment – aware of one's own vitality, aware of one's environment, and aware of the life-force of the Goddess – the Princess is consequently and simultaneously both a receiver and a conduit of the love which pulses not only throughout our planet, but throughout the entire Universe.

There is a link between the King of Wands, Fire of Fire, and the Princess of Pentacles, Earth of Earth. Spiritual fire enlivens the physical body, producing energy and enthusiasm. She is pregnant, also suggesting that the King of Wands' transformative energy ultimately returns to a new birth, and as such, renews the cycle of the Tetragrammaton. The Princess of Pentacles holds the fiery energy of Aries, symbolized by the ram on her crown, the torc around her neck, and her sheepskin cloak which protects her through the transition from darkness into light, and generates a new cycle and new growth. The trees with their yet leafless branches echo their network of roots, pulsing with the earth's blood beneath the lush green grassland, and the late winter roses signify her title of Rose of the Palace of Earth, as the background heights reflect her title of Princess of the Echoing Hills. Generous, kind, hardworking practical and reliable, the Princess of Pentacles is also gentle, sensual, fertile and beautiful to behold. Such beauty is inherent within our earth – a jewel in our solar system – both in love with life and eagerly awaiting the new beginning.

> For the anxious longing of the creation waits eagerly for the revealing of the sons of God. (2 Cor. 5:19)

> For we know that the whole creation groans and suffers the pains of childbirth together until now. (2 Cor. 5:21)

The Colour Magic of the Golden Dawn

The Golden Dawn Colour Scales exist today in several forms, from Florence Farr's colour tables of the late 1800's, to those published by Israel Regardie in the 1900's, to the more modern colour tables suggested by Pat and Chris Zalewski generated from Whare Ra colour documents, and the HOGD modifications of Chic and Tabatha Cicero. Each has their differences, yet each carries the same intention: to evoke through colour (along with the other associated symbolisms) the inherent nature of each Path or Sephira. Each version shares certain fundamental criteria, laid out in a Golden Dawn document entitled "Ritual W – Hodos Chamelionis" (*The Path of The Chameleon*).[1]

There are four Golden Dawn Colour Scales, consisting of King Scale, Queen Scale, Prince Scale and Princess Scale, which correspond to the Four Hebrew letters of the Divine Name *Yod Heh Vav Heh*. Sandra Tabatha Cicero, in her in-depth study of the Golden Dawn Colour Scales[2] wrote:

> After examining a document called "The Book of the Tomb" which describes the symbolism of the Vault of the Adepti, I came to the conclusion that the entire Princess Scale of Color was a bit of an after-thought. This is because the "Book of the Tomb" describes only three scales of color: the King Scale, the Queen Scale, and the Scale of the Child. The Child Scale is obviously the Prince Scale – a combination of the King and Queen Scales. I believe that the Princess Scale was added later to round out the divine family, so to speak, to give the King and Queen a son *and* a daughter, and make the colors correspond better to the Four Worlds and the holy name of Tetragrammaton."

---

1   Israel Regardie, *The Golden Dawn: The Original Account of the Teachings, Rites & Ceremonies of the Hermetic Order.* (Woodbury, MN: Llewellyn Worldwide, Ltd., 2002), 95-99.

2   Sandra Tabatha Cicero, *The Book of the Concourse of the Watchtowers: An Exploration of Westcott's Enochian Tablets* (Elfers, FL: H.O.G.D. Books, 2012), 58.

The Colour Scales are laid out in a table of the 32 Paths of the Western Hermetic Tree of Life. All four Scales were employed in the painting of the Major Arcana of the *Golden Dawn Temple Tarot*, which were also bordered in King Scale colours. The Minor Arcana utilized the colours of King Scale for Wands, Queen Scale for Cups, Prince Scale for Swords, and Princess Scale for Pentacles in both backgrounds and borders.

In the early stages of painting, our colour choices were loyal to Israel Regardie's Colour Scales, with reference also to the modifications within the Cicero Colour Scales.[3] Upon completion of the four Aces, I had a dream in which I was instructed by an Angel to continue painting the remaining cards using only the three primary colours and White on my palette. Primary colours are used in the formation of the Sephirothic colours in Queen Scale, affecting the colouring of the Cups cards as well as the Swords cards which are coloured in a mix of King and Queen Scale colours.

While the Tarot paintings were underway, Harry was also working upon the construction of the Vault of the Adepti. The colour structure within the Vault comes from the document entitled *The Book of the Tomb* which provides a formula in which the colours of the seven planetary walls are added to the colours associated with the Hermetic symbols placed thereon, also utilizing the relevant complementary colours. As Harry began painting the Vault Panels using the colours of traditional Golden Dawn colour theory within the mixing formula, he realized that a certain vibrancy was lacking. Coinciding with my dream to paint the Minor Arcana using the primary colours, Harry also dreamt that an Angel presented him with an empty colour wheel and told him to fill it, and indicated that the colour structure within the Vault needed to be examined. The colour wheel of 12 segments relates to the Zodiacal Paths in King Scale and is a useful tool for identification of complementary or "flashing" colours.

Our work involved updating the traditional colour assignments in accordance with modern advances in colour theory and pigment production, which affects the primary colours and complementary colours previously used within the Golden Dawn system. Alterations within the Colour Scales would result in a revised Minutum Mundum diagram (wherein the Tree of Life diagram is depicted with the first 10 Paths in their Queen Scale colours, and the latter 22 Paths in the King Scale colours. As our work focussed upon the Minutum Mundum diagram, complementary colours and Sephirothic colours, we have not produced a revision of the four colour scales in their entirety, but leave it to the individual to interpret and intuit any further alterations.

Our investigation of the nature of primary colours and the colour wheel led us to the extensive research of artist Don Jusko, creator of the *Real Color Wheel*,[4] several of whose insights have informed this study.

---

3   See Appendix IV for Regardie, Cicero, and Wendrich Colour Scales.
4   www.realcolorwheel.com

The True Primary Colours

In our modern printing age we are familiar with the three Primary Colours (i.e. colours which cannot be mixed) as Magenta (Quinacridone Magenta), Lemon Yellow, and Cyan (Pthalocyanine Blue), rather than the common Red, Yellow, and Blue theory that has been taught for centuries. A study of the emergence of colour pigments reveals that the original Golden Dawn Orders would have had a very different range of pigments on their palette than those of the 21st Century. For example, a century ago the primary colour Magenta was unavailable as a non-fading pigment. The closest available non-fading colour was Permanent Alizarin, derived from Madder Lake in 1826. The colour Magenta was discovered in 1859, but it was fugitive (it would fade in the light). Magenta only became available as a non-fugitive colour in the 1970s. Cadmium Red was available from 1909, before which time Vermilion would have been widely used (which was costly, toxic, and had a tendency to blacken in time). Primary Yellow was available since the 1800s in the form of Indian Yellow from 1800 until 1909, and Lemon Yellow in 1830. Prussian Blue was available in 1705, imitation Cobalt Blue in 1802, but the primary Pthalocyanine Blue was not discovered until 1935.[5]

> 1705: Prussian Blue became available (close to cyan when transparent)
> 1804: Cobalt Blue available
> 1826: Permanent Alizarin was discovered
> 1830: Lemon Yellow was discovered
> 1860: Cobalt Violet was made
>
> **1888: FOUNDING OF FIRST GOLDEN DAWN TEMPLE**
>
> 1909: Cadmium Red was made
> 1935: Cyan Blue (Pathalocyanine) was discovered, the true primary.
> 1970s: Liquitex made a perfect transparent primary magenta, called "Acra Violet," today called Quinacridone Magenta (code PR:122)

---

5   With reference to www.realcolorwheel.com and
Douma, Michael, curator. *Lemon Yellow, Pigments through the Ages*, 2008, http://www.webexhibits.org/pigments/ Indiv/ history/lemonyellow.html, Retrieved December 14th, 2015.

The Sephiroth in Queen Scale

The lower seven Sephirothic colours in Queen Scale are derived using a formula based upon the mixing of primary colours to make secondary colours, which are further mixed to produce the colours of Malkuth. When Magenta and Cyan are substituted for the original Red and Blue primary positions, there are repercussions throughout the lower portion of the Tree, not only in Queen Scale, but also in the colours of Prince Scale which are produced by mixing together those of King and Queen Scales. *The Path of the Chameleon* eloquently describes the colours of the Sephiroth in Queen Scale, and from these descriptions come the colour attributions.

> In Kether is the Divine White Brilliance, the scintillation and corruscation of the Divine Glory – that Light which lighteth the universe….
> In Chokmah is a cloud-like grey which containeth various colours and is mixed with them, like a transparent pearl-hued mist, yet radiating withal, as if behind it there were a brilliant glory…

Traditional GD Scales attribute the term "White Brilliance" to Kether in Queen Scale, and "Grey" to Chokmah. In our Sephirothic Queen Scale we have attributed Chokmah (Two of Cups) with "Pearl Grey." The naming of this Sephira "Pearl Grey" rather than simply "Grey" satisfies the logical formula when mixing this Queen Scale colour with the "Soft Blue" of King Scale to produce "Bluish Mother of Pearl" in Prince Scale.[9] The text describes a transparency which is important in Chokmah, wherein various pearl-hued colours can be seen. Mother of Pearl displays specific primary and secondary colours within a soft grey iridescent effect, and these delicate multi-hued colours of Pearl carry the loving life force of Two of Cups in a way that an opaque Grey does not. However, to produce a Pearl effect requires the overlapping of several translucent colours with the addition of White, so an opaque Pale Grey may at times be used for convenience: the colour Grey pertains to Wisdom (Chokmah) even as the hair of man becomes grey with age. However, wherever possible it is preferable to generate both Chokmah and Binah from the overlaying and blending of Primary colours, as both Sephiroth contain all colours, with Chokmah notably also including the White of Kether.

> In Binah is a thick darkness which yet veileth the Divine Glory in which all colours are hidden, wherein is mystery and depth and silence, and yet, it is the habitation of the Supernal Light.

---

9   Farr, Regardie and the Ciceros attributed Queen Scale Chokmah with Grey, yet described Prince Scale Chokmah as Blue pearl grey (Farr) Bluish Mother of Pearl (Regardie), Pearlish blue-grey (Cicero). Applying the colour mixing formula to Regardie's table, if Soft Blue of King Scale is mixed with Grey of Queen Scale, the result would be a Pale Bluish-grey in Prince Scale, rather than Bluish Mother of Pearl.

Regardie and the Ciceros attribute the Sephira of Binah with Black; Farr and Zalewski called it Blackish Red (the logic of which can be deduced when reading further); we have also termed it Black, which is the colour produced when the three primaries are mixed together.

The Sephiroth of Chesed, Geburah, and Tiphareth are written of thus:

> In Chokmah is the Radix of blue and thence is there a blue colour pure and primitive, and glistening with a spiritual Light which is reflected unto Chesed...

The traditional GD colour attribution for Chesed is Blue; we have updated this to Cyan, the true Primary.

> In Binah is the Radix of Red, and therein is there a red colour, pure and scintillating and flashing with flame which is reflected unto Geburah…

The 'Radix' of Red means the origin, the root, and therefore the primary nature, which whilst found in Binah, is also reflected into Geburah. This is the reason why Farr's Colour Scales label Queen Scale Binah as "Black with hidden red" and the Zalewskis' version as "Blackish-red." (Interestingly, the Radix of both Blue and Red are more obviously seen in King Scale Chokmah and Binah, in the colours Soft Blue and Crimson.) The Fifth Knowledge Lecture,[10] wherein this text can be found, goes on to describe how the force of Geburah brings war, strength and slaughter and rules the Planet Mars; this establishes an argument to retain Red as the colour of Geburah. Yet today the Radix of Red is understood to be the Primary colour Magenta, which is also the colour of the kundalini flame. Strangely enough, the colour was named after the Battle of Magenta, as the Magenta dye was discovered by a Frenchman in the same year that the battle was fought and won by the French near the town of that name (1859). Magenta is not the colour attributed to Mars, but neither does the Queen Scale colour of Chesed correspond with that of Jupiter, that of Tiphareth with the Sun, Hod with Mercury, or Yesod with the Moon. Nevertheless, to update the attribution for Geburah to Magenta within the Golden Dawn tradition seemed a monumental decision to make, especially considering the repercussions throughout the system. It was not a decision that we felt was ours to make lightly. Enquiring within meditation, Harry was shown that we had been given the task of introducing Magenta as a primary colour within Geburah and within the Golden Dawn colour system.

As a confirmation of that which Harry had been told in meditation, we experienced a magical occurrence concerning the colour Magenta. Harry had, prior to the Tarot project, been working upon a series of paintings depicting the Sephiroth of the Tree of Life. In the *Geburah* painting he pictured the Egyptian godform Horus, using a ground

10   Regardie, *The Golden Dawn*, 97.

colour of Cadmium Red Medium, with a flashing colour of Green. Usually an oil painting takes around a couple of weeks to dry if no drying medium is added to the paint and if the paint is not thickly applied. In cold weather it takes a little longer. But in the case of the Geburah painting, we hung the canvas for *two years* in a heated room, and the red paint would not dry. At this point, having dreamt of the need for change in colour theory, we decided to paint over the still tacky canvas with a ground colour of Magenta, using Phthalo Green as the complementary colour and adjusting the colours of the Tree of Life diagram within the painting to those equating with modern primary pigments. The effect of the updated flashing colours was much more powerful, and the painting dried within a few days! (Fig. 1) Such a sign from Horus himself in Geburah carried the authority to apply such changes and to present an updated colour theory to the Golden Dawn at large.

> In Kether is the Radix of a Golden Glory and thence is there a pure, primitive and sparkling, gleaming golden yellow which is reflected unto Tiphareth…

Farr and Regardie attributed Yellow (gold) to Tiphareth; the Ciceros shortened this to Yellow, being the third primary, with which we concur.

> The beams of Chesed and of Tiphareth meet in Netzach and thence in Netzach arises a green, pure, brilliant, liquid, and gleaming like an emerald.

Farr and Regardie attributed Netzach with "Emerald" which the Ciceros renamed "Green." When Cyan is mixed with Yellow, several shades lay between. In our own experiments, four intermediary shades make it difficult to choose a "middle shade." It is always best to mix colours from primaries to determine exact hues for oneself. We have retained the name "Green" for this Sephira (fig. 2).

> The beams of Geburah and Tiphareth meet in Hod and thence arises in Hod a brilliant pure and flashing orange tawny.

Tawny is an example of a colour description used in times gone by but less common in this century. It is described as being a brownish-orange colour, from the Anglo-Norman *tauné* associated with the brownish-yellow of tanned leather. Orange tawny was shortened to Orange in Regardie's Colour Scales, the colour formed by the mixing of Red and Yellow. However, with the true primary Magenta now being mixed with Yellow, we have attributed Hod with the colour of Cadmium Red Light, a very deep Orange bordering on Red, which we have termed Red-orange (fig. 2).

The beams of Chesed and Geburah meet in Yesod and thence ariseth in Yesod
a brilliant deep violet-purple or puce, and thus is the third Triad completed.

"Puce" is another colour term which is rarely used in modern language. The French word for "flea" and "flea-coloured," Puce is named according to the brownish purple or dark reddish-brown colour of crushed fleas, but although pigments have been obtained by the crushing of the bodies of insects (such as the derivation of the crimson-coloured dye carmine from the cochineal insect and the extraction of Tyrian Purple from the mucus of marine molluscs of the Murex genus[11]), we have found no reference to puce pigment being obtained from crushed fleas! However, the use of the term "Puce" within the Golden Dawn document illustrates how in the past a browning element would have resulted from the impure addition of yellow to the assumed primary Red, which was then mixed with a Blue which was not the true primary Cyan, to make what Regardie labels "Violet" within Queen Scale Yesod.

It is worth noting that in the abridged version of this text (which appears in the Adeptus Minor ceremony[12]) this same "Violet" of Queen Scale Yesod is referred to as both "Purple" and "Puce." This begins what can become a confusing dilemma when positioning the colours Violet and Purple upon the colour wheel, and when either colour is called for within the Golden Dawn Colour Scales, which shall be examined shortly. In either case, unless one replaces Red with Magenta and Blue with Cyan on one's palette, it is impossible to mix a pure Purple or Violet.

We have attributed Yesod with the colour Purple, formed from the mixing of Magenta with Cyan, which in pigment would be termed "Dioxazine Purple." (Fig. 2)

From the mixing of the three secondary colours are the four colours of the Malkuth Square derived. Our Queen Scale Sephiroth have altered colour attributions in Geburah, Hod, and Yesod, so we can expect to find further alterations within the colours of Malkuth.

From the rays of this Triad there appear three colours in Malkuth together with a fourth which is their synthesis. Thus from the orange tawny of Hod and the green nature of Netzach, there goeth forth a certain greenish 'citrine' colour, yet pure and translucent withal. From the orange tawny of Hod mingled with the puce of Yesod there goeth forth a certain red russet brown, 'russet' yet gleaming with a hidden fire. From the green of Netzach and the puce of Yesod there goeth forth a certain other darkening green 'Olive' yet rich and glowing withal. The synthesis of all these is a blackness which bordereth upon the Qlippoth.

All previous GD Colour Scales use the terms Citrine, Olive, Russet, and Black to

11   Douma, Michael, curator. *Pigments from Animals and Plants*, Cause of Color, 2008, http://www.webexhibits.org/causesofcolor/7.html; Retrieved 16th February, 2016.
12   Regardie, *The Golden Dawn*, 241.

describe the colours formed by the mixing of the secondary colours in their various combinations. Within the Golden Dawn, Citrine is sometimes taken to be a greenish-yellow colour, and sometimes a yellow-brown. The first recorded use of citrine as a colour in English was in 1386,[13] and the original reference point for the citrine colour was the citron fruit. However, it has since been used to describe the brownish-yellow colour of the variety of quartz crystal which bears its name, and we have found this colour to bear a closer resemblance to the Citrine of Malkuth, especially with the additional description of "greenish." Magenta in Geburah increases the reddening component of Hod (although this is balanced somewhat by the purity of Cyan in the Green of Netzach with which Red-Orange is mixed). The increased reddening component of this upper quadrant of the Malkuth square emphasizes its brown quality, giving "Citrine" a greenish-yellow-brown colour, as shown in figs. 3 and 4.

The Russet colour of the left-hand quadrant also has a slightly less yellow tone to it, as would be expected whenever Magenta replaces Red in a mix. Such a colour exists in rocks with iron content, such as red ochre, which takes its reddish colour from the mineral hematite, an anhydrous iron oxide. Significantly, the left-hand position links this quadrant with the Sephira of Geburah and its rulership of Mars, the red planet, attributed with the metal iron.

The term "Olive" with its additional description of "darkening green" can be misleading if associated with either actual olives or military colours. In a 1920s document on colour, the term "slate" was sometimes used as "olive" to describe an equal mix of purple and green pigments,[14] and it may be that these were common colour terms during the days of early Golden Dawn. It is important to remember that the Queen Scale "Violet" of Yesod, when taken from the text, should be a "brilliant deep violet-purple" – thus a dark shade, and *not* the Violet colour which is attributed to Jupiter and adjacent to Magenta in a modern colour wheel. When this deep Violet-Purple colour is mixed with Green, the result seems almost closer in hue to Black than the black quadrant of Malkuth. This is because there is very little Yellow in the right-hand quadrant, and a double portion of Cyan, making for a very dark result which really has to be mixed in order to be known, as words and comparisons cannot easily describe colour accurately.

The final Black, the synthesis of all the colours, is a warm earthy Black compared to the right-hand segment, due to its greater proportion of Yellow. It is the deep brownish-black of soil rich in decomposed matter – quite apt when we consider that this lower quadrant "bordereth upon the Qlippoth." (Figs. 3 & 4).

Thus the most noticeable changes that the true primaries bring to the 10 Sephiroth are within the colours of Chesed, Geburah, and Hod, affecting the colouring of the 4, 5, and 8 of Cups and Swords. Other modifications are more subtle.

---

13   A. Maerz and M. Rea Paul, *A Dictionary of Color.* (New York: McGraw-Hill, 1930), 193.

14   John Lemos, "Color Charts for the School Room", The School Arts Magazine, Volume 19 (1920): 580–584.

Violet and Purple

There seems to have been some confusion with the terms Violet and Purple within the early Golden Dawn which continues in the world at large today. Conflicting information exists in the wide variety of printed material and internet sites which examine the subject. In pigment terms, both colours are derived from the mixing of the two primaries of Cyan and Magenta. The German word for Purple, "purpurrot," ends with the German word for red "rot," which would indicate that Purple is the nearest colour to Red on the colour wheel, but this is because the French *pourpre* and German *purpurrot* have more red included in their mix and less blue, compared to the Purple of the UK and USA, lending to possible further confusion.

Within a rainbow, the colour Magenta can almost be glimpsed at the outer edge of the Violet band. When looking at light through a prism, although the colour Violet can be seen, there can be some difficulty in pinning the hue due to the phenomenon known as The Bezold–Brücke Shift, in which our perception of Violet light, with its wavelength of 380-450 nanometers, changes its hue as light intensity increases, shifting towards blue.[19]

For the sake of minimising confusion within the Golden Dawn Colour Scales, we have opted to follow the colour naming adopted by Farr, Regardie, the Ciceros, and the Zalewskis, in that of the two colours, Violet is the name we have given to the shade closest to Magenta, compared to Purple which we have placed closer to blue. This retains the results from mixing King and Queen Scales to produce Prince Scale colours, e.g.:

The 4th Path (Chesed):
> King Scale/Deep Violet + Queen Scale/Blue = Prince Scale/Deep Purple

The 9th Path (Yesod):
> King Scale/Indigo + Queen Scale/Violet = Prince Scale/Very Dark Purple

There seems to have been an anomaly in the colour scales of Farr, Regardie, and the Ciceros when it comes to Da'ath,[20] as Pure Violet mixed with Grey White would produce Lavender, not the other way around, but this reversal of the colour mixing formula is in fact symbolic of the reverse Tree of Life which is accessible through Da'ath.

> King Scale/Lavender + Queen Scale/Grey White = Prince Scale/Pure Violet.

---

19   Arne Valberg and Barry B. Lee, *From Pigments to Perception: Advances in Understanding Visual Processes*, (New York: Springer: 1991), 431.
20   The modern scales named by Christine Zalewski attribute the logical mixing sequence to the colours of Da'ath (King Scale/Blue Lavender White + Queen Scale/Very light Lavender Grey = Prince Scale/ Very light Lavender Grey) *The Magical Tarot of the Golden Dawn*, Pat and Chris Zalewski, (London: Aeon, 2008), 39-42.

Choosing paints for Golden Dawn Colour Work

When working with the Colour Scales, it is important to bear in mind that regardless of the preferred colour *term,* the correct *colour* is selected, and even then, one's intuition and intention play as important a role.

Computer screens and printed matter cannot be trusted to inform us of correct colours – even within this book the original colours of pigments, once photographed and manipulated by the computer and printing technology, have altered.

Neither is it an easy task to obtain the desired colour when purchasing paints. Worded descriptions cannot always be relied upon. The modern pigments for sale in art shops have conflicting names: one brand's violet is another brand's purple, many paints are named "primary" when they are not, and the colour on a printed label rarely matches the colour within the tube.

Therefore, it helps to prepare one's own colour chart from the three primaries in order to compare it with potential pigments before purchasing/using them. When mixing primaries to ascertain the correct secondary colours, the most accurate results will be obtained through the use of transparent paints: oil pigments are preferable in that they retain a superior sense of lightfastness than acrylic paints. Mixes of the pure transparent pigments of Lemon Yellow, Pthalocyanine Blue and Quinacridone Magenta can be used[21] to ascertain the correct secondary and tertiary shades. Once the results of mixing primaries have been obtained in this way, one has a useful colour chart for matching different brands of paints, and the nearest available acrylic pigment may now be selected for ease of colouring tools. Wherever possible, remove the lid of the paint and test a tiny amount on a piece of white paper.

Often opaque or semi-opaque acrylic paints are used for colouring tools, as transparent acrylic paints, whilst providing the most accurate hue, tend to darken when applied thickly, and the pure bright colours become lost. However, in some situations it is worth remembering that a thin application of a transparent paint upon a white base can generate the "scintillating," "gleaming," "glistening," and "brilliant," effects of colour described in the Golden Dawn text whereas an opaque pigment cannot.

The Liquitex Professional range of Heavy Body acrylics provides a wide choice of colours: their Cerulean Blue provides a close opaque match to Cyan, although their Pthalo Blue (Green Shade) is a more accurate transparent shade. The true primary Quinacridone Magenta is available, and transparent Hansa Yellow Light is closer to Lemon Yellow than the opaque Cadmium Yellow Light, although neither is the exact primary.

Dioxizine Purple is a good transparent Purple, and Prism Violet a transparent Violet which benefits from a small addition of Magenta.

---

21   Trusted brands of oil paint for this purpose are are Mussini Lemon Yellow, Mussini Translucent Cyan, Winsor & Newton Quinacridone Magenta.

The Paths of King Scale

Thus far we have examined the Minor Arcana according to the colours assigned to Paths 1 – 10 in Queen Scale. We shall now turn our attention to Paths 11 – 32 in King Scale, which equate to the 22 Paths that connect the Sephiroth – in Tarot terms, the Major Arcana. There are three main colour formulae within the King Scale which, when Tarot cards are coloured accordingly, allow the user to make astrological or elemental connections via the colour symbolism. These formulae are also used in the production of the Rose in the Rosy Cross Lamen, included as a Cover Card within the deck.[15]

The Three Elemental Colours
The three inner petals of the Rosy Cross relate to the Paths associated with the three primary colours, the elements of Air, Water, and Fire, and correspond to the three Hebrew Mother letters (*aleph* א, *mem* מ, and *shin* ש). Here, the worded colour descriptions in the Regardie and Cicero Colour Scales illuminate a difference in thought within the Golden Dawn – should these three Paths tonally suggest the elemental colours of Air, Water and Fire? Or should they carry the three primary colours, according to their status as bearing the three Mother letters?

Regardie followed the colours as laid down by Florence Farr, illustrating the *elemental nature* of these cards, as can be deduced by the additional colour descriptions of *bright, pale* (Air), *deep* (Water), and *glowing* (Fire). The Ciceros simplified the colour names with the result of slight changes which place emphasis upon the *primary* nature rather than the tonal quality.

In the *Golden Dawn Temple Tarot*, we coloured the borders of the Hanged Man and the Fool according to Regardie's tables, but used Magenta for the Spirit of the Primal Fire of the Judgement Key, rather than Glowing Scarlet-orange or Red. The colour Red lends to Judgement the energy of elemental/terrestrial fire, but the colour Magenta relates to the Spiritual Fire in man, the kundalini. This colour decision was made by the Judgement archetype in a meditation in which we specifically asked about the colour of this Path, leading us to deduce that the colours of the Paths attributed to the three Mother Letters allude to an inherent nature of the card that is neither solely elemental nor primary, but spiritual, according to their Titles:

א The Spirit of Ether
Bright Pale Yellow suggestive of the fine vibration of the higher astral

מ The Spirit of the Mighty Waters
Deep Blue associated with the subconscious waters

---

15   See inner front cover and fig. 5, p. 298

ש The Spirit of the Primal Fire
Magenta symbolic of the purifying kundalini flame.

PATH	ATTRIBUTION	HEBREW LETTER	TAROT KEY	KING SCALE: REGARDIE	KING SCALE: CICERO	KING SCALE: WENDRICH
11	Air	Aleph	The Fool	Bright Pale Yellow	Yellow	Bright Pale Yellow
23	Water	Mem	The Hanged Man	Deep Blue	Blue	Deep Blue
31	Fire	Shin	Judgement	Glowing Scarlet-orange	Red	Magenta

It is important to note that although Magenta replaces Red's primary position on the colour wheel, the Element of Fire remains coloured Red. Red is the colour which first appears when metal is heated, and it is the colour closest to the infra-red rays (heat-giving rays) of the Sun. Red is the colour of terrestrial, elemental Fire: Magenta is the colour of the Spiritual Fire, the kundalini. For this reason, we allocated the Court Cards the elemental colours of Red for Wands, Blue for Cups, Yellow for Swords, and the Malkuth colours for Pentacles.

The Seven Planetary Colours
The middle layer of seven petals of the Rose equate to the Paths of the Seven Planetary Signs in King Scale. They hold the colours of the rainbow/the electro-magnetic spectrum of light through a prism. The introduction of Magenta within the colour wheel does not affect the planetary colours, as Magenta is not visible within the electro-magnetic spectrum of light (it lays within the Violet ray). Blue, however, should be updated to Cyan.

PATH	PLANET	TAROT KEY	KING SCALE: REGARDIE	KING SCALE: CICERO	KING SCALE: WENDRICH
12	Mercury	The Magician	Yellow	Yellow	Yellow
13	Moon	The High Priestess	Blue	Blue	Cyan
14	Venus	The Empress	Emerald Green	Green	Green
21	Jupiter	The Wheel of Fortune	Violet	Violet	Violet
27	Mars	The Tower	Scarlet	Red	Red
30	Sun	The Sun	Orange	Orange	Orange
31	Saturn	The Universe	Indigo	Blue-violet	Indigo

It is important to remember that the Indigo associated with Saturn is the very deep band of Blue seen in the rainbow spectrum, between Cyan and Violet – a pure and deep Blue (Ultramarine), not the navy blue colour of the plant dye. We have retained the term *Indigo* in our work, as the rainbow colour sequence is so is well-known (ROYGBIV/"Richard Of York Gave Battle In Vain"/Red, Orange, Yellow, Green, Blue, Indigo, Violet) although in renaming "Blue" as "Cyan," perhaps we should think of Richard Of York Giving Chase in Vain!

The 12 Zodiacal Colours

The 12 outer petals of the Rose correspond with the Paths associated with the 12 Zodiacal signs of King Scale, and their colours follow the sequence of a colour wheel. Members of the early Golden Dawn would have probably been familiar with any of several colour wheel theories which inaccurately pinned Red as a primary colour, resulting in a loss of accuracy in complementary colours (although some theories were based upon concepts other than physical pigments), including:

1. 1666, *Opticks* by Isaac Newton: the first colour wheel, with seven segments of the light spectrum (in which magenta does not show up), based on the accurate observation that a prism splits white light into the colours of the visible spectrum.

2. 1708, *Traite de la Peinture in Mignature*, attributed to Claude Boutet: the oldest example of the symmetrical 12-hue artists colour wheel using Red, Yellow, and Blue as the primaries.

3. 1755, Tobias Myer: a colour triangle with primaries indicated as Red, Yellow, and Blue.

4. 1809, *Zur Farbenlehre (Theory of Colours)* by Johann Wolfgang von Goethe: depicting a 6-segment colour wheel using Red, Yellow and Blue as primaries.

5. 1880, Ewald Hering: Six primary colours, coupled in three pairs: red–green, yellow–blue, and white–black.

6. 1919, *Die Farbenfibel (Color Primer)* by Wilhelm Ostwald: a 24-segment colour wheel with Red, Yellow, Blue, and Sea-Green in the quarters.

7. 1961, *Farbkreis* by Johannes Itten: using Red, Yellow, and Blue as the three primaries.

In 1908, J. Arthur Hatt in his innovative work *The Colorist*[16] published an accurate colour wheel of 24 segments, in which he named the three primary colours Yellow, Magenta and Cyan Blue, with complementary colours of Violet, Green, and Red (fig. 6). However, because the pigments Magenta and Cyan were at that time only available in fugitive form (in Hatt's charts, personally made by himself and Mr. Coon) Hatt's accurate colour wheel had to be kept from the light, which perhaps goes some way to explain how such important colour knowledge was adopted by so few.[17]

In 1996, Don Jusko's *Real Color Wheel* (fig. 7) demonstrated how the colours of light, crystals and pigments are joined, using the true primaries of Yellow, Magenta, and Cyan in a wheel of 36 segments, with complementary colours of French Ultramarine Blue, Pthalo Green, and Cadmium Red Light.

It is important to recognise Magenta and Cyan as the True Primaries in pigment terms, and position them accordingly on a colour wheel for the following reasons:

1. They hold a unique position as Primary colours.
2. They affect the production of the Secondary colours,
3. which affects the production of Tertiary colours.
4. Their correct placement shifts the Complementary Colours away from those which are traditionally used in the GD system.
5. The colouring of Golden Dawn tools is affected.
6. Their unique vibrational frequency allows for a greater expression of colour magic relevant to our current age.

The colour wheel used by the Golden Dawn can be reproduced by analysis of the associated 12 Zodiacal colours in King Scale. As shown in the following table, the Ciceros named these colours in a logical fashion which assists in visualizing a sequence of colours around the wheel. This method of naming colours was also used in the main part by J. Arthur Hatt in his 24-segmented wheel.

The true primaries Magenta and Cyan are missing from the earlier Golden Dawn Colour Wheels, as is also the purest form of Violet, which can only be formed by the mixing of the primaries Magenta and Cyan. (Mixing Red with Blue results in a muddier violet colour, because in actuality yellow has been included in the mix.)

---

16   J. Arthur Hatt, *The Colorist*, 1908. (MT: Kessinger, 2010)
17   Hatt, *The Colorist*, xv.

12-SEGMENT COLOUR WHEEL: ZODIACAL COLOUR COMPARISONS

PATH	ZODIACAL SIGN	KING SCALE: REGARDIE	KING SCALE: CICERO	KING SCALE: WENDRICH
15	Aries	Scarlet	Red	Magenta
16	Taurus	Red Orange	Red-orange	Red
17	Gemini	Orange	Orange	Orange
18	Cancer	Amber	Yellow-orange	Amber
19	Leo	Greenish-Yellow	Yellow	Yellow
20	Virgo	Yellowish-Green	Yellow-green	Yellow-green
22	Libra	Emerald Green	Green	Green
24	Scorpio	Green-blue	Blue-green	Turquoise
25	Sagittarius	Blue	Blue	Cyan
26	Capricorn	Indigo	Blue-violet	Indigo
28	Aquarius	Violet	Violet	Purple
29	Pisces	Ultra Violet Crimson	Red-violet	Violet

The differences between the Wendrich Zodiacal Colour Wheel and previous Golden Dawn Colour Wheels are:

1. Aries becomes Magenta instead of Red.

2. Taurus becomes Red instead of Red-orange.

3. Leo, as the Ciceros stated, is coloured with the primary Yellow. Regardie and Farr labelled Leo as Greenish-Yellow, but this served to pin the yellow colour to Lemon Yellow, rather than the warmer Cadmium Yellow which tends toward Amber.

4. Sagittarius becomes Cyan instead of Blue.

5. Aquarius is named Purple instead of Violet, although the actual hue remains the same (tending towards blue). It would bring greater clarity and consistency to the GD Colour Scales if the term "Violet" for Aquarius were substituted for "Purple."[18]

5. With the introduction of Magenta as the primary colour associated with Aries, the former GD colour choices of Red-Violet, Crimson, and Ultra Violet Crimson for the 29th Path of Pisces become obselete. These colours were the midway point of mixing Violet with with Red, but as Red contains Yellow they no longer have a place upon an updated

---

18   In the Adeptus Minor Ritual, Aquarius is assigned the colour Purple, showing the Golden Dawn's interchanging of these two colour terms. (Regardie, *Golden Dawn*, 241)

colour wheel, as there should be no yellow pigment in colours between Magenta and Cyan.

6. Violet is now the adjacent colour to Magenta, and thus becomes the associated colour for Pisces.

The Wendrich Zodiacal Colour Wheel is pictured in fig. 8. Our starting point was the three true primary colours. The colours were gradated to produce the most distinct hues that lay between the three primaries. Of these, the visually centre-most hues were selected as the secondary colours, and the other distinct hues positioned accordingly. We have named the colours according to traditional Golden Dawn labels wherever possible.

The Colour Wheel and the Tarot
Aries becoming Magenta instead of Red, despite being most apt astrologically, in Tarot terms would call for an Emperor card with a predominance of Magenta. Magenta did not seem to fit with the traditional symbolism incorporated within the *Golden Dawn Temple Tarot*'s Emperor Key. Harry asked about this in meditation and was told that in the future the Emperor Key will be designed in such a way that captures the essence of the vibration of Magenta within its symbolism (in a different deck). Ironically, the Emperor's influence, while powerful, is yet temporal, suggesting the inevitable transition into a new age of which Magenta would be an appropriate herald. So we opted at this time to keep the Emperor in his traditional Red, but increased the amounts of Magenta in the borders of the two adjacent cards of the Emperor and the Moon Card (Pisces). We also highlighted Magenta as the correct complementary colour to the Green of Venus, hence the Magenta-coloured dress worn by the Empress.

The Zodiacal Colour Wheel is an accurate tool for working with modern primary colour attributions within general Golden Dawn astrological and Tarot work, and has been utilized in our updated Minutum Mundum diagram (see inner rear cover image). It provides an up-to-date colour system for colouring tools wherever zodiacal colours are called for, including the Lotus Wand, the Rose Cross Lamen, the Pastos, and the symbolic squares on the walls of the Vault. However, it is worth noting that although colours in opposition upon the Zodiacal Colour Wheel can be considered flashing colours, a greater degree of accuracy in determining complementary colours is required when following the colour mixing formula for painting the walls of the Vault of the Adepti. The 16-segment Vault Colours and Charges Chart in fig. 9 is suitable for this purpose, which lists the colours required to paint the Vault Panels along with their most accurate Charge colour.

Through the Vault of the Adepti

The updated colour wheel becomes paramount in the constructing of various tools for use within the Inner Order, and rightly so, bearing in mind that the Path of the Adeptus Minor, *Hodos Chamelionis*, is so very concerned with colour. Magenta, Cyan, and Violet may now take their rightful place upon such items as the Lotus Wand, the Rose Cross Lamen, and the Vault of the Adepti itself.

The Vault of the Adepti is a seven-sided chamber: each of the walls represents one of the visible Planets and is coloured in accordance with its associated colour.

"Now, if you take the planetary colours, affix the planets, and arrange them in the order of the Solar Spectrum; then bend the series into a ring and make the chain into a heptagon and bend the whole lot about until you get the two ends to meet at the East, you will have this Mysterium. (1), Jupiter, Violet. (2) Saturn, Indigo. (3) Moon, Blue. (4) Venus, Green. (5) Mercury, Yellow. (6) Sun, Orange. (7) Mars, Red." [22]

Seven sets of symbols are used to generate 40 squares upon each Panel, and these are:

1. the Enochian Spirit Wheel
2. the 4 Kerubic symbols
3. the 10 Sephiroth
4. the 7 Planets
5. the 12 Zodiacal signs
6. the 3 Elemental symbols of Fire, Water and Air
7. the 3 Alchemical symbols of Sulphur, Mercury and Salt.

From the Adeptus Minor Ritual:
"The colours of the varying squares may be either represented by the colour of the Planet and the colour of the Force therein mixed together, or by these colours being placed in juxtaposition, or in any other convenient manner; but the foundation of them all is the Minutum Mundum diagram." [23]

In using the expanded colour range within the Munitum Mundum diagram with pigments of our age, the Vault Panels can be completed with a greater dynamic expression than was previously possible.

---

22   Regardie, *Golden Dawn,* 267.
23   Regardie, "Adeptus Minor Ritual," *Golden Dawn,* 246.

The colouring of the Planetary Vault walls is based upon the colours of the rainbow and joins Red (Mars) with Violet (Jupiter). Magenta is a mystical colour: despite, as we have discovered, holding the position of one of the three Primary colours, Magenta is invisible within the electro-magnetic spectrum – it lays hidden within the Violet ray. In the positioning of the Red Mars Panel beside the Violet Jupiter panel, Magenta is the invisible link between them, residing at the very edge between light and darkness, as a veil – the position of the Chief Adept.

> "Modern Science teaches and reveals a great truth: that however valuable the seven colours of the prism may be, there are rays invisible (and so not demonstrable by space), beyond the red end of the spectrum and beyond the violet and that these have great chemic or Yetziratic force. These forces are present but are unseen and are represented by the Chief Adept standing at the Eastern Angle, the most powerful person in the group and the delegate of the Chiefs of the Second Order and through them of the Mystic Third Order. …. Representing the East, coming from the East, he faces the Western world, bringing Initiations with Him. The Chief Adept has Mars and Geburah at his right; and on his left hand he has Jupiter and Gedulah; and he faces Venus in the West, the Evening Star which represents the entry of the Candidate who has toiled all the day until the evening." [1]

Magenta's complementary colour is Green, which makes Magenta the charge colour for the Venus Panel – the doorway into the Vault, which faces the Chief Adept. It is worth noting that on the Inner Planes, the Door of the Vault is invisible until you are ready to open it.

Harry used Primary Magenta in the colouring of the Kerubic symbols, as it seems important to employ the purity of the Primaries at this high level. The colouring for Alchemical Sulphur was given as Pink, so he used Magenta mixed with white to make the purest form of Pink. The Geburah Square was painted fully in Magenta. The Aries Square was imbued with Magenta: asking in meditation upon this, Harry was shown that this was acceptable in that as with the Emperor card, Magenta was being included in its invisible or hidden aspect between Red and Violet. With the method adopted by Harry in the colour mixing, an accurate charge (complementary colour) was also necessary to produce the desired effect of each square. At the time that this work was underway, we found Don Jusko's Real Color Wheel to be invaluable in determining accurate charge colours, because, as was noted earlier, the 12-segmented zodiacal colour wheel lacks the pin-point accuracy of complementary colours. The colours of the full Minutum Mundum diagram and their complementaries had to be considered, along with those associated with the other symbols inscribed upon the Vault walls.

The colours required for the construction of a modern-day Vault are listed in the following table and are illustrated in the Vault Colour Chart on page 299.

---

1   Regardie, *Golden Dawn*, 267,268.

UPDATED VAULT COLOURS AND CHARGES

SYMBOL	COLOUR	CHARGE
ENOCHIAN SPIRIT WHEEL	White	Black
KERUBIC FIRE	Magenta	Green (Pthalo Green)
KERUBIC WATER	Cyan	Red-Orange (Cadmium Red Light)
KERUBIC AIR	Yellow	Indigo-Purple (Ultramarine + Purple)
KERUBIC EARTH	Black	White
KETHER	White	Black
CHOKMAH	Pearl Grey (Magenta, Pthalo Green + White, roughly mixed)	Deep Brown (Ultramarine + Amber)
BINAH	Black	White
CHESED	Cyan	Red-Orange (Cadmium Red Light)
GEBURAH	Magenta	Pthalo Green
TIPHARETH	Yellow	Indigo-Purple
NETZACH	Green (Pthalo, yellow shade)	Magenta
HOD	Red-Orange	Cyan
YESOD	Purple	Yellow-Green
MALKUTH	Citrine, Olive, Russet, Black	White
SUN	Orange (Cadmium)	Cobalt Blue
MOON	Cyan	Red-Orange (Cadmium Red Light)
MERCURY	Yellow (Lemon)	Indigo-Purple
VENUS	Green (Pthalo, yellow shade)	Magenta
MARS	Red (Cadmium Medium + Magenta, or Naphthol Red)	Turquoise
JUPITER	Violet	Green
SATURN	Indigo	Amber
ARIES	Magenta	Pthalo Green
TAURUS	Red	Turquoise
GEMINI	Orange	Cobalt Blue
CANCER	Amber	Indigo
LEO	Yellow (Lemon)	Indigo-Purple
VIRGO	Yellow-Green	Purple
LIBRA	Green	Magenta
SCORPIO	Turquoise	Red (Napthol Red)
SAGITTARIUS	Cyan	Red-Orange (Cadmium Red Light)
CAPRICORN	Indigo	Amber
AQUARIUS	Purple	Yellow-Green
PISCES	Violet	Green
FIRE	Red (Cadmium Red Light)	Cyan
WATER	Blue (Cobalt Blue)	Orange (Cadmium)
AIR	Yellow	Indigo-Violet

SYMBOL	COLOUR	CHARGE
SULPHUR	Pale Magenta (Magenta + White)	Pthalo Green (deepened with Magenta)
MERCURY	Pale Yellow (Yellow + White)	Purple-Indigo (deepened with Yellow)
SALT	Pale Blue (Blue + White)	Red-Orange (deepened with blue)

The main differences in the updated Vault colour scheme compared with the original Vault colour combinations are as follows:

- The traditional pairing of Red/Green becomes Magenta/Green. Green is associated with the Planet Venus, and Magenta is far more harmonious with the feminine Venusian force and expressions of love than is the former Red, which, although in some circles is considered the colour of the blood of the Earth, in the Golden Dawn is more commonly associated with the war-like, passionate, masculine force associated with Mars, and terrestrial fire.

- The traditional pairing of Red/Green becomes Red/Turquoise. The Turquoise of Scorpio, associated with Death, connects to the Naphthol Red of Mars.

- Red-orange (Cadmium Red Light) is the true complementary colour of Cyan and is used as the colour for the Fire element: in terrestrial fire a Cyan flame may be seen.

- Cobalt Blue is required (between Cyan and Indigo on the colour wheel) for the colouring of the Water element, with a complementary of Cadmium Orange.

- The traditional pairing of Yellow/Violet is shifted towards a bluer and hence darker shade of Indigo-Purple: the very lightest hue complementing the darkest possible hue mixed from Magenta and Cyan.

- The complementary colours of Violet and Purple become Green and Light Green respectively (not Yellow at this degree of accuracy).

- The Grey of the Chokmah square is a Light Grey formed by the rough mixing of White with Magenta and Pthalo Green, thus generating a Pearl effect.

- The Charge colour for Chokmah should be formed from the mixing of Indigo (Ultramarine) with Yellow, resulting in a deep blackish-brown.

- Similarly, the pale colours (tints) of the Alchemical Symbols find their Charge colours in the regular Charge of the specific hue mixed with a tiny amount of its opposite, thus tending to darken in contrast to the whitening of the tint.

Magenta: The Eighth Ray

Nicola dreamed that from the end of the year 2012, people would be able to see more, including colours that we currently do not see.[6] The 'Sleeping Prophet', Edgar Cayce, wrote in his essay *AURAS: An Essay on the Meaning of Colour* that our eyes seem to be gradually gaining in power: through time, humankind's ability to distinguish between different colours has increased. [7]

> In his remarkable book, Pain, Sex, and Time, Gerald Heard, speaking of the evidence for the evolution of consciousness, points out that our ability to see colours is expanding. The easiest color to see, as you know, is red. At that end of the spectrum the waves of light are long. At the other end, where the blue runs into indigo and violet, the waves are short. According to Heard, who is a reliable scholar, our ability to see blue is very recent. Natives who live on the Blue Nile in Africa do not know it by that name. Their title for it, when translated, means brown. Homer, all through the Iliad and Odyssey, describes the Mediterranean as the "wine-dark sea." Mr. Heard says that apparently Homer caught "the slight tinge of red in the purple of the Mediterranean," but did not see its predominant blue. Aristotle, moreover, said that the rainbow had only three colours: red, yellow and green."

Nicola also dreamed (in December 2011) that the world would be bathed twice in Magenta-coloured light, and then a new Light would shine in the sky, streaming white light upon people who were celebrating its presence, singing about a new day.[8] In a subsequent meditation Harry was shown that in the future there will be eight visible rays of light instead of our present seven and that Magenta will be the eighth ray.

There are currently seven visible rays of light in the rainbow/electro-magnetic spectrum, and these colours were attributed by the Mystery Schools to the seven visible planetary bodies, i.e., those visible to the naked eye, including our Sun and Earth's Moon. Our technological advances have informed us of so much more that lays beyond what we can see, but that which our naked eye beholds is of great interest to us, especially given that humankind's ability to see colour is believed to have developed in time, and may yet develop further.

A point of interest with regards to the seven-sided Vault of the Adepti is that a colour which had until recently (1970s) been unavailable in non-fugitive pigment form has now entered the physical space of this magical tool, and the frequency of Magenta is thus now able to become a part of the magical dialogue within the initiation ceremonies.

---

6   Wendrich artHouse. Accessed Feb. 27th, 2016. http://wendricharthouse.com/propheticinfo8_new.htm
7   Edgar Cayce, *Auras: An Essay on the Meaning of Colour*. (Virginia: A.R.E. Press, 1973), 8.
8   "Mystical Magenta," Wendrich artHouse. Accessed Feb. 27th, 2016.
        http://www.wendricharthouse.com/study/mystical-magenta/

The seven walls of the Vault correspond with the seven visible planets and seven visible rays of coloured light. If then an eighth ray of Magenta light becomes visible to our naked eye, could this be synonymous with an eighth planetary body becoming visible to our naked eye? Much has been written in recent years of a Planet X (Nibiru) which has entered our Solar System in the past, and is expected to do so again. Biblical scholar Tim McHyde in his study of the Book of Revelation and the prophecies of the Bible relates the emergence of such a planet to many of the dramatic situations which have been prophesied for planet Earth.[24]

The number eight is also associated with the "Eighth Day" following the Biblical Feast of Sukkoth (Tabernacles), considered by some to be a prophetic metaphor for the end of this earth and the signal for the New Earth and New Heavens. Elsewhere in the Bible, the number eight represents a new beginning or new creation and a sign of the covenant between humanity and God (eight people on the ark; circumcision on the eighth day [symbolic of mankind's circumcision of the heart]). The Greek transliteration of the name of Jesus is 888.[25]

An eighth ray is synonymous with Gnostic teachings of an ogdoad – a supercelestial eighth sphere which lays beyond the seven rays/spheres of influence of the seven planets. The path of the rising serpent upon the Tree of the Knowledge of Good and Evil follows a passage through the seven planetary spheres towards and into the Supernal Realm which borders *Ain Soph*. This is echoed in the discourse of Hermes Trismegistus with Poimandres, in the Hermetica. [26]

Hermes: "But tell me again (about) the way up; tell me how it happens."

To this Poimandres said: "First, in releasing the material body you give the body itself over to alteration, and the form that you used to have vanishes. To the demon you give over your temperament, now inactive. The body's senses rise up and flow back to their particular sources, becoming separate parts and mingling again with the energies. And feeling and longing go on to irrational nature.

Thence the human being rushes up through the cosmic framework, at the first zone [Moon] surrendering the energy of increase and decrease; at the second [Mercury] evil machination, a device now inactive; at the third [Venus] the illusion of longing, now inactive; at the fourth [Sun] the ruler's arrogance, now freed of excess; at the fifth [Mars] unholy presumption and daring recklessness; at the sixth [Jupiter] the evil impulses that come from wealth, now inactive; and at the seventh zone [Saturn] the deceit that lies in ambush.

24   Timothy McHyde, *Know the Future: A Bible Prophecy Breakthrough*, 8th ed. (2012)
25   Aristeo Canlas Fernando expounds the number of Jesus as 888 on his website, using the Greek Ionic Ciphered Numeral System, with the name of Jesus in Greek spelled I H S O U S Accessed 3rd March, 2016. http://aristean.org/jesus888.htm
26   Copenhaver, *Hermetica*, 5,6. [Wendrich notes in square brackets]

And then, stripped of the effects of the cosmic framework, the human enters the region of the ogdoad; he has his own proper power, and along with the blessed he hymns the father. Those present there rejoice in his presence, and, having become like his companions, he also hears certain powers that exist beyond the ogdoadic region and hymn god with sweet voice. They rise up to the father in order and surrender themselves to the powers, and, having become powers, they enter into god."

The rising kundalini, coloured Magenta, correlates with the individual's experience of the breaking of illusions and release into higher forms of consciousness, through which our ultimate aim is to become reunited with God – the Higher and the lower joined once more.

Colour, light, consciousness and universal love are all linked as Cayce explains:

"Where do colours come from, and what makes them shift and change? Well, color seems to be a characteristic of the vibration of matter, and our souls seem to reflect it in this three-dimensional world through atomic patterns. We are patterns, and we project colors, which are there for those who can see them."

Cayce further imagined an evolutionary step for the future of mankind when everybody would be able to see auras:

"What will it mean to us if we make this next evolutionary step? Well, it will mean that we can see auras. What will this mean?

A friend's example: Whenever a person, whether it be a stranger, an intimate friend, or a member of my family, decides to tell me an untruth, or to evade a direct and frank answer to a question of mine, I see a streak of lemony green shoot through his aura, horizontally, just over his head. I call it gas-light green, and I have never known it to fail as an indication of evasion and falsification.

Imagine what that will mean – everyone able to see when you plan to tell them a lie, even a little white one. We will all have to be frank, for there will no longer be such a thing as deceit!"[27]

27   Edgar Cayce, *Auras: An Essay on the Meaning of Colour*. (Virginia: A.R.E. Press, 1973), 8.

Epilogue

Raising the Great Dragon

by Harry Wendrich

Ain Soph means "without end, boundless." It is identified with the Aristotalian "Cause of all Causes," and in the Kabbalah is called the "Root of all Roots," it is the substance of God Himself, imminent within all Creation, and is considered pure thought or divine will. Yet little is known about this vast and sublime concept of Mind/Consciousness.

There is a seeming contradiction within *Ain Soph* as both a realm which is perceived as non-dualistic yet at the same time emanating duality from within itself. *Ain Soph* is One. One infinite Mind holding everything in its rightful place. Nothing that exists can exist without it. *Ain Soph* is the inner reality of everything in existence – all that is known and all as yet undiscovered. Our modern conscious awareness is so programmed to operate within time and space that the idea that everything is one can be difficult for our egos to accept in a world of opposites – good and evil, up and down, man and woman etc. – but within *Ain Soph* there are no such distinctions.

Here at the table, writing my notes, I am an individual, separate from other people and objects around me. The table, the chair, the walls, air – they are all separate, the outer reality of time and space. Yet if I could find the root of my self within *Ain Soph*, I would become aware that I am not actually separate from anything, but just a part of the one Mind or Consciousness. I would perceive that my body was not separated from the table, floor or air, and that I am in fact joined to my spouse, my neighbours and enemies alike, as well as everything else within Creation.

Our universe is an enormous reflection of a higher order, and within the Greater Mind nothing happens by chance. Within this Mind are other realities and more subtle intelligences which can be accessed given the right keys. The Book of Thoth holds such a key. The Tarot is one example of a vehicle used by *Ain Soph* to speak to us – guiding us through symbols designed for the purpose of transmitting a message from the realm of *Ain Soph*. Since the serpent force is everywhere, it can be seen how Tarot cards can be used as a divinatory tool: the Greater Mind is able to bring into manifestation within the realm of Time and Space the exact cards needed to portray a picture of the soul's position within the Greater Mind. Thus it is able to speak using the symbols inherent within the cards to give advice to the individual soul as to how to progress on its journey back into *Ain Soph* through the experience of its higher nature or Higher Self.

We have the freedom to explore the Tree of Life as a symbol or map of consciousness within the realm of Time and Space. This exploration occurs both at an individual level, and on the broader level of humanity, although in many cases it is unconscious. The ultimate quest of our spiritual journey is to regain our oneness in God, Who had and continues to transform Himself into the universe which is present within us as well as outside of ourselves. Yet *Ain Soph* is an enigma. If we could enter the realm of *Ain Soph* with the idea of causing change through an act of magic, everything within the entire universe would be affected to some degree, with the potential outcome that chaos could rage throughout our Solar System and beyond: hence the level of conscious awareness defined by individual egocentric will prevents one from doing so. It is only when the soul has discovered love as a universal principle that it returns to oneness with God. As it is, much of humanity's lack of understanding and love within this deeper level of Mind has brought about such atrocities as the atomic bomb, which has the potential to disturb other worlds within the universe as well as our own.

The Wisdom of the Fool and Extra-terrestrial Intellingence

The archetype of the Fool gives us a key to unlock the mystery of love as the fundamental law which is the foundation of creation: the ego is the opposite to the law of love. The Fool shows us that we need to return to a childlike awareness that has become lost in adulthood. Our journey upon the Tree of Life teaches us that the ego must be minimised so that the conscious point of the soul can rise to the highest levels of awareness occupied by the presence of the Fool.

The Fool resides in the twilight zone between time and space and non-time. He has become aware of the realm of *Ain Soph* and may have had a glimpse of its sublime nature. Although there is a desire to penetrate deeper, the realm of *Ain Soph* is an alien concept for the human perception. Yet within the Kabbalah it is hinted that we should always strive towards *Ain Soph*.

Many years ago, while studying the papers of Michael Bertiaux on astral magnetism, I explored the different frequency levels within a syzergy. The work with syzergies was a way of glimpsing the cultural evolution of man's history, influenced by planetary frequencies. As I came to the highest levels I came across alien intelligence, which at the time I blanked. I felt uncomfortable with their appearance, as they were not within my belief structure. However, the contact with higher extra-terrestrial intelligence is not new within occult exploration. As it happens, Michael Bertiaux also admitted contact with an alien being first contacted by Aleister Crowley, named Lam. Aleister Crowley first contacted Lam in 1918, during a series of magical workings called the Amalantrah Working, which apparently created a magical portal or rent in the fabric of Time and Space. Lam is a Tibetan word for Way or Path, and Bertiaux believed that Lam was part of human evolution.

I had pretty much blanked my first encounter with extra-terrestrial intelligence (which was experienced within the higher astral realms), but many years later I had another encounter which came about while meditating within a circle of standing stones. In meditation, I managed to evoke a cone of energy around the stones. As I projected the energy into a large dolmen outside the circle, I was instantly projected up into a spaceship where I encountered a being who was thin, tall, and very human-like, and wearing a silver, tight-fitting suit, among others of his kind. I was so shocked (because they knew I was there and were even expecting my presence), that I jumped back into my body. My further attempts to create a similar cone of power within the circle met without success. This seems to suggest that it was the influence of the extra-terrestrial beings which worked the energy of the cone that day and which brought me to them. From that time on, as it was such a strong experience, I began to look into the UFO phenomenon.

In 1955, a small book was published called *The Secret of the Saucers* by Orfeo M. Angelucci, in which Orfeo gave detailed descriptions of his encounters with extra-terrestrial entities. He was not an occultist, but leaned more towards science. His descriptions included conversations in which it was explained to him that the extra-terrestrial beings (or more accurately, extra-dimensional beings) are from a dimension beyond Time: "Approaching the speed of light the time dimension as known on Earth becomes non-existent."[1] They went on to say that we three-dimensional beings can have no concept of extra-dimensional beings. They see us as we really are, not as we perceive ourselves. They hold records of every human being on this earth, and they consider us brothers, giving an indication of our connection within *Ain Soph*. They consider the speed of light to be the speed of truth. At one point Angelucci described how he was projected into an alien body and that it felt amazingly light and ethereal, vibrant with life. Orfeo was told that flying saucers are powered and controlled by tapping into universal magnetic forces, again hinting at an awareness of *Ain Soph*.

In the book *Ami, Child of the Stars* by Enrique Barrios, Ami tells the author, "... our spaceships have been flying around here (the Earth) for eons, but it was only after the first atomic bomb that we allowed you to see us." Ami explained further: "...we want you people to understand that atomic energy is something very delicate, something that could even affect other nearby worlds."[2]

Thus we can consider Ain Soph to have a voice with the phenomenon that we call extra-terrestrial (or extra-dimensional) intelligence, which seems to suggest that their natural conscious domain lies within *Ain Soph*, and that they are trying to wake us up to the importance of attempting a shift in consciousness within humanity. Gerard Aartsen on the front cover of his book *Here to help: UFOs and the Space Brothers* encapsulated their message to humanity and our planet:

"Message from space: Life is One, so live as one... or perish." [3]

1   Orfeo Angelucci: *The Secret of the Saucers.* (Forgotten Books, 2008), 21.
2   Enrique Barrios: *Ami: "Child of the Stars."* (1986)
3   Aartsen, Gerard. *Here to Help: UFOs and the Space Brothers, 2nd ed.* Amsterdam, Netherlands: BGA Publications, 2012.

Raising the Great Dragon

The deeper mysteries taught their initiates that the Universal Life Force was symbolized as a dragon. Energy moves in a similar way to the movement of a serpent, and within *Ain Soph* this holy serpent can be seen weaving through the crystalline structure as a living pulse generating a magnetic field from which the Four Worlds begin to form. The dragon has two aspects to itself: it is the will or desire to evolve through the experience of duality, and yet also to remain as one, creating a tension or frequency of a magnetic quality that brings about the crystallization of light into the Four Worlds of the Kabbalah. The dragon's body is the manifested universe, and the in-dwelling light/life is the Christos.

The Great Dragon is bound by the soul's desire to experience, and this desire is akin to the sexual energy. As we focus outwardly upon the objects of our desire, it has the effect of fragmenting our consciousness into separate archetypes: this fragmentation creates the concepts of good and evil, and from the perspective of one within duality we seek to understand the creative laws that govern our reality within time and space.

The balancing of archetypes frees the serpent so that it may rise. The rising of the kundalini is closely linked to magical work and is associated with rising the consciousness of an individual, bringing about greater awareness of love throughout creation. The action of kundalini or serpent power raises awareness through the focus of the Third Eye and the opening of the Heart Chakra (which is the seat of the soul and where love is experienced at its most profound). Once the Heart Chakra is fully opened, the soul of the individual connects to the Soul of the Earth, which in turn takes us into an inner universe. This inner universe is held together by the Great Dragon; in other words, the inner universe within us is underpinned by Love which has become conscious of itself. The Great Dragon is connected to the oneness experienced during orgasm. It is the Contradiction of Unity described by Crowley. This oneness is experienced within, and, as a result, we reflect Love out into our physical universe. The identification and understanding of a unifying principle that is expressed as love has the long-term effect of creating communities and building for the common good of all, as consciousness is not individualized, but is experienced as a whole within all created beings.

About 30 years ago, I was meditating on the 19th Key of the Sun. My guide took me deep into the Peruvian Andes and into the Monastry of the Seven Rays, which holds the golden Disk of Mu, which once hung in the Sun Temple of Cusco and was moved when the Conquistadors arrived. The monastery is said to be suspended in the fourth dimension until humanity awakens, upon which it will reveal humanity's true history. The enormous disk is made of a transparent gold not of this world. It is said that it can be used to teleport and cause environmental changes when played in a certain key. The priest in charge asked me to put my hands on the disk. They instantly became locked to the disk as if energy began to attune me to itself. As I looked up at its beautifully decorated surface, an image appeared which showed all the rivers of our beautiful planet spewing out black, polluted water into the sea. That was 30 years ago. Today, here in Wales, whales are being beached with mercury poisoning. This is a direct reflection of our level of consciousness as a species, and there are many who desire for humanity to remain at this level of consciousness as slaves to the will of those who crave power and wealth.

The rising of consciousness occurs both at an individual level, and on the broader level of humanity. The raising of the Great Dragon is not so much an event in time and space but rather a gradual awakening in consciousness as a universal principle of life. To raise the Great Dragon is the essential work of all creative, magical peoples around our beautiful planet – to expand consciousness beyond the boundary of the intellectual arrogance which blinds to the deterioration of our natural world for profit and self-adulation, and to raise the consciousness of humanity to the point of becoming one with the underlining principle of Love throughout the universe, ultimately shifting our perception into the realm of *Ain Soph*.

The Orphic Egg, by Harry Wendrich

GLOSSARY

Amazonian Women
A legendary race of female warriors chosen to represent the Princess force of the Tarot.

Anima Mundi
The Soul of the Earth herself.

Archetypes
Living energies interlocked within nature: magnetic frequencies which interact with our personal universes. Archetypes which are weak within us attract life situations which enable interaction with their specific frequencies for the purpose of becoming strengthened and balanced.

Azoth
The Azoth (Essence) is related to the concept of Ain Soph being deeply rooted within matter and generating its existence within the manifested universe. The Azoth invokes the drive which pulls us towards perfection through the transformation of consciousness. The word is formed from the first and last letters of the Latin, Greek, and Hebrew alphabets (A-Z, A-O, A-TH).

Book T
A Golden Dawn document consisting of "A Description of the Cards of the Tarot with their Attributions; Including a Method of Divination by Their Use." Provides detailed descriptions of the Minor Arcana including the Court Cards.

Conscious Point
The focus of the soul.

Cosmic Egg (Orphic Egg)
Traditionally seen in creation myths, experienced in the second birth into spirit. It can also be associated with the alchemical Philosopher's Stone, in which lead is transformed into gold.

Disk of Mu
A mythical golden disk that once hung in the Sun Temple of Cusco in Peru, now in the Monastery of the Brotherhood of Seven Rays.

Elemental Serpents
Forces used in the devic realm for the maintenance of the elements, found beneath the thrones of the Elemental Rulers. Once the elemental serpents are risen, a higher frequency is obtained within the corresponding element.

Enochian Aethers
The Enochian Aethers are comprised of 30 realms inhabited by angelic and demonic entities, ultimately held together by the Great Dragon.

Great Dragon
A universal, all-encompassing Mind/Superconsciousness.

Great Work (Magnum Opus)
The discovery of one's true potential/devotion to Self-realization.

Kundalini Fire (serpent fire, serpent power)
One of the first stages of spiritual awakening, often perceived as a fire rising within the body, usually in stages in accordance with the balancing of archetypes. The rising kundalini fire is a purifying experience which creates a path for the Kundalini ("Coiled Serpent") and other serpents to rise.

Minutum Mundum
The Tree of Life diagram in its usual depiction with the first 10 Paths (the 10 Sephiroth) in their Queen Scale colours, and the latter 22 Paths in the King Scale colours: together they represent the forces of the Paths in the masculine, active King Scale of Atziluth uniting the Sephiroth in the feminine, passive Queen Scale of Briah. (See inner rear cover.)

Qlippoth ("Shells")
An aspect of creation that is opposed to evolution and even its own existence.

Saturn Return
The completion of Saturn's orbit of the Sun, returning to any specified zodiacal degree every 30 years. Its influence upon an individual is to align one's life path to one's True Will, and is often associated with the conscious commencement of one's spiritual path.

Serpent Force
The rising of serpents which, before being risen, have held the conscious point of an individual in an area of illusion.

Sheela-na-Gig

Celtic in origin, Sheela-na-Gig is believed to have been an image connected to the legend of Niall, son of the High King of Ireland, Eochaid. The story revolves around Niall and his four brothers looking for water on a hunting trip. The brothers find a well, but it is guarded by a hideous old hag. She demands a kiss from the brothers before water can be drawn from the well. Only Niall kisses her with passion, upon which she is transformed into a beautiful woman. She grants Niall water from the well and kingship over the land for many generations.

Tetragrammaton

The Hebrew name of God transliterated in four letters as *YHVH – Yod, Heh, Vav, Heh*
(יהוה)

Third Eye

Positioned on the forehead between the eyes, when activated produces the ability to see into the spiritual realms, guided by spiritual entities. When fully opened, it is perceived as an intense and beautiful flower.

Veil of Paroketh

A division on the Tree of Life which separates the Sephiroth of Tiphareth and above from those below. The ego has difficulty penetrating this division, allowing the soul to assert its True Will.

Vault of the Adepti.

A seven-sided chamber, with ceiling, floor, walls, and all furniture specially inscribed with symbols of the Western Mysteries, used during the initiation ceremony into the Inner Order of the Hermetic Order of the Golden Dawn.

WatchTowers

Governors of environmental and elemental balance; their work is to maintain a stable environment for life to succeed on Planet Earth, but they are not concerned with humanity as such.

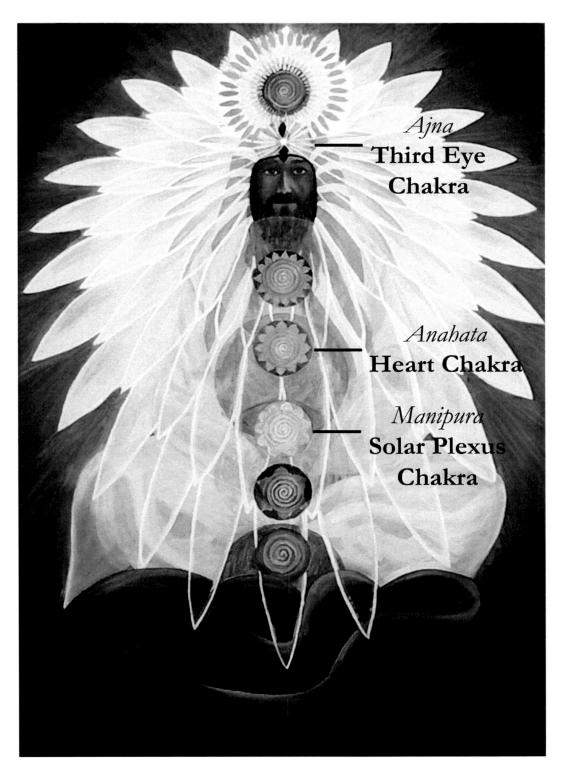

Ajna
**Third Eye
Chakra**

Anahata
Heart Chakra

Manipura
**Solar Plexus
Chakra**

APPENDIX I

The Shem ha-Mephorash

The Shem ha-Mephorash is known as the 72-fold Divine Name of Extension. The Names of the Angels of the Shem ha-Mephoresh are derived from three verses in the book of Exodus (Chapter 14, verses 19, 20, and 21). In Hebrew, these verses contain 72 letters each.

> 19 And the Angel of God, which went before the camp of Israel, removed and went behind them; and the pillar of the cloud went from before their face and stood behind them:
>
> 20 And it came between the camp of the Egyptians and the camp of Israel; and it was a cloud and darkness to them, but it gave light by night to these: so that the one came not near the other all the night.
>
> 21 And Moses stretched out his hand over the sea; and the LORD caused the sea to go back by a strong east wind all that night, and made the sea dry land, and the waters were divided.

These three verses demonstrate the divine presence, guidance, and protection in the figure of the Angel of God, and three forms of separation:

(i) the simultaneous expression of both light and darkness, forming

(ii) the separation between Israel and her enemies, and

(iii) the separation of the waters of the sea, allowing for safe passage and deliverance.

In the Universe Key of the *Golden Dawn Temple Tarot*, the circuit of Celtic Knotwork reveals the separation between the physical realm of Time and Space and the astral angelic realms beyond. On the journey from our conscious awareness into an awareness of the greater subconscious, the Shem ha-Mephorash carries the light of divine presence, guidance, and protection.

When these three verses are written one on top of each other in the original Hebraic language (the first verse from right to left, the second from left to right and the third from right to left) and then read from top to bottom, 72 three-lettered Names are formed: these further generate 72 angelic names by adding either *Yod Heh* (*YAH*), or *Aleph Lamed* (*EL*) to the end of each, as can be seen in the following table:[1]

---

1   Material derived from table in Agrippa, Henry, Cornelius, trans. James Freake, ed. Donald Tyson. *Three Books of Occult Philosophy: The Foundation Book of Western Occultism.* (Woodbury, MN: Llewellyn Publications, 2009), 540.

THE 72 ANGELS OF THE SHEM HA-MEPHORASH

18	17	16	15	14	13	12	11	10	9	8	7	6	5	4	3	2	1	
כ	ל	ה	ה	ם	י	ה	ל	א	ה	כ	א	ל	ם	ע	ס	י	ו	v. 19
ל	א	ק	ר	ב	ו	ה	א	ל	ו	ה	כ	ל	ה	ל	י	ל	ה	v. 20
י	ו	ם	י	ה	ל	ע	ו	ד	י	ת	א	ה	ש	ם	ט	י	ו	v. 21

1. Vehuiah 2. Ieliel 3. Sitael 4. Elemiah 5. Mehasiah 6. Lelahel
7. Akaiah 8. Cahethel 9. Haziel 10. Aladiah 11. Lauiah 12. Hahaiah
13. Ieiazel 14. Mebahel 15. Hariel 16. Hakamiah 17. Leviah 18. Caliel

36	35	34	33	32	31	30	29	28	27	26	25	24	23	22	21	20	19	
ם	כ	ל	י	ו	ל	א	ר	ש	ע	ה	נ	ה	ם	י	נ	פ	ל	v. 19
נ	ו	ה	ח	ש	כ	ו	י	א	ר	א	ת	ה	ל	י	ל	ה	ו	v. 20
ר	ק	ח	ו	ר	ב	ם	י	ה	ת	א	ה	ו	ה	י	כ	ל	ו	v. 21

19. Leuuiah 20. Pahaliah 21. Nelkael 22. Ieaiel 23. Melahel 24. Chahuiah
25. Nithhaiah 26. Haaiah 27. Ierathel 28. Seehiah 29. Reiiel 30. Omael
31. Lecabel 32. Vasariah 33. Iechuiah 34. Lehachiah 35. Kavakiah 36. Monadel

54	53	52	51	50	49	48	47	46	45	44	43	42	41	40	39	38	37	
נ	נ	ע	ה	ד	ו	ם	ע	ע	ם	י	ו	ם	ה	י	ר	ח	א	v. 19
י	נ	ם	ה	ב	ה	י	ש	ר	א	ל	ו	י	ה	י	ה	ע	נ	v. 20
ת	א	ם	ש	ה	ו	ה	ל	י	ל	ה	ל	כ	ה	ו	ע	ם	י	v. 21

37. Aniel 38. Chaamiah 39. Rehael 40. Ihiazel 41. Hahahel 42. Mikael
43. Veveliah 44. Ielahiah 45. Sealiah 46. Ariel 47. Asaliah 48. Mihael
49. Vehuel 50. Daniel 51. Hachasiah 52. Imamaih 53. Nanael 54. Nithael

72	71	70	69	68	67	66	65	64	63	62	61	60	59	58	57	56	55	
ם	ה	י	ר	ה	א	ם	ר	א	ם	ע	י	ו	ם	ה	י	נ	פ	v. 19
ו	י	ב	א	ב	י	נ	ם	ל	ח	נ	ה	ם	צ	ר	י	ם	ו	v. 20
ם	י	ם	ה	ו	ע	ק	ב	ר	ד	י	ו	ה	כ	ר	ח	ל	ם	v. 21

55. Mebahiah 56. Poiel 57. Nemamiah 58. Ieialel 59. Harachel 60. Mizrael
61. Umabel 62. Iahhel 63. Annauel 64. Mecheiel 65. Damabiah 66. Menkiel
67. Eiael 68. Chabuiah 69. Raehel 70. Iibamiah 71. Haiaiel 72. Mumiah

Zodiacal Correspondences

The Golden Dawn applies zodiacal correspondences to each of the Angels of the Shem ha-Mephorash through aligning the sequence of 72 Angelic Names to the Wheel of the Zodiac. The 12 Zodiacal signs are divided into 3 Decans (consisting of 10 degrees) each, making 36 Decans. Over each quinance (half of a decan: five degrees), an Angel of the Shem ha-Mephoresh rules, thus for each Decan are two associated Angels. The Golden Dawn commences the Zodiac from its brightest star, Regulus, in the constellation of Leo, and the sequence of Angelic Names begins at 0 degrees Leo then follows the wheel through the signs until the last of the 72 Angels are allocated to the decans of Cancer.

The 36 Decans are assigned to the 36 cards of the Minor Arcana (the 2's to the 10's of each suit), thus are there two Angels associated with each card of the Minor Arcana (from the 2's to the 10's), again beginning from 0 degrees Leo, which equates to Five of Wands, and completing the 360 degree circuit at 30 degrees Cancer, equating to Four of Cups.

The Decans are attributed with Planetary Rulers,[2] the allocation of which follows the order of the corresponding planetary placement upon the Tree of Life glyph, from Binah to Yesod. The outer rim of planetary symbols in the diagram opposite illustrates this. Beginning at 0 degrees Leo (5 of Wands), Saturn (Binah) is followed by Jupiter (Chesed), Mars (Geburah), The Sun (Tiphareth), Venus (Netzach), Mercury (Hod), and the Moon (Yesod). This sequence of the Seven Planets also follows the Chaldean method of delineating the planets in descending order of their orbital speed. However, each of the seven planets fits only five times around the Zodiacal Wheel, accounting for only 350 degrees. The Golden Dawn allocated Mars the extra division of ten degrees, the explanation being that Mars brings the necessary fiery boost for the passage of Winter into Spring at the Vernal Equinox. Thus Mars both ends and begins the solar year, ruling over the consecutive decans of 20-30 degrees Pisces and 0-10 degrees Aries, completing the Planetary Rulership of the Decans.

Meanings of the Angelic Names

The Golden Dawn taught that the meanings of the Angelic Names are, with the exception of the 70th Name, derived from verses of the Psalms in which the Divine Name *YHVH* appears, although Mathers postulated that the first 72 Psalms (collectively known as The Psalms of David) are the related verses. Within our own study we intuitively selected occasional Biblical verses which related to our experience of the field of consciousness within a Sephira, hence in this book some of the cards of the Minor Arcana are accompanied by Scriptures chosen from our personal perspective.

The Golden Dawn also teaches that the suffix of *Yod Heh* (Yah) in the formation of an Angelic name signifies mercy and benevolence, while the suffix *Aleph Lamed* (*El* – strength, might, power) signifies severity and judgement. In our experience in writing upon the

---

2 Each circle of the knotwork in the Universe Key represents an angel and five degrees of a Zodiacal sign, coloured according to the positive aspects (King Scale) and negative aspects (Queen Scale) of the Planetary Rulers of the Decans.

journey of consciousness through the Sephiroth up the Tree we found that of the cards which proved to be challenging in some way (the Fives, some of the Sevens, several of the suit of Swords), the Angels would actually serve as great forces of encouragement and fortitude, often pointing to a brighter future or sense of reward that lay just beyond the realm of the card in question. In the cards which held a more comfortable experience, the Angels seemed to join with the soul in ecstatic expressions of joy and praise. So whilst severity may have been part of the experience of a Sephira, the Angels themselves were a source of succour and stability – indeed, they offered divine presence, guidance, protection, and deliverance.

It is worth noting that within both the painting of the deck and the writing of this book, we worked with the Angelic correspondences as applied by the Golden Dawn,[3] beginning the Shem ha-Mephorash sequence from 5 of Wands and ending on 4 of Cups. However, upon the completion of the written journey through the Minor Arcana, additional material in the form of an essay by Aaron J. Leitch came to our notice, shedding new light upon our understanding of the Shem ha-Mephorash.[4] I then dreamed that it was important that we should in this study also examine the Shem ha-Mephorash in its rectangular, tabular form as presented in Leitch's essay, which is reproduced from Agrippa[5], and follows the instructions within The Key of Solomon the King.[6]

"The Schema is one, its columns are two, its power is three, its form is four, its reflection giveth eight, which multiplied by three giveth unto thee the twenty-four Thrones of Wisdom. Upon each Throne reposeth a Crown with three Rays, each Ray beareth a Name, each Name is an Absolute Idea. There are Seventy-two Names upon the Twenty-four Crowns of the Schema.

Thou shalt write these Names upon Thirty-six Talismans, two upon each Talisman, one on each side. Thou shalt divide these Talismans into four series of nine each, according to the number of the Letters of the Schema.

Upon the first Series thou shalt engrave the Letter Yod, symbolised by the Flowering Rod of Aaron. Upon the second the Letter Hé, symbolised by the Cup of Joseph. Upon the third the Letter Vau, symbolised by the Sword of David my father. And upon the fourth the Hé final, symbolised by the Shekel of Gold.

These Thirty-six Talismans will be a Book which will contain all the Secrets of Nature. And by their diverse combinations thou shalt make the Genii and Angels speak."

---

3   With particular reference to *The Magical Tarot of the Golden Dawn* by Pat and Chris Zalewski
4   Aaron J. Leitch, *Shem ha-Mephoresh, The Divine Name of Extension*:
      http://www.hermeticgoldendawn.org/leitch-shemhamephoresh.html
5   Agrippa, Henry, Cornelius, trans. James Freake, ed. Donald Tyson. *Three Books of Occult Philosophy: The Foundation Book of Western Occultism.* (Woodbury, MN: Llewellyn Publications, 2009), 540.
6   S.Liddell MacGregor Mathers, trans., *The Key of Solomon the King* (Escondido, CA: The Book Tree, 1999), 128.

FOUR SERIES OF NINE NAMED TALISMANS (Solomonic arrangement)
WITH GD ASTROLOGICAL ATTRIBUTIONS

The 36 Talismans equate to the 36 pip cards of the Minor Arcana, discounting the Aces. The "four series of nine" named Talismans correspond to the 2's – 10's of Wands, Cups, Swords, and Pentacles of the Tarot. Solomon described how each group corresponds to one of the letters of the Divine Name *YHVH*, and is associated with a potent symbol corresponding with our modern elemental tools. Thus each pair of Names corresponds with a card of the Minor Arcana (from the 2's to the 10's) to which they are assigned as Wand (Rod), Cup, Sword, and Pentacle (Shekel).

The crucial difference between this arrangement and the circular, Zodiacal arrangement of the Golden Dawn is that the Angelic Names follow the Yetziratic sequence of the Path of Emanation, from Chokmah in Atziluth (Two of Wands), to Malkuth of Assiah (Ten of Pentacles). When the translations of the Angelic Names are considered, it is fitting that (Heyaiel) Lord of the Universe and (Mavamiah) End of the Universe should complete the sequence of 72 Names in the final card of the Minor Arcana, Ten of Pentacles.[7] It is also worth noting that in applying this sequence of Names to the Zodiacal Wheel, the sequence presents a pattern which orders the 12 constellations according to element, beginning with their Cardinal Signs, i.e., Aries, Leo, Sagittarius (FIRE), Cancer, Scorpio, Pisces (WATER), Libra, Aquarius, Gemini (AIR), Capricorn, Taurus, Virgo (EARTH).

It is clear that there are many layers of complexity to the Kabbalistic system, and there is not one absolute method either in its presentation or interpretation. What is of import when working within a chosen system is one's own intention.[8]

For My thoughts are not your thoughts, nor are your ways My ways, says the LORD.
For as the heavens are higher than the earth, so are My ways higher than your ways
and My thoughts than your thoughts.

Isaiah 55:8-9 (NKJ Bible)

---

7   The Angelic Names within the *Golden Dawn Temple Tarot* follow the Golden Dawn sequence beginning at 0° Leo. Their meanings are listed within the Minor Arcana texts, and were sourced from *The Magical Tarot of the Golden Dawn* by Pat and Chris Zalewski.

8   The song *Celestial Spheres* by Wendrich artHouse intones the 72 Angelic Names and their meanings in an alternative order: the 2's of each element, followed by the 3's, and so on until the 10's. Free download and video available from http://www.wendricharthouse.com/study/music/

APPENDIX II

Joint Meditations:
Meeting the Archetypes of the Major Arcana

The following recorded meditations have been included for the sake of those readers who may be interested in performing similar meditations to more fully understand the nature of these complex and ever-changing archetypes as they help to shape our lives. Information gleaned in this way can help to balance the archetypal forces on the Inner Planes, thereby bypassing the magnetizing of seemingly negative circumstances into our physical realm which would otherwise have been necessary to ensure that balance is achieved in our lives.

THE HERMIT
(by Harry Wendrich)

Many years ago, I first started meditating on the Tarot archetypes using a simple method of visualizing the cards before me with as much detail as possible: visualizing the Hebrew letter above and the name of the card clearly below, then bringing the image forward until the card became a doorway into a landscape of which the particular archetype could be met.

Meeting the archetypes individually can sometimes be dangerous: if their frequency is unstable it can flare up and endanger the enquirer, so for this type of interaction it is wise to seek the assistance of one's personal inner guide. But this doorway method is generally considered to be a safe way to engage with the Tarot archetypes, as the landscape is part of the archetypal energy and the archetypal frequency being met is diffused throughout the landscape.

I was systematically working my way through the deck, one card a week. I had been looking forward to meeting with the Hermit, as I identified with his archetypal concept. When the time came to meet with him, I was so excited that I jumped straight through the card without looking at the landscape before me. I landed in the middle of a main road and was hit by a car travelling at high speed. My astral body was thrown into the air in two parts. As I recovered from the shock and the two halves of me were re-magnetized together, I saw the Hermit standing on the pavement next to the road. Furiously, I asked why he had let that happen to me. He replied:

"Look before you jump..."

– advice that I have never forgotten when entering the Inner Planes.

JOINT ARCHETYPAL MEDITATIONS

Three years before our painting of the *Golden Dawn Temple Tarot* began, Harry and I embarked upon a series of joint meditations, calling upon our inner guides to facilitate meetings with the archetypes of the Major Arcana. The archetypes would be met not as their individual frequency within each of us, but with the frequency that they hold within us as a married couple. This sequence of meditations took five years in all, the last two of which overlapped with the painting of the *Golden Dawn Temple Tarot* deck. Much of that which was communicated was personal, shedding light upon our past lives and future work. Many of the insights gleaned are shared here, to demonstrate the kind of information which can be imparted through such meditations.

Upon entering our Inner Temple in meditation, our guides would be met and permission would be sought to meet with an archetype of the Major Arcana, during which meeting we would ask questions relating to how we could balance the energy of that particular archetype. Their appearance was related to how the archetype existed within us at that time. We could ask any questions on our mind, perhaps related to a recent dream, illness in the body, ideas we may have had, and if the answer was within the archetype's domain, advice would be offered. We could request alternative solutions if we felt it necessary. Questions would at times need to be repeated, or permission given to the archetype to answer if their response seemed vague. Often the archetypes would gift us with something to strengthen an aspect of our being under their region of influence. At the close of each meeting, we would check with our guides if we should ask any more questions, hold hands with our guides and the archetype to allow for a fuller attunement to their energy at work within us, and then give the archetype permission to return from whence they came in the name of Yeshua.

THE FOOL: JOINT ARCHETYPAL MEDITATION

The Fool appeared as a young man holding a tandem bicycle.

His advice was to do yoga and to eat clean foods. He said that he could tell us to drink only water, but we wouldn't do it.

He gave us the tandem and placed it between our legs. It would help us as we work together to rise the kundalini energy.

The Fool asked Harry three times if he loves Jesus, and Harry said yes.
The Fool said that we need a greater awareness of Jesus, and that the Fool can help by aligning us with his (the Fool's) energy.

THE MAGICIAN: JOINT ARCHETYPAL MEDITATION
The Magician appeared as a businessman, with short hair, wearing a black suit, collar and tie, and carrying a briefcase.

Harry: How can we balance your energy?
The Magician: I am already very close to you.
Harry: How do we experience your energy?
The Magician: I am with your analytical mind, aligning it with God's will. You just need to keep on as you are.
Nicola: Do you have anything to give us?

He gave us a silver sphere and placed it on the left-hand side of our brain.

Harry: What is the silver sphere for?
The Magician: It is for a holistic understanding. You do not need to use it – it works for you.

In his briefcase is a clear plastic triangle in two pieces, and some papers. Harry is asked to eat the papers. They will help in his Golden Dawn studies, helping to assimilate and recall the knowledge when necessary.

The Magician: The triangle represents a pyramid, the top of which is God. You are in the pyramid, which is without a top because you have not yet formed the top, neither can you or have you visualized it. The studies form the base, where you are. You need to study because there is certain knowledge of the way things are which will help you to build the pyramid.
　　Jesus is the top, and He will help you to get to the top, but you must make the effort to get near it. Harry, you need to also study the Torah under the guidance of your former tutor. It is very important – it will help to balance everything.

THE HIGH PRIESTESS: JOINT ARCHETYPAL MEDITATION
The High Priestess appeared as a lady with long black hair and a flowing translucent negligée. She held a sceptre with symbols of the phases of the Moon on the top.

Harry: What can we do to balance your energy within us?
High Priestess: Become more aware of the Moon and her phases. Not just intellectually, but with an awareness that really feels the phase of the Moon. It is an awareness that much of humanity has moved away from, but it is very connected to the Earth and her cycles.

She gave us the sceptre and placed it in our awareness.

Harry: How long will it take?

High Priestess: If you put your effort into it, one full yearly cycle will bring you into the awareness I speak of. I am already working with you.

THE EMPRESS: JOINT ARCHETYPAL MEDITATION

The first time that we met with The Empress, she gave Harry a sceptre with a white orb on the top, and told us to concentrate upon the orb when making love.

The Empress: Doing so will drive your energies towards God. Physical sensations can make it difficult, but persist, even if you don't fully understand.

She asked us to meet with her again, so we returned two months later.

Harry: What can we do to balance your energy?

The Empress: You are already doing what you need to do for me. It is important to focus on the sceptre during lovemaking. Doing so will help the conception of a new life.

Nicola: Is this a good time for me to conceive?

The Empress: It would be unwise at present to allow for pregnancy. You have a lot of work to do.

(We deduced from this that the conception of new life of which The Empress spoke was not connected to physical conception.)
We met with the Empress a third time, having been instructed to do so by our guides. The Empress appeared wearing a beautiful sparkly dress and a crown of stars.

She held something – it is a gift which is for Nicola, but she places it in Harry's mouth and he passes it to Nicola through kisses. It looks like stardust.

Nicola: What is this gift for?

The Empress: It will help to strengthen you to bear the energies which will be passing through you. The kundalini energy is beginning to awaken, and you will notice effects in your bodies – some temporary, some permanent.

Nicola: Is the kundalini energy the cause of my nausea?

The Empress: Your nausea is not to do with energies. It is a food imbalance. You should eat less dairy and more salad. I have more to tell you but it is not relevant yet. You are doing well, but there is still much work ahead.

THE EMPEROR: JOINT ARCHETYPAL MEDITATION

Harry: How does your energy manifest in our lives?

The Emperor: My energy helps to organize and bring order to your lives.

Harry: What can we do to balance your energy?

The Emperor: Drink more milk in order to allow my energy to flow easier.

Nicola: The Empress said that I should consume less dairy.

The Emperor: Drink milk in tea etc.

Harry: Is there anything else we can do?

The Emperor: You should work in the garden. Be faithful and true in word and deed with one another. Think carefully about the things you want to do. There is no reason why you cannot achieve them.

THE HIEROPHANT: JOINT ARCHETYPAL MEDITATION

The Hierophant appeared as an impressive figure wearing a robe and a headpiece.

Harry: What should we do to balance your energy?

The Hierophant: Make love regularly. My energy is connected with the serpent energy and the physical pleasure sensation felt in lovemaking.

Harry: Do you have anything to give us?

The Hierophant: No. You have all you need for the serpent to rise.

THE LOVERS: JOINT ARCHETYPAL MEDITATION

The Lovers archetype appeared as a young boy and a man.
The young boy seemed needy, wanting.

The archetype told us that we were being too restricted in our choices, for example, with music. In being less restricted, we would make choices that would help us to see ourselves more clearly.

THE CHARIOT: JOINT ARCHETYPAL MEDITATION

The Chariot appeared as a young teenage boy wearing clothes like a jester, with shoes that pointed upwards, one black and one white. He was playing the tin whistle.

Harry: What do we need to do to align your energy within us?

The Chariot: Walk with me. You are two parts of one body, like twin souls. Harry is like one foot and Nicola the other. One is in front, the other behind. They are not in the same place, but on the same path, and of the same body. Above you is the greater body of Jesus of which many are a part. You have a job to do in your body. I can help to balance energies in preparation for your work.

Harry: Why were you playing the tin whistle?
The Chariot: It helps you to walk with me and to become aware of the one body.
Nicola: Are our sons part of our body?
The Chariot: You carry them for now, but they will one day find the other parts of the bodies to which they belong.

He plays the whistle again and says it will help in balancing our energies.

As the meeting comes to its close, Nicola's guide points back to the Chariot archetype who is now half male and half female – a boy playing a flute and a woman with long, black hair and a green dress. The guide says that every person has the duality of male and female.

STRENGTH: JOINT ARCHETYPAL MEDITATION

When we met with the archetype of Strength in a joint meditation, it was our intention to ask the same questions that we put to each archetype. However, that which was communicated by the Strength archetype had a somewhat cryptic form of its own.

Strength appears sitting on a white horse. She is a beautiful, naked woman with hair that reaches to the ground as she sits on the steed. She has total control over the horse: he obeys her. As she approaches, there is a shaft of energy around us all. There is a power coming from her.

Harry: What can we do to balance your energy?
Strength: There is no balance or imbalance. Strength is strength.

My steed is my strength, but you will not find strength in my steed.
My hair is my strength, but you will not find strength in my hair.
My hips and breasts are my strength, but you will not find strength in them.

You are mine to play with.

To Harry, she says, "I love you."
To Nicola, she says, "I love you too."

Strength: I will give you strength.

260

Strength gives Harry a hammer.

Strength: Your strength is your strength but you will not find strength in your strength.

She gives Nicola a pearl hair clip.

Strength: Your beauty is your strength, but you will not find strength in your beauty.

Nicola: Are you able to help to banish the depression from which I suffer ?

Strength: Depression comes from darkness. Strength is of the light. But in darkness, there is light to be found. Remember me, and my steed, in times of weakness. But you will not find me if you look for me. I will just come to help you in your weakness.

         *   *   *   *   *

Our gleanings from this communication:

Physical strength, beauty, and fertility are among the manifestations of strength, but the essence of strength may not be found in such qualities. Strength is a gift, and we are at the mercy of the giver. The giver of this gift is of the light and loves us. Strength will appear when needed.

THE HERMIT: JOINT ARCHETYPAL MEDITATION
The Hermit appeared wearing a hooded cloak, carrying a lamp in one hand
and a stick in the other.

The Hermit: Why have you called me?

Harry: What do we need to do to balance your energy within us?

The Hermit: You already follow my light. My energy does not need balancing because you follow.

Nicola: Do you have anything to give us to help us to work better with your energy?

The Hermit gives us two flutes, but they are not placed on our body. They are symbolic.

The Hermit: The two of you are like two flutes being divinely blown. You are in harmony.

Harry: Do you have any more advice for us?

The Hermit: Follow my light.

THE WHEEL OF FORTUNE: JOINT ARCHETYPAL MEDITATION
The Wheel of Fortune appeared as an Irish leprechaun figure.

Harry: What can we do to balance your energy?

The Wheel of Fortune: Drink at least one glass of milk per day because of the energies at work in you.

He gives Nicola a crystal ball and places it in her chest.

Nicola: What is it for?

The Wheel of Fortune: It will illuminate areas and talents that were hidden in the earth element. When you look for them you will see them. It will benefit Harry as it happens in you.

Harry: In what way does your energy manifest in our lives?

The Wheel of Fortune: My job is to bring you prosperity. You have more coming to you than you imagine.

Harry: Is your energy a marriage of both our Wheel of Fortune energies?

The Wheel of Fortune: No, I am over you both, even over the whole family as a group energy.

JUSTICE: JOINT ARCHETYPAL MEDITATION
On our first meeting with Justice, the archetype appeared as a woman wearing a green dress, carrying scales. (She represented the balancing aspect of the archetype).

Harry: What do we need to do to balance your energy?

Justice: In Harry it is already in balance, but Nicola has an imbalance of male and female energies. The female aspect is over-emphasized.

Nicola: How can I redress the balance?

Justice: Drive a car.

Nicola: I don't want to drive a car. Can you suggest something else?

Justice: You could write. Perhaps about the changes taking place in Harry and yourself.

Nicola: I document my dreams in writing – does that count?

Justice: It is not enough to document dreams. The writing needs to be from the analytical, conscious mind, not the subconscious.

(As a result of this meditation, I wrote the short autobiographical story of how Harry's and my spiritual journeys led to the setting up of our business, called About Us)

In our second meeting with the Justice archetype, she appeared as a woman with a sword, wearing a green cloak.

Justice:	My job is to help you to use words effectively.
	Words are not for you, they are for those who hear them,
	and they need to come from the heart.

Harry saw a lion walking on a tightrope, and asked Justice about the image.

Justice:	The lion's strength is of no use in walking on this path. Balance is needed.
Nicola:	Is the story *About Us* adequate for its purpose?
Justice:	It will benefit some who read it. You have mastered many things, but not the use of words.

Justice gave us a remote-controlled aeroplane and put it over our mouths. She said that it would help to direct our words to their targets. She also left us her double-edged sword.

THE HANGED MAN: JOINT ARCHETYPAL MEDITATION
The Hanged Man appeared as Jesus on the cross, then reappeared as a young boy, about five years old, so as not to be confused with Jesus.

The Hanged Man:	Listen to the voice of intuition, meditate, and be aware of your feelings. Be active in the realm of the subconscious because that is where things are created, birthed.
	Some things are destined, some are created, some require physical effort. Intuition will show you the difference. For example, you want a van. You should both affirm what you want and discuss the details. On the New Moon, draw it or plan it on paper in some way and then burn it. That will activate its creation in the astral.
	You are joined in the subconscious. The important thing is to affirm.

He gave us a ball of light and placed it in our foreheads, to help us to see the subconscious area.

(Note: Harry and I followed the advice. The van that we hoped for arrived one month before the birth of our fourth son, when our need for a six-seater vehicle became paramount.)

DEATH: JOINT ARCHETYPAL MEDITATION
Death appeared as a beautiful woman with blonde hair and red lipstick. She was dressed in black, from a black mask to basque, suspenders, stockings and high heels. She held a whip.

Death:	Are you surprised to see me in this form?
Harry:	Yes.
Death:	I represent an aspect of life which needs to die in you both.
Harry:	Could you expand?
Death:	You should not place importance on outward appearances – the desire of the eye.
Nicola:	What can we do to balance your energy?
Death:	You do not understand my energy properly.

She gave us a cigarette holder and held the cigarette under our nose, to show that, despite the elegance of the holder, the reality was the smell of the smoke and the deadly consequences.

TEMPERANCE: JOINT ARCHETYPAL MEDITATION

Temperance appeared as a thin, vertical, silver line. The line was vibrating. It transformed into a figure of an Egyptian woman wearing a nemyss, no top, and a short, pleated skirt. She held an ankh in one hand and a cup in the other.

Harry:	How can we balance your energy within us?
Temperance:	It is already in balance.
Harry:	How can we strengthen it?
Temperance:	Stay in love and communicate with each other.
Nicola:	What did the silver line represent?
Temperance:	It represents the connection between you and higher forces, i.e., the Higher Self. It is the line that should not be crossed, the boundaries that you have been given.
Nicola:	How might the connection be broken?
Temperance:	By trespassing.
Harry:	Why the Egyptian guise?
Temperance:	Because in a former lifetime you were together in Egypt.

She places the ankh between us to show our life together.

Temperance:	The cup represents your work. It is similar to work that you had to do in Egypt. The work has carried over; you have to do a similar type of work now.

We are each given of the cup to drink.

Temperance:	The work was given to you in the beginning – it is part of who you are. You have certain information to communicate to others which will act as a trigger, to bring about a new state of consciousness.

THE DEVIL: ARCHETYPAL MEDITATION

The primeval, totemic aspect of the 15th Key was made apparent in the following recorded joint meditation. The Devil jumps into the scene as a black panther. Harry asks it to move back a bit. It represents a huntress.

Harry: How do we balance your energy?

The Devil: It doesn't need balancing – it needs using.

Harry: How do we use it?"

The Devil: Pounce on prey, material and spiritual. Stalk prey; focus in silent concentration, and pounce. The silence is important. Without it, the prey would be long gone.

Nicola: Do you have anything to give us to help us?

The Devil looks directly at Nicola and gives her an ornamental axe with a handle of bone shaped like an animal's leg, a metal head, and feathers and thongs around the join of head and handle.

The Devil: It is to be used for receiving and cutting thoughts received from ancestors.

(One of the titles of this archetype is Child of the Forces of Time).

The ancestors may appear as departed relatives. It is a link to the spirit world, like the True Will, but in a lower form. The axe is a link – you do not need to use it consciously.

Harry: Should we focus on a particular prey?

The Devil: Spiritual. Silence is absolute concentration on prey with every fibre of your being. Without it, you won't get the prey.

THE TOWER: ARCHETYPAL MEDITATION

The Tower appeared as a kitten, playing with a ball of wool.

Harry: Why have you appeared in this form?

Tower: Because I am the image that represents The Tower in both of you at this time.

Harry: In what way does a kitten represent that?

Tower: I am a deadly hunter. As cute as I may appear and as playful as I am, my eyesight is keen, my claws are sharp, and death surrounds me. The archetypal energy of the Tower through you both is not so visible, but it nevertheless resides as a lightning impulse to overcome any problem or break down any blocks.

Harry begins to see a unicorn before the kitten and asks why.

Tower: The Unicorn is very much suited to the Tower. But it is not quite applicable to you both.

Harry: What is the difference between Unicorn energy and that of the kitten?

Tower: Unicorn is more Uriel. Kitten is more Mars.

Nicola: How can we balance or strengthen your energy?

Tower: It is not wise to strengthen it too much. It needs to be a sublime energy, an undercurrent, menacing but not threatening.

Nicola: Do you have anything to give us to remind us of you?

She gives each of us one of her claws.

Tower: Don't forget, I have the power to destroy and to build up. I can help to strengthen your finances.

Nicola: Do you have any advice for us?

Tower: Put a Unicorn in the Tower Tarot painting.

THE STAR: ARCHETYPAL MEDITATION

The Star appeared from above as a naked woman holding something above her head, swirling around. It was a cloak which covered her once she had descended. Only her head could be seen beneath the cloak. She had long, blonde hair. She seemed cold.

Harry: Can you help us to understand how your energy works in us, and how to balance it?

The Star: Be patient.

Harry: What is your energy, and how does it work in us?

The Star: I cannot tell you.

Harry: Why not?

The Star: You are not ready to know. That is why I am veiled.

Nicola: Is there anything we can do to become ready to know?

The Star: With patience comes hope. Hope has a magic.

Harry: I've met you before, unveiled, so why won't you show yourself now?

The Star: Harry, this is a different level.

The Star showed us something in her hand. It was a piece of foil. She closed her hand, around it and it became shaped as a house. She did it again and it was a piece of foil again. She tore it in half and gave half to each of us. It was absorbed into us.

The Star: This will help you to know yourselves. You will move into the new and bigger home that you have dreamed of. I am Hope. Your hope for the house has never faded. Patience is necessary.

Nicola: Is there some way that Harry can depict your influence within the Tarot painting?
The Star: There should be an upwards energy or movement within the card.

(Hence in the Golden Dawn Temple Tarot card, the Venusian Star figure is depicted on tiptoes with her arms stretched upwards.
Five years after this meditation, we were gifted with a larger house – perfect timing for the accommodation of our growing family).

THE MOON: ARCHETYPAL MEDITATION

The Moon appeared as a woman with enormous breasts, abnormally huge. She wore a crown, a mini-skirt and white boots.

Harry: May we ask you some questions?
Moon: Yes. (*Smiling, she sits down).* If you like, I'll take my clothes off.
Harry: No. In what areas of our life may your influence be felt?
Moon: In the home, in the kitchen, as a mother energy, fertility, abundance.

Her breasts now have milk pouring from them.

Harry: Do you have large breasts because it is full moon?
Moon: Yes. I would have a different appearance on a different phase of the Moon.
Harry: Are there any negative tendencies to your energy that we would feel?
Moon: Feeling spiritually lost, and depression.
Harry: How can we counteract these tendencies or turn them into positive energy?
Moon: It comes and goes with the phases of the Moon. Be centred in God to bypass the negativity.
Harry: Why did you say you would take your clothes off?
Moon: They are not comfortable – I do not need them.
Harry: Okay. You may take them off.

Her clothes disappear.

Harry: What do we need to do for your energy to work positively and creatively in our lives?
Moon: You are beginning to understand the relationship between the phases of the Moon and my energy. Spend more time beneath the sky at night.
Nicola: Can you help Harry as he paints the Moon Tarot painting?
Moon: Yes.

Nicola: Is there anything in particular that should be in it?

Moon: The feminine influence, even a woman.

She gives us something like a diamond. It is a star. She places it between the two of us. It is shining, and has solid rays.

Harry: What is it?

Moon: It is the two of you as one.

Harry: Why did you give us that?

Moon: Because that is your centre, now visible outside of yourselves and between you both. You can concentrate upon it to beat depression.

Nicola: Can you help us to understand the phases of the Moon and your energy better?

Moon: It is not to do with focussing on the phases, more feeling and going with the feeling. The Moon is very changeable, never the same, therefore the feeling is always different. Attunement to your feelings is important to remain in the flow or current of life.

Nicola: Is it like intuition?

Moon: It is more than intuition. It is already in you. The feeling needs to be allowed to make itself known.

THE SUN: ARCHETYPAL MEDITATION

The Sun appeared as a six-year-old boy, with a green suit and a Robin Hood style hat. He wears a medallion of the sun, and has a walking stick with a crystal on the top.

Harry: Are we attuned to your energy?

The Sun: Yes.

Harry: What is your influence in our lives?

The Sun: Play, energy, and love.

Nicola: How can the healing energy be strengthened?

The Sun removes the medallion and puts it around Nicola's neck. Harry wants one too, so the Sun gives one to Harry!

Nicola: How can we feel your energy in the home?

The Sun: In the love you show your children and one another, in creative work, and by going for walks in nature.

JUDGEMENT: ARCHETYPAL MEDITATION

Judgement appeared as a princess, wearing a long, pointed hat and veil, and a flowing dress. She had long, blonde hair and was very beautiful.

Harry: Why have you appeared in this form?

Judgement: My natural state would consume you. You see me as I am within both of you, as a feminine form. I am the feminine intuition and the form of the serpent fire that rises up the spine.

Harry: What are the effects of it rising?

Judgement: The flames are what you would call Holy Spirit. When they flare, it is like a deeper insight into God – rapture. *Kundalini* is the Eastern term, but in the West *kundalini* is not understood in religious terms.

Nicola: Can we help your energy to rise more quickly?

Judgement: Yes, but there are too many levels to be consciously aware of. It will rise when you are ready, and no sooner.

Harry: Is there anything you can give us to bring us into a deeper awareness of these levels?

Judgement gives us the Ace of Wands painting of the Golden Dawn Temple Tarot Deck. She says that it is a symbol of Fire on all levels.

Harry: How does the Ace of Wands benefit us?

Judgement: It makes you more sensitive to the spiritual and to inner guidance, and it gives you a deeper yearning for an understanding of God and His ways. Also, it frees you of karma, and you can become free of bondage to many earthly things.

Nicola: Do you have any other advice for us?

Judgement: Feel the essence of love. When you have found the essence of love you have found my energy, and I burn within you.

THE UNIVERSE: JOINT ARCHETYPAL MEDITATION

We met with the archetype of the Universe on three occasions over these years of meditation. On each occasion the archetype had a different appearance and presented us with different information.

The first time, at the beginning of our series of joint meditations, we met with a Robin Hood-type figure, with a bow and arrow and a horn. He gave us each an arrow, placing them in our bodies pointing upwards. He said that it would help to direct the sexual energy upwards.

Harry: What can we do to balance your energy?

The Universe: Be in the garden, and collect wood from the woods. Walk and work within the garden and the woods. As you do this, it will allow unconscious things to balance.

Harry: Why have you appeared like Robin Hood?

The Universe: Because he helped to balance great imbalances.

Nicola: I dreamed of a spider on my throat. Can you explain the dream?

The Universe: Currently the sexual energy rises as far as your throat. This is a powerful place of communication. The energy needs to rise higher, and the arrow placed within you will help it to do so. When the energy reaches your forehead, you will be able to communicate divine truths. At present, you can communicate earthly things in a divine way.

Harry: Do you have anything else to tell us?

The Universe: There is much hard work before you.

18 months later, we had our second meeting with the Universe, at the suggestion of our guides. She appeared as a naked woman carrying flowers.

Harry: Why did we need to meet with you again?

The Universe: I have a gift for you, from the flowers. It will bless you and it will help you to prosper.

She has a jug of liquid flower essence which she pours upon us.

The Universe: It will bless your business. You do not need to know how.

Nicola: Do you have any other advice for us?

The Universe: You should drink more milk.

In our third meeting with the Universe, just over two years later, she appeared as a beautiful naked woman with blonde hair. She holds a long golden wand with a gold rim on the top, and wears a bracelet on her right arm of consisting of many spheres in sequence on a thread.

Harry:	Why have you appeared in this form?
The Universe:	Because you are a beautiful couple. You have ended one cycle and are beginning a new cycle.
Harry:	In what way has it ended?
The Universe:	A cycle in your relationship and in your life in general.
Harry:	How will a new cycle develop?
The Universe:	It may take many forms, but it will be more beautiful than I am now.
Nicola:	Why do you have a wand?
The Universe:	It is the Hierophant's Wand. It belongs to Harry for the next cycle. Remember to use it in the work ahead.
Nicola:	Why do you wear a bracelet?
The Universe:	It is a symbol of eternity. Each ball represents a new cycle. The string links them. The cycles are connected by one straight road.
Nicola:	How will we know when we are in the new cycle?
The Universe:	It has already begun by calling on me. I am the past and the future.
Harry:	Can you tell us how to proceed with our spiritual work?
The Universe:	You will need an obsidian ball. It will work on you as you work with it.
Harry:	For what purpose do we need it?
The Universe:	It will give you clearer vision and help to penetrate deeper and hold your focus. Take this wand and hold it while I tell you the form of your next meditations…You will start with Kether, and work through the 4 Aces, then the 2's, the 3's, and so on. Document everything. This will be your learning phase. You will be taught how to work together. But remember this wand. It opens and closes. It gives you authority over proceedings. Use it each time you use the obsidian ball. Keep it in your right hand.
Harry:	Should I have a wand in the physical?
The Universe:	If you wish you may have one in the physical as a reminder of its presence here, but it is here that it is important. It can command spirits and help protect you both from any violation by them.
Harry:	I have a sword.
The Universe:	Yes, the sword is a symbol of power. It should not be used until necessary. The wand is authority which you have earned. Use it wisely.
Nicola:	How can we balance your energy?
The Universe:	Make love. In your lives, I am Time. I am the time it takes to complete the work. I am the time it takes to make love. I am the time it takes to be born and to die. I am the time it takes to transform.

She takes her bracelet off and throws it to Harry. It is for Nicola.

APPENDIX III

Divinatory Meanings from the *Golden Dawn Temple Tarot*

0 THE FOOL
Spirit of Aether
The Great Work. Spiritual birth. Great creative potential. Wisdom in spiritual matters. Innocence. Leap of faith. Ability to rise to the higher astral realms. Planting a seed. New undertakings. Search for truth. Sacrifice. Saturn Return.
Ill-dignified: Many lessons to learn. Folly. Danger. Loss and despair. Confusion. Hedonism. Vanity.

1 THE MAGICIAN
The Magus of Power
Creative potential. Power. Magic or magical ritual. Strong will. A unique individual. Self-confident and intelligent. Developing magical skills. Subtleties. Achieving one's goals. Creating your own universe. Meditation and ritual activity under the direction of the Higher Self. A complex situation.
Ill-dignified: Misuse of power. Head-games. Trickery. Manipulative. Clever tactics to bring about selfish results. Lacking the concentration to carry out one's plans. Deceptive energies. A black magician.

2 THE HIGH PRIESTESS
Priestess of the Silver Star
Unconditional Love. Purity of intent. Right actions driven by the unconscious. An indication of a period of gestation. High, intense spiritual energies. Well-balanced. Inner silent voice. Skilled in the Occult Arts. Spiritually awakened individual.
Ill-dignified: Fear of the unknown. Drawn by sexual magnetism rather than controlling it.

3 THE EMPRESS
Daughter of the Mighty Ones
Emotional security. Love. Love affair. Marriage. Pleasure. Motherhood. Birth. Creative Genius. Illumination. Material security. Abundance. A woman with powerful influence. A woman whose inner depths are concealed. Magnetic attraction

of both love and wealth. Aspirations of fulfilling ones True Will.
Ill-dignified: Barrenness. Poverty. A woman unaware of her personal power.

4 THE EMPEROR
Son of the Morning; Chief among the Mighty
Will-power. A successful man. Great courage. Stability in a situation. Challenges won. Energy and endurance. Kundalini force. Good fortune. Worldly status. Self-sacrifice. A man with spiritual aptitude.
Ill-dignified: Loss of control. Selfishness. An angry man. Immaturity.

5 THE HIEROPHANT
Magus of the Eternal Gods
Striving to find Truth. Developing occult abilities. Finding your own way. Upholding a tradition. A Teacher. Intuition. Servitude. Marriage, perhaps on different levels. Commitment to others. Material stability.
Ill-dignified: Gullibility. Self-indulgence. Stubbornness. A strong desire for material security over spiritual growth.

6 THE LOVERS
Children of the Voice Divine; Oracle of the Mighty Gods
Union. Attraction. Love. Influenced by beauty. Art, creative writing. Careful analysis of a situation. Important choice to be made. Overcoming chaos through divine guidance. Inner voice. Twin souls.
Ill-dignified: Sensual addiction. Impulsive decisions. Separation and loss of love. Disagreement. Divorce.

7 THE CHARIOT
Child of the Power of the Waters; Lord of the Triumph of Light
Triumph over obstacles. Success in any undertaking. Help and protection by Providence. Unconscious sexual drive. Moving forward, promotion. Inner drive to succeed. Travel. Strong will and self-control. Conception. The Chariot almost always indicates a good omen.
Ill-dignified: Success will only materialise with continued effort. Unprepared. Lack of discipline. Failure due to lack of direction.

8 STRENGTH
Daughter of the Flaming Sword; Leader of the Lion
Strength of character. Righteousness. Transformation. Mercy. Love. Magnaminity. Union. Perfect balance. Faith. Physical health. Spiritual potential. Lust for life. Kundalini rising.
Ill-dignified: Abuse of power. A dictator. Discord. Weakness.

9 THE HERMIT
The Magus of the Voice of Light; The Prophet of the Gods
Look before you jump. Awakening to inner calling. Following one's hunch. Life's work and research. Stepping out of the mainstream. Journey or change of residence. The need to be alone to understand an important problem. Viewing a problem from above. Meditation. Inner guides. Self-discovery. New understanding of the universe around you. The Hermetic Path.
Ill-dignified: Resistant to inner calling. Overly confident. Disguise. Fear.

10 THE WHEEL OF FORTUNE
Lord of the Forces of Life
Good fortune. Natural change. Things will get better. The cycles of life. Taking control of one's life; starting a new course. Increase of awareness and understanding through experience. Fate and destiny. Magnetism. Karma. Travel.
Ill-dignified: Fatal attraction. Bad luck. Life turning for the worse.

11 JUSTICE
Daughter of The Lord of Truth; The Holder of the Balances
Justice, balance and harmony. A favourable outcome in legal matters. Tension. Doing the right thing.   Artistic impulse. Adjusting one's path according to Divine Will. Disciplined.
Ill-dignified: Unbalanced situation. Unfavourable influence in court. Excessive severity.

12 THE HANGED MAN
The Spirit of the Mighty Waters
Baptism by water. The descent of Spirit into matter. Wisdom. Prophecy. Sacrifice and loss. Punishment. Restriction. Restraint. Spiritual growth through suffering. Stilling the mind. Deep spiritual insights. Awakening of the higher nature.   In material matters, a reversal.
Ill-dignified: Selfishness. Following the crowd.

13 DEATH
The Child of the Great Transformers; Lord of the Gates of Death
Transformation. Sexuality. Old age. Death. Framed within the syntax of Time. Letting go of unnecessary or outmoded influences. The breaking down of the ego. The process of the surrender of the self to something bigger.
Ill-dignified: Fear of change. Not engaging in life.

14 TEMPERANCE
Daughter of the Reconcilers; The Bringer Forth of Life
Unification of opposites. Mixing. Moderation. Meditation. Polarity. A safe environment for growth and adjustment. Realization. Quiet inner drive to succeed. Steady force. Connection with the True Will. Healing.
Ill-dignified: Competing interests. Disunion.

15 THE DEVIL
Lord of the Gates of Matter; Child of the Forces of Time
Puberty. Strong, sexual desires. Obsession. Magnetism. Material focus. Limitation. Authoritative father figure. Link to ancestors. Secrets. Great occult power. The divine locked within matter. Commitment and endurance. Focussed concentration on spiritual or material need. The astral realms. Serpent fire.
Ill-dignified: Fear. Resistance. Projection of will without love. Evil. Pettiness.

16 THE TOWER
Lord of the Hosts of the Mighty
Disaster. Divorce. Accidents and bad health. Emotional pain. Unexpected shock. Sudden insight. Moving home. A new path in life. A flash of inspiration after which nothing can remain the same. Destruction which contains within it a new universe.
Ill-dignified: As upright meanings, but to a lesser degree.

17 THE STAR
Daughter of the Firmament; Dweller between the Waters
Sexual magnetism. Self-awareness. Inspiration. Meditation. The rising feelings of wonder for Creation. Astrological influences. Hope for the best outcome. Altruistic love. A period of calm and reflection. Going within to find the answers. Healing.
Ill-dignified: Unable to summon the courage to continue. Loss of hope. A person unaware of their magical potential.

18 THE MOON
Ruler of Flux and Reflux; Child of the Sons of the Mighty
Subconscious yearnings. Important decisions. Guidance through dangerous waters. Influenced by dreams and intuition. Deception. Depression. Difficulty in holding on to one's True Will due to the pull of the illusionary power of the material. Illusion and delusion caused by the flux and reflux of unconscious forces. The evolution of the querant through life experience. Unconscious evolution.
Ill-dignified: Lunacy. Pretentious façade.

19 THE SUN

Lord of the Fire of the World   Reflection of the soul's essence. Love. Freedom. Friendships. Creative endeavours. Riches on the physical. Spiritual purity. Children. Youthfulness. Good health. Success.

Ill-dignified: Old age. Life not lived to its full. Lack of vitality.

20 JUDGEMENT

The Spirit of the Primal Fire

Awakening. Kundalini. Hearing the Voice of the Spirit. A birth. Spiritual rebirth. Opening of the third eye, revealing the hidden. Crossroads. Important decision to be made. Divine Judgement.

Ill-dignified: Postponement. Bad judgement.

21 THE UNIVERSE

The Great One of the Night of Time

Travel. Breaking through constraints. Completion of a cycle and the beginning of a new one, according to our karmic imprint, into a higher evolutionary pattern. Love of life.

Ill-dignified: Fear of change. Permanency. Inertia. Stagnation.

MINOR ARCANA:

KING OF WANDS

The Lord of the Flame and the Lightning/King of the Spirits of Fire

King and Throne of the Salamanders

Fire of Fire

Sphere of Influence: Above 20° Scorpio – 20° Sagittarius

An initiating force. Dynamic energy. Activity. Generosity. Pride. Swiftness. Impulsiveness. A noble and strong man; a leader. A catalyst. An innovator. Passionate. Loving. Open-hearted. Sense of humour. Deep respect for life. Abrupt. Aggressive. Courageous. Daring. Impetuous. Fierce. Sudden.

Ill-dignified: Destructive. Evil-minded. Cruel. Bigoted. Brutal. Illness.

QUEEN OF WANDS

Queen of the Thrones of Flame

Queen of the Salamanders

Water of Fire

Sphere of Influence: Above 20° Pisces – 20° Aries

A steady force. Adaptability. Persistent energy. Calm authority. Self-assertive and self-assured. Generous. Warm-hearted. A successful woman in business and at home. Attractive. Social. Popular. Impatient of opposition. Impulsive. Proud.

Ill-dignified: Obstinate. Vengeful. Intolerant. Domineering. Tyrannical. Apt to turn suddenly against another without a cause.

PRINCE OF WANDS
The Prince of the Chariot of Fire
Prince and Emperor of the Salamanders
Air of Fire
Sphere of Influence: Above 20° Cancer – 20° Leo
Swiftness. Strength. Eager for action. A young man who is quick, noble, fair, generous, aggressive, rather violent. Warm. Generous. Friendly. Gregarious. Optimistic. Good sense of humour. Rising confidence levels.
Ill-dignified: Inflated ego. A force that cannot easily be stopped.

PRINCESS OF WANDS
Princess of the Shining Flame/The Rose of the Palace of Fire
Princess and Empress of the Salamanders
Earth of Fire
Sphere of Influence: Quadrant of the area around Kether; Throne of the Ace of Wands
Brilliance. Strong-willed. Enthusiasm. Courage. Daring. Vigour. Initiating the result of a situation. Capable of creating and destroying. Desire for power. Beauty. Sudden in anger or love. Faithful. Trustworthy. Outspoken. Revenge. A virgin. Threshold of a new career ambition. Ill-dignified: Cruel. Domineering. Stubborn. Theatrical.

ACE of Wands: Root of the Powers of Fire; Kether of Atziluth
Force. Strength. Vigour. Energy. Rush. Life force. Momentum behind a new beginning or enterprise. Initiated into spiritual awareness. Abstract idea, as yet not understood. Ill-dignified: False start. Decadence. A need to exercise the body and mind to allow the flow of divine force within.

2 of Wands: Lord of Dominion
Chokmah of Atziluth
Mars in Aries, 0° – 10°
Primeval urge to succeed. Strength. Dominion. Harmony of rule. Justice. Boldness. Courage. Generous. Ambitious. Well-balanced individual. Good business sense. Pride. Ill-dignified: Domination by others. Turbulence. Obstinacy.

3 of Wands: Lord of Established Strength
Binah of Atziluth
Sun in Aries, 10° – 20°
Completion of labour. Realisation of hope. Success. Nobility. Wealth. Power. Author-ity. Generosity. Enterprise. Successful business venture. Pride. Self-assertion. Ability

to delegate.
Ill-dignified: Unreliable allies. Failure in business venture. Inability to communicate one's ideas.

4 of Wands: Lord of Perfected Work
Chesed of Atziluth
Venus in Aries, 20° – 30°
Perfection of one's affairs. Rest after labour. Material and emotional blessings. Prosperity. Subtlety. Beauty. Mirth. Reasoning faculty. Graceful in manners. Ability to govern. Shangri-La.
Ill-dignified: One's ideal not yet birthed. Unreadiness. Unsteady. Insincere.

5 of Wands: Lord of Strife
Geburah of Atziluth
Saturn in Leo, 0° – 10°
Violent strife and contest. Conflict. Obstacles. Competition for material gain or recognition. Reorganisation of one's life or affairs. Letting go of unwanted baggage. Possible improvement in business affairs. Boldness. Rashness. Lust and desire. Generosity.
Ill-dignified: Trickery. Restrictions. Complications.

6 of Wands: Lord of Victory
Tiphareth of Atziluth
Jupiter in Leo, 10° – 20°
Victory after strife. Success through energy and industry. Hopes realized. Triumph. Love. Pleasure gained by labour. Carefulness. Sociability. Charisma. Magnetism.
Ill-dignified: Vulnerability. Fear of enemy. Delay. Pride of riches and success. Arrogance.

7 of Wands: Lord of Valour
Netzach of Atziluth
Mars in Leo, 20° – 30°
Possible victory, depending upon the energy and courage exercised. Valour. Opposition, obstacles, and difficulties, yet courage to meet them. Financial good fortune. Integrity.
Ill-dignified: Anxiety. Confusion. Hesitancy. Pretence. Undue optimism in business. Violence.

8 of Wands: Lord of Swiftness
Hod of Atziluth
Mercury in Sagittarius, 0° – 10°
Too much force applied too suddenly. Very rapid rush, but too quickly passed and expended. Swiftness. Rapidity. Activity. Courage. Boldness. Confidence. Freedom.

Travel. Swift communication. Thirst for knowledge.
Ill-dignified: Disputes. Theft and robbery. Guilt. Jealousy. Untrustworthiness. Difficulty in travel and communication.

9 of Wands: Lord of Great Strength
Yesod of Atziluth
Moon in Sagittarius, 10° – 20°
Tremendous and steady force that cannot be shaken. Inner strength crystallized by opposition. Apprehension and doubt before victory. Strength. Power. Hard-working. Good health and recovery. Realisation of what can and cannot be accomplished.
Ill-dignified: Obstacles. Adversity. Distress. Illness and disability. Obstinacy.

10 of Wands: Lord of Oppression
Malkuth of Atziluth
Saturn in Sagittarius, 20° – 30°
Overbearing force and energy, applied to material ends. Inability to delegate, resulting in too great a burden. Breaking point. Success under oppression. Generosity. Self-sacrifice. A turning point in one's outlook.
Ill-dignified: Selfishness. Unwillingness to take on responsibility. Difficulties. Injustice.

KING OF CUPS
Lord of the Waves and the Waters/King of the Hosts of the Sea
King and Throne of the Undines
Fire of Water
Sphere of Influence: 20° Aquarius – 20° Pisces
The power of the Ocean. Power of Water.
A strong force working behind the scenes. Instinctive. Intuitive. A visionary. Complex and emotional. Noble. Gallant. Sensitive. Deep, quiet power. Capable of a high level of spiritual development. Good sense of humour. Graceful. Poetic. Artistic. Venusian. Passionate. Romantic. Attractive. A man in love. A kind, considerate man. Responds to desire. Inspires others. Illuminates thoughts and ideas.
Ill-dignified: Sensual. Idle. Untruthful. Inconstant. Unfaithful. Selfish.

QUEEN OF CUPS
Queen of the Thrones of the Waters
Queen of Nymphs and Undines
Water of Water
Sphere of Influence: 20° Gemini – 20° Cancer
Reflective. Dreamy. Psychic. Prophetic. Intuitive. Imaginative. Moody. Passive. Tranquil. Affected by and reflecting of surrounding influences; sometimes invisible as a result yet in this way a revealer to others. Great attunement to one's Higher Self. Priestess of

the Goddess. A loving, kind-hearted, nurturing mother figure. A woman in love. Gentle. Creative. Hopeful. Sometimes unreliable.
Ill-dignified: Weak. Resentful. Feelings of dependency. Losing oneself in the energies of others, with resultant instability and ungroundedness.

PRINCE OF CUPS
Prince of the Chariot of the Waters
Prince and Emperor of Nymphs and Undines
Air of Water
Sphere of Influence: 20° Libra – 20° Scorpio
Intellect acting upon Emotions. Volatile force. Travel. Changeable. Mysterious. Subtle. Secretive. Self-contained. Impression of calm, masking hidden passions. Clever. Intense. Creativity, inspiration. Control over emotions. Perceptive and intuitive. Objective. An opportunity. A man troubled by a new romantic relationship.
Ill-dignified: Evil and merciless. Superficial, false. Untrustworthy, crafty. Emotionally turbulent. Aloof.

PRINCESS OF CUPS
Princess of the Waters/Lotus of the Palace of the Floods
Earth of Water
Sphere of Influence: Quadrant around Kether; Throne of the Ace of Cups
Creative energy. Generation and crystallization of ideas. Harmonious and beneficial change. Birth. Artistic. Gentle and caring. Dreamy. Romantic. Intuitive. Warm. Fragile. Difficulty coping with conflict. Conception. A woman falling in love. The aspirations of the Soul. Reliable. Strength of purpose and the energy to accomplish goals.
Ill-dignified: Indolent. Selfish. Self-indulgent. Hormonal imbalance.

ACE of Cups: Root of the Powers of Water; Kether of Briah
Love. Joy. Fertility. Productiveness. Beauty. Pleasure. Happiness. The eternal Mother principle. The Muse. Spiritual awakening of one's soul's path.
Ill-dignified: Revolution, change. A need for emotional empathy.

2 of Cups: Lord of Love
Chokmah of Briah
Venus in Cancer, 0° – 10°
Love. Spiritual union. Friendship. Harmony of masculine and feminine united. Pleasure. Mirth. Subtlety. Marriage. Reflection of one's true nature.
Ill-dignified: Jealousy. Disharmony. Folly. Dissipation. Waste. Narcissism.

3 of Cups: Lord of Abundance
Binah of Briah
Mercury in Cancer, 10° – 20°
Abundance. Success. Pleasure. Sensuality. Good fortune. Love. Kindness. Hospitality. Merriment. Social gathering. New friends. Pregnancy. Healing.
Ill-dignified: Excess of physical and sensual pleasures.

4 of Cups: Lord of Blended Pleasure
Chesed of Briah
Moon in Cancer, 20° – 30°
Taking charge of a situation. Success or pleasure approaching an end. Pleasure, but some discomfort and anxieties therewith. Dissatisfaction with environment or self. Longing for change.
Ill-dignified: Good omen for something new entering the querant's life.

5 of Cups: Lord of Loss in Pleasure
Geburah of Briah
Mars in Scorpio, 0° – 10°
Disappointment. Sorrow and loss in those things from which pleasure is expected. Sadness. A love affair that cannot be. A bitter and frustrating marriage. Deceit, treachery, ill-will. Charity and kindness ill-requited. All kinds of anxieties and troubles from unexpected and unsuspected sources.
Ill-dignified: Renewed hope. Return of a friend or relative. A new alliance. Cleansing.

6 of Cups: Lord of Pleasure
Tiphareth of Briah
Sun in Scorpio, 10° – 20°
Happiness, success and enjoyment. The commencement of steady increase, gain and pleasure. Amiable. Patient. Sexual attraction. Depth of understanding.
Ill-dignified: Contention, strife, arising from unwarranted self-assertion and vanity. Thankless. Presumptuous.

7 of Cups: Lord of Illusionary Success
Netzach of Briah
Venus in Scorpio, 20° – 30°
Lethargy. Limited attainment. Disappointment in the moment of apparent victory. Promises unfulfilled. Lacking the tenacity to turn ideas into reality. Illusion. Error. Drunkenness. Vanity. Promiscuity. Deception in love and friendship.
Ill-dignified: Love of nature. Action. Occult or psychic gifts. Sexual magnetism.

8 of Cups: Lord of Abandoned Success
Hod of Briah
Saturn in Pisces, 0° – 10°
Temporary success, but without further result. Indolence in success. Lack of interest.
Seeing through illusions. Journeying from place to place.
Ill-dignified: Materially-minded. Striving for success, albeit illusionary.

9 of Cups: Lord of Material Happiness
Yesod of Briah
Jupiter in Pisces, 10° – 20°
Complete success. Wish fulfilled. Material, emotional and spiritual well-being. Pleasure.
Happiness. Good luck. A good, generous, but maybe foolish nature. Sensuality. A good
omen.
Ill-dignified: Over-emphasis on material and physical aspects of life. Imperfections.

10 of Cups: Lord of Perfected Success
Malkuth of Briah
Mars in Pisces, 20° – 30°
Permanent and lasting success. True happiness inspired from above. Perfection of human love and friendship. Love of family life. Contentment. Attainment of the heart's
desires. Kindness. Generosity. Peace-making.
Ill-dignified: Disharmony. Guilt. Anger. Bitterness. Waste.

KING OF SWORDS
Lord of the Winds and Breezes/King of the Spirit of Air
King and Throne of the Sylphs
Fire of Air
Sphere of Influence: 20° Taurus – 20° Gemini
Will applied to intellect. He is active, clever, subtle, fierce, delicate, courageous, skilful,
but inclined to domineer. Intuitive. Intelligent. Capable of making difficult decisions. A
man who gives orders and directives. A brilliant mind. Enquiring, analytical, a keen observer. Patient and careful, yet ruthless. High ideals. Elusive, ethereal, with a strength
and fascination. Distant.
Ill-dignified: Tyrannical. Deceitful. Crafty. Pig-headed. Manipulative. Unprincipled.
Self-seeking. One who has been emotionally hurt, and thus angry and vengeful. Physically violent. Mentally cruel. Cold. Harsh.

QUEEN OF SWORDS
Queen of the Thrones of Air
Queen of the Sylphs
Water of Air
Sphere of Influence: 20° Virgo – 20° Libra
Emotions acting upon Intellect. Keen perception. Clarity. Subtle. Quick. Confident. Often perseveringly accurate in superficial things. Graceful. Social. Strong-minded. Capable of going it alone. Independent in thought and judgement. Upfront and honest. Far-sighted. Intuitive. Analytical. Intelligent. Dry sense of humour. Cool demeanour. Private. A level head when under pressure.
Ill-dignified: Cruel, sly, deceitful, unreliable. Cold, judgemental, critical. Hard towards others. Cynical, sharp, embittered, resentful. Uptight. A woman scorned. A widow, or one recently divorced.

PRINCE OF SWORDS
Prince of the Chariots of the Winds
Prince and Emperor of Sylphs
Air of Air
Sphere of Influence: 20° Capricorn – 20° Aquarius
Intellectual. Open-minded. Full of ideas and thoughts and designs. Distrustful. Suspicious. Firm in friendship and enmity. Challenging. Stimulating. An abstract thinker. Careful. A private person. Someone who prefers to work alone. Unemotional. Independent.
Ill-dignified: Harsh. Plotting. Obstinate. Unable to make a decision. Day-dreaming. Erratic. Unreliable (Bad judgement). Cold. Angry. Violent.

PRINCESS OF SWORDS
Princess of the Rushing Winds/Lotus of the Palace of Air
Princess and Empress of the Sylphs
Earth of Air
Sphere of Influence: Quadrant around Kether; Throne of the Ace of Swords
The materialization of ideas. Practical understanding. Wisdom. Strength. Keen vision. Grace. Dexterity and agility. Bringing clarity and insight. Keen observer of life. Honest and frank. Objective and rational. Sees through the smokescreen, cuts away the unnecessary and gets to the heart of things. Ruthless. A skilled arbitrator.
Ill-dignified: Frivolous. Cunning. Unfortunate circumstances. Angry. Vicious. Spiteful. Heartless. Hiding behind dogma. Vengeful. Juvenile.

ACE of Swords: Root of the Powers of Air; Kether of Yetsirah
The Higher Self. Triumph of Divine Law. One's True Will. The light of Truth. Invoked force for good.
Ill-dignified: Divine wrath and punishment. Invoked force for evil.

2 of Swords: Lord of Peace Restored
Chokmah of Yetsirah
Moon in Libra, 0° – 10°
Peace restored. Balance. Justice. A truce. Divine intervention/guidance. Making peace with oneself. Acceptance.
Ill-dignified: Mental block. Friendships and truces built upon deceit.

3 of Swords: Lord of Sorrow
Binah of Yetsirah
Saturn in Libra, 10° – 20°
Separation. Delay. Sorrow. Sadness through change brought about by the ending of a cycle. Pain followed by readjustment and fresh understanding.
Ill-dignified: Troubles due to misjudgement or misconduct of the querant.

4 of Swords: Lord of Rest from Strife
Chesed of Yetsirah
Jupiter in Libra, 20° – 30°
Rest and recuperation following sorrow and strife. Peace after war or conflict. Voluntary seclusion for spiritual development. Going on a retreat. Relaxation. Cessation of anxiety. Developing new ideas.
Ill-dignified: Prison cell. Dogma.

5 of Swords: Lord of Defeat
Geburah of Yetsirah
Venus in Aquarius, 0° – 10°
Defeat. Loss. Dishonesty. Dishonour. Anxiety. Trouble. Avarice. Slander. Malice. Spite.
Ill-dignified: Triumph over one's enemies. Cutting away out-moded habits.

6 of Swords: Lord of Earned Success
Tiphareth of Yetsirah
Mercury in Aquarius, 10° – 20°
Success following trouble. Resolution of difficulties. Application of one's will to realise one's hopes. Groups working together towards common goal. Study. Voyage. Arrival of a messenger or news.
Ill-dignified: Unexpected help or gain.

7 of Swords: Lord of Unstable Effort
Netzach of Yetsirah
Moon in Aquarius, 20° – 30°
Plans, hopes and expectations. One-pointed focus, but unable to grasp the moment. Un-reliable. Compromise.

Ill-dignified: Plans unfulfilled due to lack of sustained effort. Failure and irritations. Opponents in a stronger position.

8 of Swords: Lord of Shortened Force
Hod of Yetsirah
Jupiter in Gemini, 0° – 10°
Concentrated focus on detail, perhaps at expense of more important things. Unable to see a way through difficult circumstances. Indecision. Conflict. Pettiness. Intelligent. Clever. Lacking in feeling. Academically-minded. Change of fortune.
Ill-dignified: Forcing another to comply. Sudden clarity. Accident. Release.

9 of Swords: Lord of Despair and Cruelty
Yesod of Yetsirah
Mars in Gemini, 10° – 20°
Male principle dominating the feminine. Bullying. Cruelty. Stress-related illnesses. Nightmares. Heavy depression. Despair. Misery. Drastic split in a relationship.
Ill-dignified: Divine retribution.

10 of Swords: Lord of Ruin
Malkuth of Yetsirah
Sun in Gemini, 20° – 30°
The complete ending of a matter. Finality, such as death. Ruin. Defeat. Physical illness resulting from mental overload. The darkness before the dawn. A turning point towards Truth.
Ill-dignified: A seed of hope for a new beginning. An awakening.

KING OF PENTACLES
Lord of the Wild and Fertile Land/King of the Spirits of Earth
King and Throne of the Gnomes
Fire of Earth
Sphere of Influence: 20° Leo – 20° Virgo
A generative force. A quiet man, with deep passion. Laborious, clever, and patient in material matters. Prudent with the Earth's resources. A wealthy man. Spiritually rich. Earthy. Steady. Dependable. Helpful. Faithful. A good manager.
Ill-dignified: Avaricious. Too materialistic. Dull. Jealous. Not very courageous. Stubborn. Boring.

QUEEN OF PENTACLES
Queen of the Thrones of Earth
Queen of Gnomes
Water of Earth
Sphere of Influence: 20° Sagittarius – 20° Capricorn

Fertility of the Earth. Home environment. Family. Fecundity. She is impetuous, kind, timid, rather charming, great-hearted, intelligent, melancholy, truthful, yet of many moods. Warm and generous. Loyal. Nourishing. A facilitator. A hard worker. Practical. In tune with Nature. Working together with the Earth to bring about abundance.
Ill-dignified: Undecided. Capricious. Foolish. Changeable (fear of failure). Too dependent. Untrusting.

PRINCE OF PENTACLES
Prince of the Chariot of Earth
Prince and Emperor of the Gnomes
Air of Earth
Sphere of Influence: 20° Aries – 20° Taurus
Increase of matter. Increase of good and evil. Solidifies. Practically applies things. Steady, reliable. Slow to anger, but furious if roused. Intolerant of dishonesty or unfaithfulness. Deeply passionate. Sensual. A quiet and meditative man. Strong yet gentle. Dedicated. Resourceful. Learning to take on responsibility.
Ill-dignified: Stubborn. Bloody-minded. Unspiritual.

PRINCESS OF PENTACLES
Princess of the Echoing Hills/Rose of the Palace of Earth
Earth of Earth
Sphere of Influence: Quadrant around Kether; Throne of the Ace of Pentacles
Generous. Kind. Diligent. Benevolent. Quiet. Gentle. Reserved. Careful. Reliable. Hardworking. Practical. Capable. Courageous. Persevering. Concerned with nature, domestic matters, pregnancy. A practical manager. Accountancy. A young woman on the threshold of life – marriage, motherhood. New beginnings. Growth. Change. In love with life. In tune with the moment. Connected to one's Higher Self and the Forces of Love. Aware of the creative force of the Goddess.
Ill-dignified: Wasteful. Prodigal. Unable to conceive.

ACE of Pentacles: Root of the Powers of Earth; Kether of Assiah
Complete happiness. Sudden clarity regarding ones true desire. A new path unfolding. Financial gain. Wealth and power.
Ill-dignified: Querant may be following the wrong path.

2 of Pentacles: Lord of Harmonious Change
Chokmah of Assiah
Jupiter in Capricorn, 0° – 10°
Love of life. Heightened awareness. Fluctuations in finances and/or health. Pleasant change. Harmony in the midst of conflict. Control. Balance.
Ill-dignified: Lack of control. Argumentative. Indecisive.

3 of Pentacles: Lord of Material Works
Binah of Assiah
Mars in Capricorn, 10° – 20°
Constructive force. Increase of material things. Mastery of a skill. Building up a business. Renown. Community welfare.
Ill-dignified: Narrow and prejudiced. Overly concerned with gain at cost of craft.

4 of Pentacles: Lord of Earthly Power
Chesed of Assiah
Sun in Capricorn, 20° – 30°
Material gain. Rank and dominion. Law and Order. An inheritance or gift. Possessive. Covetous. Avaricious.
Ill-dignified: The giving of tithes.

5 of Pentacles: Lord of Material Trouble
Geburah of Assiah
Mercury in Taurus, 0° – 10°
Material trouble. Illness or operation generating physical difficulties and long-term inaction. Attuning to the land. Spiritual or material poverty. A decision to live lightly upon the earth. Financial difficulty. Loneliness. Toil, labour. Worry.
Ill-dignified: Money regained following hard labour. New employment. Small monetary gain.

6 of Pentacles: Lord of Material Success
Tiphareth of Assiah
Moon in Taurus, 10° – 20°
Success and gain in material matters. Gain in power and rank. Well-established in one's field. Nobility. Fair and generous.
Ill-dignified: Wasteful. Prodigal. Arrogant from success. Desire. Avarice. A bad debt.

7 of Pentacles: Lord of Success Unfulfilled
Netzach of Assiah
Saturn in Taurus, 20° – 30°
Disappointment, but temporary. Cultivating the land. Little gain for much labour. A collector. Do not give up hope – heralds improved fortunes!
Ill-dignified: Loss of hoped-for harvest. Bad investments. Hardened disposition. Emotions closed to the natural world.

8 of Pentacles: Lord of Prudence
Hod of Assiah
Sun in Virgo, 0° – 10°
A well-ordered, tranquil period. Spiritual growth due to stable material environment. Prudence. Hardworking. Attention to detail. Cultivating the land. Preparatory groundwork. Accountancy.
Ill-dignified: Likely disruption of plans.

9 of Pentacles: Lord of Material Gain
Yesod of Assiah
Venus in Virgo, 10° – 20°
Material gain. The attainment of ones wishes. Inheritance on the horizon. A gift or imbursement. Reward for past efforts. Short-term monetary solutions.
Ill-dignified: Still well-omened, but may take longer to reap benefits.

10 of Pentacles: Lord of Wealth
Malkuth of Assiah
Mercury in Virgo, 20° – 30°
Wealth. Inheritance. Fortune. The pinnacle of success. Hereditary line. Karma.
Ill-dignified: The weight of material success. Monetary gain less than expected.

APPENDIX IV

Golden Dawn Colour Scales

The Colour Scales of the Ten Sephiroth in the Four Worlds
(Wendrich Version – changes in **bold**)

SEPHIRA	YOD - FIRE	HEH- WATER	VAV - AIR	HEH final - EARTH
	King Scale	Queen Scale	Prince Scale	Princess Scale
	Atziluth	Briah	Yetzirah	Assiah
	Wands	Cups	Swords	Pentacles
1 KETHER	Brilliance	White brilliance	White brilliance	White, flecked gold
2 CHOKMAH	Soft Blue	**Pearl Grey**	Bluish Mother of Pearl	White, flecked **magenta**, cyan, yellow
3 BINAH	Crimson	Black	Dark brown	Grey, flecked pink
4 CHESED	Deep Violet	**Cyan**	Deep Purple	Deep azure, flecked yellow
5 GEBURAH	Orange	**Magenta**	**Red**	Red, flecked black
6 TIPHARETH	Clear Pink Rose	**Yellow (Lemon Yellow)**	**Salmon**	Gold-Amber
7 NETZACH	Amber	**Green**	**Yellow-green**	Olive, flecked Gold
8 HOD	Violet-purple	**Red-orange**	**Russet**	Yellow-brown, flecked white
9 YESOD	Indigo	**Purple**	**Indigo-purple (Fr. Ultramarine Blue, red shade)**	Citrine, flecked Azure
10 MALKUTH	Yellow	Citrine, Olive, Russet, Black	Citrine, Olive, Russet, Black, flecked gold	Black rayed yellow

The Four Colour Scales
(Regardie Version)

SEPHIRA	YOD - FIRE	HEH- WATER	VAV - AIR	HEH final - EARTH
	King Scale	Queen Scale	Prince Scale	Princess Scale
	Atziluth	Briah	Yetzirah	Assiah
	Wands	Cups	Swords	Pentacles
1 KETHER	Brilliance	White brilliance	White Brilliance	White flecked gold
2 CHOKMAH	Soft Blue	Grey	Bluish Mother-of-Pearl	White, flecked red, blue, yellow
3 BINAH	Crimson	Black	Dark brown	Grey flecked pink
4 CHESED	Deep violet	Blue	Deep purple	Deep Azure flecked yellow
5 GEBURAH	Orange	Scarlet-red	Bright Scarlet	Red flecked black
6 TIPHARETH	Clear PinkRose	Yellow (gold)	Rich Salmon	Gold Amber
7 NETZACH	Amber	Emerald	Bright yellow-green	Olive, flecked gold
8 HOD	Violet-purple	Orange	Red russet	Yellow-brown flecked white
9 YESOD	Indigo	Violet	Very dark Purple	Citrine, flecked blue
10 MALKUTH	Yellow	Citrine, Olive, Russet, Black	4 colours flecked gold	Black rayed yellow
11 AIR	Bright Pale Yellow	Sky-blue	Green	Emerald flecked gold
12 MERCURY	Yellow	Purple	Gray	Indigo rayed violet
13 MOON	Blue	Silver	Cold Pale Blue	Silver, rayed sky-blue
14 VENUS	Emerald Green	Sky-blue	Early Spring Green	Bright Rose of Cerise, rayed pale yellow
15 ARIES	Scarlet	Red	Brilliant Flame	Glowing Red
16 TAURUS	Red-orange	Deep Indigo	Deep Warm Olive	Rich Brown

17 GEMINI	Orange	Pale mauve	New Yellow	Reddish grey inclined to mauve
18 CANCER	Amber	Maroon	Rich bright russet	Dark Greenish Brown
19 LEO	Greening-yellow	Deep Purple	Grey	Reddish-amber
20 VIRGO	Yellowish-green	Slate grey	Green grey	Plum Colour
21 JUPITER	Violet	Blue	Rich Purple	Bright blue rayed yellow
22 LIBRA	Emerald Green	Blue	Deep Blue green	Pale green
23 WATER	Deep Blue	Sea-green	Deep olive green	White, flecked purple like mother of pearl
24 SCORPIO	Green-blue	Dull brown	Very dark brown	Livid indigo brown-black beetle
25 SAGITTARIUS	Blue	Yellow	Green	Dark vivid blue
26 CAPRICORN	Indigo	Black	Blue-black	Cold dark grey near black
27 MARS	Scarlet	Red	Venitian red	Bright red, rayed azure or emerald
28 AQUARIUS	Violet	Sky blue	Bluish Mauve	White tinged purple
29 PISCES	Ultra Violet Crimson	Buff, flecked silver-white	Light translucent pinkish brown	Stone Colour
30 SUN	Orange	Gold Yellow	Rich Amber	Amber rayed red
31 FIRE	Glowing Scarlet-orange	Vermilion	Scarlet flecked gold	Vermilion flecked crimson and emerald
31 SATURN	Indigo	Black	Blue black	Black, rayed blue
32 EARTH	Citrine, Olive, Russet, Black	Amber	Dark Brown	Black, flecked yellow
32 SPIRIT	White, merging gray	Deep Purple (nearly black)	7 Prismatic colours, violet outside	White, red, yellow, blue, black (outside)
DA'ATH	Lavender	Gray white	Pure Violet	Gray flecked gold

The Four Colour Scales
(Cicero Version)

SEPHIRA	YOD - FIRE	HEH- WATER	VAV - AIR	HEH final - EARTH
	King Scale	Queen Scale	Prince Scale	Princess Scale
	Atziluth	Briah	Yetzirah	Assiah
	Wands	Cups	Swords	Pentacles
1 KETHER	Brilliance	White brilliance	Brilliant White	White, flecked gold
2 CHOKMAH	Soft Blue-grey	Grey	Pearlish blue-grey	White, flecked red, blue, yellow
3 BINAH	Deep Crimson (deep red-violet)	Black	Dark brown	Grey, flecked pink
4 CHESED	Deep violet	Blue	Deep purple	Deep blue, flecked yellow
5 GEBURAH	Orange	Red	Red-orange	Red, flecked black
6 TIPHARETH	Rose Pink	Yellow (gold)	Salmon	Yellow-orange
7 NETZACH	Yellow-orange	Green	Amber-green	Olive, flecked yellow
8 HOD	Violet	Orange	Red russet	Yellow-brown, flecked white
9 YESOD	Blue-violet	Violet	Dark Purple	Citrine, flecked blue
10 MALKUTH	Yellow	Citrine, Olive, Russet, Black	Citrine, Olive, Russet, Black, flecked gold	Black rayed yellow
11 AIR	Yellow	Sky-blue	Green	Green, flecked yellow
12 MERCURY	Yellow	Violet	Gray	Blue-violet rayed violet
13 MOON	Blue	Silver	Silver Blue (Pale blue)	Silver, rayed sky-blue
14 VENUS	Green	Sky-blue	Blue-green	Rose Cerise, rayed pale green
15 ARIES	Red	Red	Red	Red
16 TAURUS	Red-orange	Deep Blue-violet	Deep Warm Olive	Rich Brown

17 GEMINI	Orange	Pale mauve	Light tan brown	Reddish grey inclined to mauve
18 CANCER	Yellow-orange	Maroon	Rich bright russet	Dark greenish brown
19 LEO	Yellow	Deep violet	Grey	Reddish Amber (Light Orange)
20 VIRGO	Yellow-green	Slate grey	Green grey	Plum
21 JUPITER	Violet	Blue	Blue-violet	Bright blue. rayed yellow
22 LIBRA	Green	Blue	Blue green	Pale green
23 WATER	Blue	Sea-green	Deep olive green	White, flecked purple
24 SCORPIO	Blue-green	Dull brown	Very dark brown	Brownish blue-violet
25 SAGITTARIUS	Blue	Yellow	Green	Dark blue
26 CAPRICORN	Blue-violet	Black	Blue-black	Cold dark grey near black
27 MARS	Red	Red	Venitian red	Bright red, rayed blue or green
28 AQUARIUS	Violet	Sky blue	Bluish Mauve	White tinged violet
29 PISCES	Red-violet	Buff, flecked silver-white	Light pinkish brown	Stone (dark grey)
30 SUN	Orange	Yellow	Yellow-orange	Yellow-orange, rayed red
31 FIRE	Red	Vermilion red	Red, flecked gold	Vermilion, flecked red-violet and green
31 SATURN	Blue-violet	Black	Blue black	Black, rayed blue
32 EARTH	Citrine, Olive, Russet, Black	Yellow-orange	Dark Brown	Black, flecked yellow
32 SPIRIT	White, merging gray	Deep Purple (nearly black)	7 Prismatic colours, violet outside	White, red, yellow, blue, black (outside)
DA'ATH	Lavender	Gray white	Violet	Gray, flecked yellow

Bibliography

Agrippa, Henry, Cornelius, trans. James Freake, ed. Donald Tyson. *Three Books of Occult Philosophy: The Foundation Book of Western Occultism.* Woodbury, MN: Llewellyn Publications, 2009.

Angelucci, Orfeo M. *The Secret of the Saucers: How UFOs work.* 1955. Reprint, Forgotten Books, 2008.

Antoine de Saint-Exupéry, *Airman's Odyssey.* Florida: Harcourt, 1942.

Aartsen, Gerard. *Here to Help: UFOs and the Space Brothers, 2nd ed.* Amsterdam, Netherlands: BGA Publications, 2012.

Bain, Derek, with Marcus Katz and Tali Goodwin. *A New Dawn for Tarot: The Original Tarot of the Golden Dawn.* Forgewick Press. 2014.

Barrios Enrique. *Ami: Child of the Stars.* Twin Lakes, WI: Lotus Press, 1989.

Brother Philip. *Secret of the Andes,* 4th ed. London: Neville Spearman, 1970.

Cayce, Edgar. *Auras: An Essay on the Meaning of Colour.* Virginia: A.R.E. Press, 1973.

Cavali, Thom F. *Embodying Osiris: The Secrets of Alchemical Transformation.* Wheaton, IL: Quest Books, 2010.

Cicero, Sandra Tabatha. *The Book of the Concourse of the Watchtowers: An Exploration of Westcott's Enochian Tablets.* Elfers, FL: H.O.G.D. Books, 2012.

Cicero, Chic and Sandra Tabatha. *Self-Initiation into the Golden Dawn Tradition.* St. Paul, MN: Llewellyn Publications, 2003.

Cicero, Chic and Sandra Tabatha. *The New Golden Dawn Ritual Tarot: Keys to the Rituals, Symbolism, Magic & Divination.* St. Paul, MN: Llewellyn Publications, 1996.

Copenhaver, Brian P., trans. *Hermetica.* Cambridge, UK: Cambridge University Press, 1992.

Crowley, Aleister. *The Book of Thoth: Egyptian Tarot.* York Beach, ME: Red Wheel/Weiser, 2006.

Davidson, John. *The Gospel of Jesus: In Search of His Original Teachings.* UK: Clear Press Ltd., 2004.

Devereux, Paul. *Stoneage Soundtracks.* London: Vega, 2001.

Farrell, Nick, and Harry Wendrich. *Golden Dawn Temple Tarot Deck Meditation Guide.* Llanelli, Wales: Wendrich artHouse, 2011.

Ginsburg, Rabbi Yitzchach. *The Hebrew Letters: Channels of Creative Consciousness.* Jerusalem: Linda Pinsky Publications, 1990.

Godwin, David. *Godwin's Cabalistic Encyclopedia, 3rd ed.* St. Paul, MN: Llewellyn Worldwide, Ltd. 2004.

Hatt, J. Arthur H. *The Colorist.* 1908. Reprint, Whitefish, MT: Kessinger Publishing, 2010.

Jasmuheen. *Pranic Nourishment: Living on Light.* Buderim, Australia: Self Empowerment Academy, 2012.

Kaplan, Aryeh. *Sefer Yetzirah: The Book of Creation: In Theory and Practice.* Rev. ed. York Beach, ME: Red Wheel/Weiser, 1997.

Knight, Gareth. *A Practical Guide to Qabalistic Symbolism.* York Beach, ME: Red Wheel/Weiser, 2001.

Lemos, John. *"Color Charts for the School Room", The School Arts Magazine,* Volume 19, 1920.

Maerz A.J. and M. Rea Paul. *A Dictionary of Color.* New York: McGraw-Hill, 1930.

Mathers, Moina, and W.W. Westcott. *The Golden Dawn Court Cards.* Ed. Darcy Kűntz. Sequim, WA: Holmes Publishing Group, 2006.

Mathers, S. Liddell MacGregor, trans., ed. *The Key of Solomon the King.* Escondido, CA: The Book Tree, 1999.

McHyde, Timothy. *Know the Future: A Bible Prophecy Breakthrough.* 2012.

Montalban, Madeline. *The Prediction Book of the Tarot.* Poole, UK: Javelin Books, 1985.

Munk, Rabbi Michael L. *The Wisdom in the Hebrew Alphabet: The Sacred Letters asa Guide to Jewish Deed and Thought.* New York: Mesorah Publications, Ltd., 2002.

Parker, Julia and Derek. *Parkers' Astrology.* London: Dorling Kidersley Ltd. 2003.

Regardie, Israel. *The Golden Dawn: The Original Account of the Teachings, Rites & Ceremonies of the Hermetic Order.* Woodbury, MN: Llewellyn Worldwide, Ltd., 2002.

Roads, Michael J. *Journey Into Oneness: A Spiritual Odyssey.* Tiburon, CA: H. J. Kramer Inc. 1994.

Samael Aun Weor. *Treatise of Sexual Alchemy.* New York: Glorian Publishing, 2012.

Scholem, Gershom. *Kabbalah.* Jerusalem: Keter Publishing House Jerusalem Ltd, 1987.

Skinner, Stephen. *The Complete Magician's Tables.* Singapore: Golden Hoard Press. 2006.

Steinbrecher, Edwin C. *The Inner Guide Meditation: a Spiritual Technology for the 21st Century.* York Beach, ME: Samuel Weiser, 1988.

Temple, Robert. *The Sirius Mystery: New Scientific Evidence of Alien Contact 5,000 Years Ago.* Vermont: Destiny Books. 1998.

Valberg, Arne and Barry B. Lee, *From Pigments to Perception: Advances in Understanding Visual Processes.* New York: Springer: 1991.

Waite, A.E. *The Pictorial Key to the Tarot.* New York: Dover Publications Inc. 2005.

Werner, Michael and Thomas Stöckli. Life from Light: Is it possible to live without food? UK: Clairview, 2007.

Wang, Robert. *The Qabalistic Tarot: A Textbook of Mystical Philosophy.* Canada: Marcus Aurelius Press, 2004.

Zalewski, Pat and Chris. *The Magical Tarot of the Golden Dawn.* London, UK: Aeon Books Ltd. 2008

Websites:

Aquarian Path.
    http://www.aquarianpath.com/
Bible Hub.
    http://biblehub.com/
Douma, Michael, curator. "Pigments through the Ages." (2008).
    http://www.webexhibits.org/pigments.
Gal Einai Institute: The Inner Dimension Website
    http://www.inner.org/
Jusko, Don. Real Color Wheel
    http://www.realcolorwheel.com
Leitch, Aaron. Shem ha-Mephoresh, The Divine Name of Extension:
    http://www.hermeticgoldendawn.org/leitch-shemhamephoresh.html
Wendrich artHouse
    http://www.wendricharthouse.com

COLOUR PLATES

Fig. 1: Geburah (original and amended) by Harry Wendrich

Mixing the Malkuth Square From Primaries

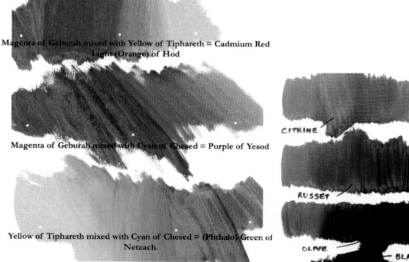

Magenta of Geburah mixed with Yellow of Tiphareth = Cadmium Red Light (Orange) of Hod

Magenta of Geburah mixed with Cyan of Chesed = Purple of Yesod

Yellow of Tiphareth mixed with Cyan of Chesed = (Phthalo) Green of Netzach.

Fig. 2: Finding Hod, Netzach, and Yesod

CITRINE

RUSSET

OLIVE ——— BLACK

Fig. 3: Mixing the Malkuth Colours

Fig. 4: The Malkuth Square

CITRINE

RUSSET

OLIVE

BLACK

Fig. 5: Rose Ankh
(Cover Card, Golden Dawn Temple Tarot)

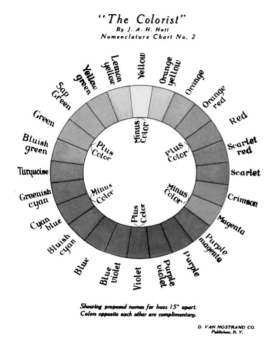

Fig. 6: Hatt's Colour Wheel (1908)

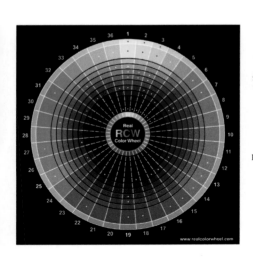

Fig. 7: Don Jusko's Real Color Wheel

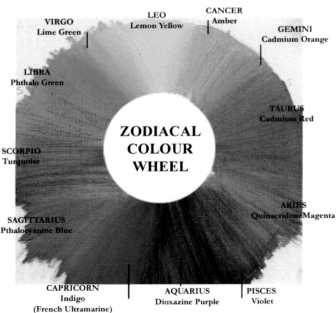

Fig. 8: Zodiacal Colour Wheel

Fig. 9: Vault Colours and their Charges

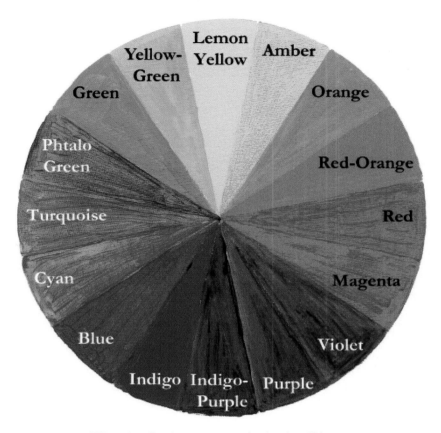

Vault Colours and their Charges

Additional Colours & Charges (from left):
Spirit Wheel, Alchemical Mercury, Alchemical Sulphur,
Alchemical Salt, Chokmah.

Also published by Wendrich artHouse:

Golden Dawn Temple Tarot Deck

Nick Farrell, Harry Wendrich, and Nicola Wendrich
A modern Golden Dawn Tarot deck of 80 cards, based upon the descriptions of *Book T*, with designs influenced by Golden Dawn ritual and archetypal meditations.

ISBN 978-0-9927479-0-9

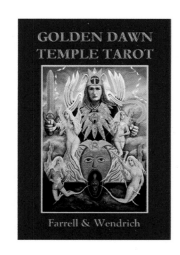

The Golden Dawn Temple Tarot Meditation Set

Nick Farrell & Harry Wendrich

A set comprising of 23 cards (sized A5) of the Major Arcana from the *Golden Dawn Temple Tarot* deck, for use with meditation and ritual. An accompanying hand-book provides an introductory study of the attributions of the Major Arcana, including full descriptions of the traditional symbolism incorporated within each Key. Preparatory exercises and a consecration ritual are followed by several tried and tested meditation techniques for exploration into how the archetypal Tarot energies function in your life.

ISBN: 978-0-9927479-1-6

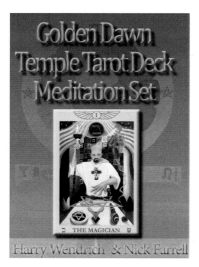

By Nicola Wendrich
ABOUT US: The Story of Wendrich artHouse

An autobiographical story giving a fuller picture behind the business, which was set up to paint images of both spiritual and prophetic content. The story follows the spiritual awakenings and life paths of the artists Harry and Nicola Wendrich, and it details some of their unusual spiritual experiences and understandings.

Published by lulu.com
ISBN-10: 184728258X
ISBN-13: 978-1847282583